# THE ENGLISH SPIRIT

D1499600

# BOOKS BY A. L. ROWSE

## Literature

WILLIAM SHAKESPEARE: A BIOGRAPHY

SHAKESPEARE'S SONNETS:

*Edited with an Introduction and Notes*

CHRISTOPHER MARLOWE: A BIOGRAPHY

SHAKESPEARE'S SOUTHAMPTON: PATRON OF VIRGINIA

THE ENGLISH SPIRIT

TIMES, PERSONS, PLACES

A CORNISH CHILDHOOD

A CORNISHMAN AT OXFORD

POEMS OF A DECADE, 1931–1941

POEMS CHIEFLY CORNISH

POEMS OF DELIVERANCE

POEMS PARTLY AMERICAN

WEST-COUNTRY STORIES

## History

BOSWORTH FIELD AND THE WARS OF THE ROSES

THE ENGLAND OF ELIZABETH

THE EXPANSION OF ELIZABETHAN ENGLAND

THE ELIZABETHANS AND AMERICA

RALEGH AND THE THROCKMORTONS

SIR RICHARD GRENVILLE OF THE 'REVENGE'

TUDOR CORNWALL

THE EARLY CHURCHILLS

THE LATER CHURCHILLS

THE SPIRIT OF ENGLISH HISTORY

THE USE OF HISTORY

THE END OF AN EPOCH

ALL SOULS AND APPEASEMENT

ST. AUSTELL: CHURCH, TOWN, PARISH

A HISTORY OF FRANCE

By Lucien Romier

*Translated and completed*

*Douglas Glass*

A. L. Rowse was born in Cornwall in 1903; he went to Oxford as a Scholar in English Literature at Christ Church, and won a Fellowship in History at All Souls.

He has written a classic of its kind in **A Cornish Childhood,** with its sequel **A Cornishman at Oxford,** two portraits of a society with his **Tudor Cornwall** and **The England of Elizabeth,** which also has a sequel in **The Expansion of Elizabethan England,** and a pendant, **The Elizabethans and America.** Two biographical studies, **Sir Richard Grenville** and **Ralegh and the Throckmortons,** complement each other, while **The Early Churchills** and **The Later Churchills** set a model for family history. The quartet consisting of his epoch-making biography, **William Shakespeare,** his edition of **Shakespeare's Sonnets, Christopher Marlowe** and **Shakespeare's Southampton,** with his volumes of essays, **Times, Persons, Places** and **The English Spirit,** and his poems, display his equal gifts as a man of letters.

A Fellow of the British Academy, he divides his time between Oxford, Cornwall and California, where he is a Senior Fellow of the Huntington Library.

# The English Spirit

ESSAYS IN LITERATURE
AND HISTORY

BY

A. L. ROWSE

REVISED EDITION

MACMILLAN
London · Melbourne · Toronto
1966

To
G. M. Trevelyan
admirable exemplar of
the English spirit

© A. L. Rowse 1966

MACMILLAN AND COMPANY LIMITED
*Little Essex Street London WC2*
*also Bombay Calcutta Madras Melbourne*

THE MACMILLAN COMPANY OF CANADA LIMITED
*70 Bond Street Toronto 2*

*First Edition 1944*
*Reprinted 1945 (twice), 1946, 1950*
*Second Edition (revised and reset) 1966*

PRINTED IN GREAT BRITAIN

# CONTENTS

v

39810

# CONTENTS

# PREFACE

THIS book was originally published in the heroic days of 1944 — its essays and articles gathered together in the last months before the liberation of Europe from the island springboard — and owed something of its success to the circumstances of the time: it seems to have caught the mood of the moment.

After some five impressions in this country, it has long been out of print, and the time has come for a thorough revision. It is now by nearly half a new book and, I hope, as much improved. The general scheme remains, but I have omitted the topical essays that made the first third of the book: there is now far less about politics and much more about the (more durable) arts, particularly literature.

Some of the new pieces were written for special occasions. 'The Personality of Shakespeare' and 'Sir Winston Churchill as an Historian' were delivered as Founder's Day addresses at the Huntington Library and Art Gallery in California — a unique honour to have been invited twice for the occasion. 'The Problem of Shakespeare's Sonnets Solved' was given in its original form as the Giff Edmonds Memorial Lecture to the Royal Society of Literature. I am much indebted to these distinguished institutions in America and Britain for the honour they did me. 'Queen Elizabeth and the Historians' is the sole piece I have rescued from a little book I have allowed to go out of print, *An Elizabethan Garland*.

The earlier pieces have been heavily revised — some of them shortened, others expanded, some much added to — I found that the earlier written the more the revision necessary. However, continuity and theme have been retained.

A. L. ROWSE

Trenarren,
St. Austell.
*Easter, 1966.*

# ACKNOWLEDGMENTS

THE author and publishers wish to thank Mrs. Bambridge for permission to quote extracts from the works of Rudyard Kipling issued either by the present publishers or by Messrs. Methuen & Co. Ltd.; and Messrs. Jonathan Cape Ltd. for permission to quote the extracts from *Kilvert's Diary*, edited by William Plomer.

# THE PERSONALITY OF SHAKESPEARE

IN *The Importance of Being Earnest* Lady Bracknell reproves Mr. Worthing, 'to lose one parent may be regarded as a misfortune; to lose both looks like carelessness'. To be invited to give the Founder's Day Address twice within three years is not only an unprecedented honour, but must look like favouritism. However, it happens that a Shakespeare biography of mine has achieved some notice; so it must have been thought, in the Quater-centenary year, not altogether inappropriate to draft me.

I realise that, if I were wise, I should not attempt such a subject; I should offer you something uncontroversial, such as 'The semi-colons in Shakespeare'. Or would you like a whole lecture on his use of the double reflexive? — You know the form,

> Narcissus so himself himself forsook;

or

> Thou of thyself thy sweet self dost deceive.

This usage was rather characteristic of Shakespeare in the early 1590s, and there is something to say about it — would you like me to carry on about it all one afternoon? I prefer to rush on, where the angels fear to tread, and assail a more significant subject. Of the comments on my book many and varied, some sensible, some even laudatory, others wholly idiotic, one that I much value comes from a leading Canadian writer, Hugh MacLennan: 'No learned man should ever overlook (as most of them do) the great merit of the good policeman, who never fails to recognise the importance of the obvious!' Here the policeman is a simple historian, breaking into the sacred enclosure of the 'experts' — in itself sufficiently scandalous; all I can provide is the plain common sense of the historian: I offer you my simplicity.

The first and most obvious thing about Shakespeare is that he was not only a dramatist but also an actor. Shakespeare's work is full of comments on his profession from the inside. These offer an extended criticism of his craft, more to the point than any other dramatist of his age. We may sum it all up in Hamlet's advice to the players on 'the purpose of playing — whose end, both at the first and now, was and is to hold, as 'twere, the mirror up to nature'. And that, we shall see, offers us a clue to his own personality — his naturalness, ease, and spontaneity, his fidelity to nature. Ben Jonson, who knew him well, pays him the tribute we all might envy for ourselves: 'he was indeed honest, and of an open and free nature'. Nothing secretive, or contorted, or inhibited about him: a normal man in his make-up, very much in line with nature, but whose nature was il-lumined by, under the pressure of, the abnormal fact of genius — giving that return upon oneself (the double reflexive), the redoubled awareness, the creative energy that drove him to people a world of imagination before he died, like Balzac, at the age of fifty-two.

Shakespeare seems to have resented the necessity he was under of earning his living by the ungentlemanly profession of acting:

> Alas, 'tis true I have gone here and there,
> And made myself a motley to the view,
> Gored mine own thoughts, sold cheap what is most dear . . .

Then,

> O, for my sake do you with Fortune chide,
> The guilty goddess of my harmful deeds,
> That did not better for my life provide
> Than public means, which public manners breeds.

'Sold cheap what is most dear' — evidently his own thoughts, his poetry, what he cared for most. He would have preferred to be a gentleman and a poet. It is not the first or the last time that a man of genius has kicked against the traces of the necessary vehicle that has carried his genius, given him the best everyday chance of its expression. William Shakespeare was very keen on being regarded as a gentleman — as indeed his carriage of him-self merited in that violent, swaggering age: one of the few among the theatre folk who did not get involved in the broils and fights that frequently ended in manslaughter. And it may be that not even yet have we fully appreciated the tenacity and extent of his literary and poetic ambition. Nevertheless, the last word on his profession is a charitable one — as charity was of the marrow of his nature: the touching reflection on the country bumpkins who get themselves up to perform their play before the gentlefolk, 'the best in this kind are but shadows, and the worst are no worse, if imagination amend them'.

There he is, calling upon the power of charity that resides in, but also depends upon, the imagination.

We observe the effect of his lifelong profession upon his genius — though what is cause and what is effect? — as expressed in his work: the mimetic faculty of getting inside other people's skins, of all sorts and conditions, men and women, doubled in him, in addition to his instinctive perception and sympathy. There is, indeed, a certain double-mindedness — akin to the mirror effects of Leonardo: the capacity to hold contraries in mind at the same time and to state them justly. What more fundamental equipment could there be, as well as a surface grace, for a dramatist?

There was an essential normality in his nature, he was well grafted into life — unlike so many writers, whose genius is bound up with and dependent on their abnormality. (We have only to think, in their varying ways, of Byron or Proust, Whitman or Henry James.)

The world's most lovable writer, we can discern, was a lovable man. Ben Jonson, who was apt to be so difficult — so grumpy and tetchy and critical — put this aside when he thought of his friend: 'for I loved the man, and do honour his memory, on this side idolatry, as much as any'. It is clear that Shakespeare had been good to his junior, Ben, gave him his chance with the Lord Chamberlain's company, and acted in his first comedy for it, *Every Man in His Humour*. In return, after Shakespeare's comparatively early death, Ben Jonson must have helped considerably with the First Folio, to which he prefixed the long biographical poem, which tells us much about Shakespeare — and no writer ever received a more generous tribute from another: 'To the memory of my beloved, the author.'

The charm of Shakespeare's nature in all its variety, its ups and downs, is exposed most fully in the Sonnets, most auto-biographical of works. No time to go into it here, except to mention its salient feature — the modesty of Shakespeare's opinion of himself, contrasted with his confidence in himself as a poet. There is besides the loyalty of his nature, his watchful tenderness for his young patron, his readiness always to set himself aside for another. It is strange, yet perhaps significant, that the world's great writer should have been the least egoistic of men.

He was, and always remained, a countryman, though with the busy and diverse life of a country town to grow up in, on the high road to Wales and the West, not far from Oxford and the highway to London. Stratford was on the threshold of woodland country, the Forest of Arden, from which his people on both sides came. On the other side of the river Avon, one sees from the town the blue sickle-shape extending of the high Cotswolds — marvellous country for coursing the hare. As a young man he was obviously addicted to country sports (quite unlike the intellectual Marlowe) — hunting and coursing, archery and bowls, and with a perfect fixation on hunting the deer. I think there is something in the old and tenacious tradition about his poaching in some deer-park near Stratford. Like a sportsman he had an instinctive sympathy for animal creation, especially for horses and deer, even for the hare he coursed, all except dogs, which he does not seem to have so much liked.

Then there was the background of London at its most exciting — the Armada years, the last years of the Queen, the Essex conspiracy and incoming Scottish James — crowded with crafts and foreign tongues, brilliant with colour, music, pageantry, rancid with the stink of humanity, and the actor-poet had a very sensitive nose. All three of the Shakespeare brothers took the high road to London: the second brother, Gilbert, was a haberdasher there, though as a bachelor he was free to move between London and Stratford. The youngest brother, Edmund, followed his eldest brother into the acting profession and died in Southwark, near the theatres, at only twenty-seven. None of the brothers lived to be old.

William divided his time mostly between London and Stratford; John Aubrey tells us that 'he was wont to go to his native country once a year'.[1] He would not have had the where-withal to maintain two households; in London he lived in lodgings. In his earlier years there he lived in Shoreditch, just outside Bishopsgate, where the early theatres were and the roistering, quarrelling, fighting theatre-folk lived. In a sense, he was not one of them: he passed through this unscarred, but watching, observing it all. Aubrey tells us, 'the more to be ad-mired, *quia* [because] he was not a company-keeper . . . would not be debauched, and if invited to, writ he was in pain'.[2] His plays indicate that he disliked drunkenness. He was evidently a quiet, tactful, prudent man, not one for getting into trouble, intent on his own affairs — and with how much to occupy him: acting, producing, taking his share in the business affairs of the company, touring, writing one and sometimes two plays in a year. No wonder we do not hear of him bumbling about the town!

What we do hear about him, from Aubrey, was that he 'did act exceedingly well; now Ben Jonson was never a good actor, but an excellent instructor'. That is convincing; and the tradi-tion is that Shakespeare acted 'kingly parts' — as he well might with his appearance, as described by Aubrey: 'he was a hand-some, well-shaped man: very good company, and of a very ready and pleasant smooth wit'. We all know quite well what Shakespeare looked like from the one authentic portrait of him, the engraved frontispiece to the First Folio. The whole impres-sion is dominated by that magnificent bald cranium, like an-other dome of St. Paul's — plenty of room there for the most lively (and living), the most universal brain among the Eliza-bethans. It is absolutely convincing. Then there are the arched eyebrows, the large fine eyes that we can see would easily be capable of a wide range of expression, full of intelligence. The nose is large and rather sensual, yet with sensibility indicated in the flare of the nostril — and we know that he had an acute sense of smell. The mouth small and well-formed, with a sug-gestively feminine curve of the lips, almost a Cupid's bow. The well-rounded cheeks suggest the mobile face of an actor, with

[1] John Aubrey, *Brief Lives*, ed. A. Clark, ii. 226.
[2] E. K. Chambers, *William Shakespeare*, ii. 252, which corrects Clark.

easy changes of expression; the face rather hairless, with light moustache and little tuft beneath the lower lip, the hair worn long. What a powerful impression it gives: that searching look of the eyes understanding everything, what a forehead, what a brain!

Such gifts, such capacity, such charm, once they began to achieve the attention and success they merited, were bound to attract the jealousy of the less successful. Shakespeare understood all about jealousy, as he understood every human motive. We remember in *Othello*:

> But jealous souls will not be answered so:
> They are not ever jealous for the cause,
> But jealous for they are jealous.

The moment Shakespeare began to be successful in London — he was spitefully attacked by one of the tribe of literary journalists. Robert Greene, who was dying in want, wrote to warn his fellow-writers against 'the upstart crow beautified with our feathers' — that is, the mere player turned playwright — who 'supposes he is as well able to bombast out a blank verse as the best of you, and, being an absolute Johannes Factotum, is in his own conceit the only Shake-scene in a country'.

We sometimes learn something even from the attacks of our enemies; and it is clear that Shakespeare was a perfect Johannes Factotum, able to turn his hand to anything — not only plays, poems, sonnets, but to acting, producing, taking his part in the business affairs of the company, receiving the proceeds as a shareholder, prudently investing, building up a position as a country gentleman.

But that he resented the attack on him is clear from the apology he exacted from the editor, Henry Chettle, upon whom Shakespeare evidently called. For Chettle, who had not known him before, was afterwards able to say, 'myself have seen his demeanour no less civil than he excellent in the quality he professes', i.e. as an actor. He added, 'besides, divers of worship have reported his uprightness of dealing, which argues his honesty, and his facetious grace in writing, that approves his art'. Everything we hear of Shakespeare from his contemporaries testifies to his 'honesty', which in those days meant honourable character, uprightness — which was far from the case, I need hardly say, with Robert Greene who had attacked him.

This is one of the handsomest testimonials that anyone received in that querulous, biting age. What it indicates is that he kept rather to himself and his own concerns, and that he did not share the life of the literary Bohemia of London: he preferred the company of his social superiors, the cultivated society, with their more refined sensibilities, of the circle around the young Earl of Southampton. However, at the time when he was writing the French scenes of *Henry V*, we know that he was lodging in the house of the Mountjoys, the French tire-makers (or head-dress-makers) to the Queen. We know that he was on terms of confidence with Madame Mountjoy — and that the Mountjoys were no better than they should be. It is fairly clear that Shakespeare lived a double life — more exciting to the imagination, among other things.

His 'sportive blood' had led him to an early hurried marriage, at eighteen, to a country wife eight years older than himself. By the time he was twenty-one he had a wife and three children to support — unlike his contemporary Marlowe, who was still at the university. There had been no university for Shakespeare. When he was a boy of thirteen, the affairs of his father, alderman and bailiff of Stratford, began to go downhill — the father evidently neglected his own affairs for the town's. All this made for family difficulties, for a much harder struggle and longer apprenticeship for the son than has hitherto been realised. When Shakespeare ultimately emerged and found his feet financially, we find that the hard lessons of his youth had not been lost on him: he turned out a good man of business, unlike his father, very prudent about his investments. And need we regret that he did not go to the university? It could hardly have improved him; it might even have spoiled him a little, and made him more of an intellectual, like Marlowe. Shakespeare's university was life, and that mirror of life, the stage.

Nevertheless, he could not be prudent about women: he was extremely responsive, susceptible, inflammable. Unlike any other dramatist in the age, he shared the woman's point of view;

B

like Tolstoy, he knew things about women that only a woman would know. Consider the rewards he reaped from this: his plays offer a marvellous gallery of women's characters; can we remember many female characters from the other dramatists of the age to set beside his? In *Love's Labour's Lost* he tells us what he thought, through the mouth of Berowne, who is something of a self-portrait: that book-learning was little compared with learning from life and love, which

> Courses as swift as thought in every power,
> And gives to every power a double power . . .
> From women's eyes this doctrine I derive;
> They sparkle still the right Promethean fire:
> They are the books, the arts, the academes,
> That show, contain and nourish all the world.

With his extreme susceptibility corroborated by this belief it is the less surprising that he should have been dragged through the mud by his mistress, the dark lady of the Sonnets. It has been said that there is no woman like her in all the sonnet-literature of the Renaissance. Though we do not know who she was, she is a real woman, no feebly idealised Celia, or Caelica, of Idea. This was no romantic affair — no illusions about her; it was a case of sex-infatuation, without illusion on either side:

> O, from what power hast thou this powerful might
> With insufficiency my heart to sway,
> To make me give the lie to my true sight? . . .
> Whence hast thou this becoming of things ill,
> That in the very refuse of thy deeds
> There is such strength and warrantise of skill
> That, in my mind, thy worst all best exceeds?
> Who taught thee how to make me love thee more,
> The more I hear and see just cause of hate?
> O, though I love what others do abhor,
> With others thou shouldst not abhor my state.

No doubt the lady was the social superior of the actor-poet; and we may conclude from this that she not only took it out of him, but also looked down on him and did not disguise it from others.

But Shakespeare knew others for what they were as well as he knew himself:

> For why should others' false adulterate eyes
> Give salutation to my sportive blood?
> Or on my frailties why are frailer spies,
> Which in their wills count bad what I think good?

He gives his own answer:

> 'Tis better to be vile than vile esteemed,
> When not to be receives reproach of being;
> And the just pleasure lost, which is so deemed
> Not by our feeling, but by other's seeing.

That is to say, why live our lives in the light of other people's eyes, instead of in accordance with our own intrinsic feeling? And there follows the magnificent affirmation:

> No, I am that I am, and they that level
> At my abuses reckon up their own.

There's for the fundamental honesty and candour of the man — bearing out in his own words Ben Jonson's tribute to his 'open and free nature'.

But when it came to love, he thought that a man couldn't help himself. It is rather endearing that the world's great dramatist agreed with Hollywood about that. He would hardly have agreed with a quip of mine, in reply to Sir Winston Churchill's deprecation to me of his 'notoriety', 'Just as in the emotion of love there is an element of volition, so in great fame there is an element of merit.'

This feeling of his about love is a part of his general attitude to life — that one must go along with life's flow. If one attempts to hold it up, thwart it, tries to get more out it than one is ready to give, it means a deformation of the spirit. In the end, it cannot be done without ill consequences to oneself and others. This is what is brought home in and to a character such as Angelo in *Measure for Measure*; and it is a part of the wickedness of Iago. I suppose this conviction came from Shakespeare's scepticism about being able to control life at all. In this he stands at the opposite pole from Henry James, who was determined not to live life, not to give hostages to fortune, not to entangle himself with women — marriage he regarded as fatal — all for the sake of his art. The irony is that ultimately the art suffers. There is a coldness at the heart of Henry James in consequence: he sees life too discreetly from the outside, he has never been involved in it, and come through the way of enjoyment, but also suffering, as Shakespeare had. I suppose there was a strong Puritan inheritance in Henry James's nature; Shakespeare was the least Puritan of writers.

Shakespeare was evidently willing to pay the price, as Henry James was not, of going along with life's flow in full enjoyment of it. His affair with the dark lady of the Sonnets evidently gave him as much anguish as ever it did pleasure. Some of the later plays, *Hamlet* and *Troilus and Cressida*, *King Lear* and *Timon of Athens*, betray an obsession with sex and disease, the revulsion of a man who has perhaps had too much and had to pay. The last plays enforce the notes of lost innocence found and restored, of forgiveness for wrongs committed and endured, of repentance and reconciliation. We must not make the mistake of a crude transcription from the plays to the circumstances of their author's life; but neither must we forget that the dramatist is a real writer writing in the real world of his environment and of events. Those notes form the atmosphere and feeling of the last plays, and they coincide with his being much more at Stratford in his last years.

That attitude to love and life goes along with the profound loyalty of Shakespeare's nature, that of a man rooted in life, in family and soil, with its obligations. (If life in London gave him a release, it added to his double vision.) He would have agreed with the view that the solitary man is either a beast or a monster — and there is Timon to point the moral. In *Coriolanus*, along with *Julius Caesar* the most political of his plays, we come upon the telling reflection,

> As if a man were author of himself
> And knew no other kin.

So, throughout his work, as in the conduct of his life, he takes his stand squarely in the norms and obligations of family and society. Stratford, Warwickshire, exert a constant pull upon him. In this also he is exceptional among the theatre-folk of the time.

Wherever they come from, when they make their money in London they invest it in London property. Not so Shakespeare: he invests the bulk of the money he made out of the theatre in property in Stratford. The moment he achieves financial security, and at long last a surplus, what does he do? He buys the best property in the town, New Place, across the way from the grammar-school he attended as a boy. His father had failed to make the grade in applying for a coat of arms. What does the son do? He obtains the grant of a coat of arms — not without telling a tall story about the family descent (but what is the point of having imagination if it cannot be put to use?) — and the grant is made out to the father, so that the son should have been *born* a gentleman.

Actually there was some social disparity between the father, the glover of Stratford, and the mother, Mary Arden, who was probably descended from the old family of Warwickshire gentry of that name. This circumstance usually makes for a sharpened social sensibility in a clever child, nor was it diminished, we may suppose, by the father's set-backs and the son's hard struggle to establish himself. One other thing that the commentators seem to have overlooked is the extent of the resentment expressed in the Sonnets at the cross-blows of fortune, the buffets he had received. Nevertheless, none of this seems to have spoiled his good humour, his good nature, or his neighbourliness. A late reminiscence of his father in his shop credits the merry-cheeked old boy with saying, 'Will was a good honest fellow, but he durst have cracked a jest with him at any time.' The sense of neighbourliness crops up again and again: if you have

> . . . ever been where bells have knolled to church,
> If ever sat at any goodman's feast . . .

Shakespeare appears in neighbour Combe's will at Stratford — £5 for a remembrance. His own will not only remembers his fellows of the King's men — Burbage, Heminges and Condell — but quite a number of his friends: some of them like Hamnet Sadler — after whom his own little boy, who died young, had been called — lifelong acquaintance. Then there are remembrances to some of his gentlemanly friends round about, his sword to Thomas Combe near by, £10 to the poor of the town, lastly 20s. in gold to Henry Walker's little boy, 'my godson, William Walker'. This man of genius, so busy, so hard pressed with work, so crowded with his imaginings, was not above being a neighbourly man.

Neighbourliness, good cheer, good humour: these are recognisable notes of the man. The comic spirit is liable to well up at any moment in his work, even in tragedy, in the cosmic miseries and despairs of *King Lear*, for example — as Dr. Johnson noted with some disapprobation. Nevertheless, the Doctor was the best critic Shakespeare ever had, for he was a man of genius in his own right, on a level with his subject. And Johnson perceived that Shakespeare's natural disposition was for comedy: 'in his comic scenes he seems to produce without labour what no labour can improve. . . . His tragedy seems to be skill, his comedy to be instinct.' I must not turn critic; I confine myself to pointing out how this is borne out of the man in Rosaline's portrait of Berowne, which offers our one self-portrait of the author, laughing at himself:

> a merrier man . . .
> I never spent an hour's talk withal.
> His eye begets occasion for his wit;
> For every object that the one doth catch
> The other turns to a mirth-moving jest,
> Which his fair tongue (conceit's expositor)
> Delivers in such apt and gracious words
> That agèd ears play truant at his tales,
> And younger hearings are quite ravishèd,
> So sweet and voluble is his discourse.

And he goes on to laugh at his well-recognised characteristics — his fondness for women, for bed in both senses of the word, for plenty of sleep and good cheer, not too much study and certainly no fasting.

The inflexion of his tastes may be seen in the kindness with which he treats his comic characters and their foibles, all the way from Lance and his dog at the beginning to Autolycus, rogue and cut-purse, at the end. Again, as with his women, what a marvellous gallery of characters he created for our enjoyment — Dogberry and Verges, constable and headborough, so true to Elizabethan life, Justice Shallow and his crony Silence, Sir Toby Belch and the ninny Aguecheek, Falstaff, the greatest comic creation in our literature. Open Shakespeare's plays where you will and there you have his handwriting, his very signature. Here is Falstaff, who has been dumped in a dirty linen-basket in the Thames and well soused for his sins:

> If I be served such another trick, I'll have my brains ta'en out, and buttered, and give them to a dog for a new year's gift.

Here is Sir Nathaniel the curate apologising to a pedant of a schoolmaster for the dullness of Dull, another constable:

> Sir, he hath never fed of the dainties that are bred in a book; he hath not eat paper, as it were; he hath not drunk ink; his intellect is not replenished; he is only an animal, only sensible in the duller parts.

Shakespeare's high spirits constantly effervescent, bubbling up, the mercurial temperament of an actor and poet, the kindness of his nature, the charm of his disposition, along with his natural courtesy and tact, must have much recommended him to the aristocratic circle of the young Earl of Southampton, who became his patron. To that chance Shakespeare owed so much more than has been realised — not only maintenance and support at the most critical juncture in his life, the plague years of 1592 and 1593, but in the refining of the senses, the increase of social awareness and subtlety, the opportunity to observe high society and the ways of politics and politicians at close quarters, without being committed himself. For him it was the opening out of a world of refinement and culture such as his instinctive tastes, his own nature, yearned for.

His view of society was a profoundly conservative one. It is what one would expect from someone who did not believe in abstractions —

> Hang up philosophy,
> Unless philosophy can make a Juliet! —

who was all concrete observation and common sense as to the facts of human nature (no-one has ever understood human beings better than he, or had a more just picture of humanity);

who combined a sceptical intelligence, seeing through all men's pretences and their humbug, with imagination and poetry. And this makes a better combination for the understanding of politics and society than any amount of ethical illusions, making people out what they are *not* like. He was a natural Aristotelian, not an idealistic Platonist. A sceptical man, a humane man, and also — it hardly needs saying — a very clever man, he well knew how stupid and childish people are when it comes to politics, how violent and cruel, how thin the ice of ordered society is above the primitive passions that lurk beneath. He observed that any upset to the social order only brings about more suffering than before.

In his day England had only just emerged from the wars of the Roses, with all their cruelty and bloodshed, to fall, not long after he was dead, into the worse horror of the Civil War — fighting about what? In his day the contemporary world was divided from top to bottom by ideological conflict — as in ours. In the age of the Counter-Reformation, people were killing each other, burning each other and assassinating each other, over issues and doctrines as to which, in their very nature, there could be no certainty. The efforts of Rome and the Christian Churches to come together again today throw an ironic light on the trouble they took to knife each other in the sixteenth and seventeenth centuries, with the unspeakable wastage of human energy and loss of life. I doubt if that quiet man William Shakespeare thought it was worth while fighting for anything — except, perhaps, against an indisputably evil thing. You remember the wisdom of the boy in *Henry V*, when the braggart Pistol offers him immortal fame before Harfleur:

Would I were in an ale-house in London! I would give all my fame for a pot of ale and safety.

And in the searching discussion as to the rights and wrongs of war that took place between the King in disguise and his men the night before Agincourt, the last word is uttered by an ordinary soldier:

I am afeared there are few die well that die in a battle; for how can they charitably dispose of anything, when blood is their argument?

It has been made a criticism of my book that I have not gone into Shakespeare's religion and philosophy. The truth is that there is not very much to be said about it. His universe was the universe of human beings, his theme universal human nature. You remember that, when Falstaff was dying, the hostess of the Boar's Head said,

'a cried out God, God, God! three or four times. Now I, to comfort him, bid him 'a should not think of God: I hoped there was no need to trouble himself with any such thoughts yet.

This is, of course, a joke; but it may very well stand for William Shakespeare all the same. It is perfectly obvious that he was not interested in dogmas or doctrines; it is equally obvious that he had no use for fanatics on either side, Puritans or Jesuits. He was a middle-of-the-road man, a conformist, ready to take his chance, or not, with the rest. He was baptised and brought up and died, like the great bulk of his countrymen, in the bosom of the Church of England. His plays show that all the services of the Church, but especially the Bible and the Prayer Book version of the Psalms, made a deeper impression on his heart and ear than any other dramatist of his time. That was the way he was brought up. And when he came to his death-bed, his will recites the regular Protestant formula: 'I commend my soul into the hands of God my Creator, hoping and assuredly believing through the only merits of Jesus Christ my Saviour to be made partaker of life everlasting.' There is no reason to suppose that he was an unbeliever, or a Catholic — one thing we can be certain about: he was certainly not a Puritan. But I do not suppose that he was much interested in these issues, there is no evidence that he was: in general his wisdom was acceptance, no point in quarrelling about things one can't be certain about. He clearly did not think that the mystery of life could be boxed up in the compass of a dogma. First and foremost and last a poet, it is likely enough that what he thought about the creatures of his imagination applied to the creatures of this world, for it comes at the end of his life's work, in that valedictory play, *The Tempest*:

> We are such stuff
> As dreams are made on, and our little life
> Is rounded with a sleep.

But it is certain that he had a deeply moral view of life and of the universe. There is no *renversement des valeurs* in him: evil is always evil, cruelty cruelty, wrongdoing is never condoned though, as in life, it does not always receive its proper reward, any more than the ills of life are necessarily requited. The nature of things is what it is; what stands out in Shakespeare, perhaps above all other writers, is his extraordinary, his essential, justice of mind. So characteristic of him as to be another signature is his way of holding the contraries of life together in one statement:

> We, ignorant of ourselves,
> Beg often our own harms, which the wise powers
> Deny us for our good: so we find profit
> By losing of our prayers.

A frequent turn of thought with him is something we find in the experience of each one of us: just as out of good harm may sometimes come, so out of the ills of life something good turns up, or we may attain to good. He sums up what we know to be true:

> The web of our life is of a mingled yarn, good and ill together; our virtues would be proud if our faults whipped them not; and our crimes would despair if they were not cherished by our own virtues.

It is clear that what he hated most was cruelty, and perhaps next to that ingratitude, any sort of stonyheartedness, that obdurate quality that freezes the flow of feeling in man's heart:

> I hate ingratitude more in a man
> Than lying vainness, babbling drunkenness,
> Or any taint of vice whose strong corruption
> Inhabits our frail blood.

I fear he must have had experience of it.

I have said nothing by way of criticism of him. Heaven forfend that I should be a critic. (I remember too well the fierce disclaimer of the greatest Latin scholar of our time, A. E. Housman, of any title to be regarded as a literary critic: he had too high an opinion of the real thing, the rarest of literary *genres*.) Any fool can criticise; but can he do the job? The world is full of people standing on the side-lines, offering their invaluable advice; but can they run a railway and create a great institution, manage a bank or a factory, or govern a country; can they paint the picture they talk so glibly about, or even write the book? The criticism of Shakespeare made by the two Jo(h)nsons — Ben and the Doctor — is worth attending to, for they were men of genius who had proved themselves in their own work. What they said boils down to this, that he was insufficiently critical and that he wrote too fast. I dare say he did, for the pressure upon him was so great — both the internal pressure of his creative energy as well as the external demands upon him — that we can see the next play sometimes forming in his mind before the one in hand was properly finished. Dr. Johnson said that 'he sacrifices virtue to convenience, and is so much more careful to please than to instruct, that he seems to write without any moral purpose. . . . It may be observed that in many of the plays the latter part is evidently neglected. When he found himself near the end of his work and in view of his reward, he shortened the labour to snatch the profit.'

There were many pressures upon him in his so busy, crowded, hard-working life — unlike that of the lazy Doctor. And the Doctor may not have perceived that there were advantages also that accrued from the speed at which he worked — the generation of ideas that comes from working at pressure, the proliferation of poetic images that run from one into the other with the ink not yet dry on the paper. Never was there a writer with whom the sub-conscious worked night and day so powerfully for him: *there* is the ultimate reward, for a writer, of giving oneself to life and following its flow.

At heart was the world of fact and dream that nourished his imagination, the layers of the unconscious from which all artistic creation springs. What the world saw was the exterior: the Stratford boy who went to London and made good, the man of the theatre who became the gentleman of New Place, 'our countryman Master Shakespeare', as neighbour Sturley and neighbour Quiney write. The family he hoped to found in his name was shorn of its hope by the death of his only boy, Hamnet. In the play he was writing at the time we find:

> Grief fills the room up of my absent child,
> Lies in his bed, walks up and down with me,
> Puts on his pretty looks, repeats his words,
> Remembers me of all his gracious parts,
> Stuffs out his vacant garments with his form . . .

His elder daughter Susanna inherited something of his spirit and wit; Judith's little boy, Shakespeare Quiney, died young. There remained only a granddaughter Elizabeth, whose husband became a baronet and she Lady Barnard; she died, leaving money to her grandmother's family, the Hathaways, and he leaving to his family all the books and pictures, 'old goods and lumber at Stratford-upon-Avon'. What would we not give, if only it had survived, to have it here!

Nothing in the ordinary family way was able to perpetuate his name. Today the whole world is full of his name. For him there are no Iron Curtains — he penetrates through them all, with his profound and loving observation of humanity, the greatest of writers in our speech. Yet it is all understandable enough as we think of him today — rooted in normal family life, having experienced its trials, shared to the full its joys and sorrows — there in the church at Stratford where he was baptised and brought up all the days of his youth, buried with his family alongside of him within the sanctuary before the altar, and all round the wreaths from all over the world.

# THE PROBLEM OF SHAKESPEARE'S
# SONNETS SOLVED

Fie upon him! He will discredit our mystery.
Abhorson the executioner, *Measure for Measure*.

## I

THE questions relative to Shakespeare's Sonnets have been
blown up into the greatest problem in our literature. This is a
comparatively recent phenomenon, going back only to the senti-
mentalism of the later Victorians and so on into this century.
The question of the Sonnets did not much disturb the mind of
the sensible eighteenth century — Edmund Malone, for example. But the amount of rubbish written since on this subject
is hardly believable — I mean, by reputable Shakespearean
scholars, for I am not wasting time on the lunatics and crack-
pots. By the injudicious use of anagrams and acrostics, along
with much misdirected ingenuity, one can arrive at anything.
You remember Ronald Knox's plausible demonstration that
Tennyson's *In Memoriam* was written by Queen Victoria in
memory of the Prince Consort, and that Alfred Tennyson was
in fact Queen Victoria.

Much of what has been written even by Shakespearean
'experts' is on the same level. What is wanting is a little of the
historian's plain common sense — provided that he is intimately
familiar with the Elizabethan age, its everyday circumstances,
social conditions and usages; otherwise one's opinion on these
matters is not of much value. And this applies to most people:
a consideration that saves one time and energy. However, they
can use their common sense, of more use than any amount of
misdirected ingenuity.

For the first psychological consideration is perfectly simple,
yet of decisive importance. Shakespeare never wrote the Sonnets to create a puzzle at all: he wrote them directly and
straightforwardly for another person. The subject of the Sonnets

is that of his relations with that person, the young man and, hardly less important, with the Dark Lady, Shakespeare's mistress.

So the solution to the problem that has been created should be equally simple, straightforward and obvious. As, in fact, it is.

The second point is that there are *two* inspirers of the Sonnets: the young man and Shakespeare's mistress. So the phrase, 'the only begetter', which has been sentimentalised *ad nauseam*, cannot possibly mean 'the only inspirer', for there were two — one cannot omit the lady: she is almost as important in the story as the young man. The phrase, in any case, is not Shakespeare's; for the dedication is the publisher's, Thomas Thorpe's, who was somewhat effusively grateful to the one and only person who got the manuscript for him, instead of having to collect the Sonnets from here, there and everywhere. That is what the phrase means. Thorpe had reason to be grateful to Mr. W. H., who had got the manuscript for him; for in Elizabethan days the publisher who obtained a manuscript by publishing it might claim the copyright.

No wonder Thorpe was somewhat effusive, his dedication a little clumsily inflated and over-written. We, too, have reason to be grateful to him: without him should we have had the Sonnets?

Nearly all the trouble has arisen from Thorpe's dedication. It is this that has muddled people up, led them along false scents, created a needless mystery. They have for the most part been looking, quite mistakenly, for a Mr. W. H. as the inspirer of the Sonnets, instead of the only person who had got the manuscripts. If you search for a needle in a haystack, you naturally emerge with hayseeds in your hair; if you insist on looking for a mare's nest, you are quite likely to find one.

Alas, there is perhaps nothing surprising in this though it is very boring. For, as a great scholar, A. E. Housman, knew well: 'Now to detect a *non sequitur*, unless it leads to an unwelcome conclusion, is as much beyond the power of the average reader as it is beyond the power of the average writer to attach ideas to his own words when those words are terms of textual criticism.' In other words, most people are incapable of thinking, strictly speaking; they merely think what they want to think. As Housman says, men's opinions are not determined by their reason, but by their passions, and 'the faintest of all human passions is the love of truth'.

Now it is perfectly possible to make Thorpe's dedication clear to you, and to explain every phrase in it, as I propose to do be-before I have finished. For the moment, keep in your mind that but for the dedication there would be no problem (except for the identity of the mistress); that all the trouble has arisen from mistakenly looking for a Mr. W. H. as the inspirer of the Sonnets. This is a fool's errand; to follow this track, as so many have done, is the cause of the trouble. It is these people who have created the problem for us to clear up.

An indispensable condition to answering the questions posed by the Sonnets is to settle their dating. Where would you expect an historian, an Elizabethan historian, to help you more authoritatively than in matters of dating? A leading American textual scholar, Hyder Rollins, in his *New Variorum* edition, tells us: 'the question when the sonnets were written is in many respects the most important of all the unanswerable [*sic*] questions they pose. If it could be answered definitely and finally, there might be some chance of establishing to general satisfaction the identity of the friend, the dark woman, the rival poet (supposing that all were real individuals), of deciding what contemporary sources Shakespeare did or did not use, and even of determining whether the order of the Quarto is the author's or not. In the past and at present such a solution has been and remains an idle dream.'

There is no reason whatever for such defeatism; as we have seen, it is not in the least likely that Shakespeare, in writing the Sonnets, intended to pose unanswerable questions. Moreover, such defeatism is undiscriminating. This eminent scholar has not seen the elementary distinction to be drawn between the dark woman, as to whom we have no external evidence whatever, of whom we know nothing except what is internal to Shakespeare's work, and, on the other hand, both the young friend and the rival poet, with regard to whom there is not only what Shakespeare tells us within his work but a mass of converging evidence from outside.

You see the difference? Hyder Rollins did not. There is

every chance of achieving fair certainty with regard to the young friend and the rival poet; there is none whatever with regard to the dark woman, Shakespeare's mistress. There is no chance whatever of establishing the identity of this woman until one finds some point of junction with the external world, some external evidence. With regard to her all is internal and sub-jective. And yet Shakespearean scholars as well as, of course, the general public go careering off in pursuit of this will-o'-the-wisp.

To mix all three up and think they are on a comparable level, when they are not *in pari materia*, is intellectually confused. We *can* discover who the young friend and the rival poet are; as things are, and as they are likely to remain, we can *not* discover who Shakespeare's mistress was. Stupid to mix them up.

It is with me, *mutatis mutandis*, as it was with Housman: 'if you suppose yourself able to distinguish a true reading from a false one . . . they are aghast at your assurance. I am aghast at theirs: at the assurance of men who do not even imagine themselves to be critics, and yet presume to meddle with criticism. . . . It may be asked whether I think that I myself possess this outfit, or even most of it; and if I answer yes, that will be a new example of my notorious arrogance. I had rather be arrogant than impudent.'

Very well: you would expect an historian to know about dat-ing, and an Elizabethan historian — one who has spent his whole working life in that age — to be able to read the topical references to contemporary events incorporated in the Sonnets, more dependably than anyone else.

In fact, there is no real difficulty in dating the Sonnets at all. Everything — the topical references, the parallelism with *Venus and Adonis* and *The Rape of Lucrece*, the affiliations with the plays of those years, the circumstances of the time and of Shakespeare's life — everything points with entire consistency to the years 1592–5 being the years when the Sonnets were written. And this consistency holding all the evidence together cannot at any point be faulted.

## II

We should start from the consideration of overwhelming importance — the objective, public, acknowledged fact — that Shakespeare's one and only literary patron was the young Earl of Southampton. There wasn't anyone else: as Shakespeare tells us in Sonnet 105:

> Since all alike my songs and praises be
> To one, of one, still such, and ever so.

We all know that Shakespeare dedicated *Venus and Adonis* to Southampton in 1593: it would have been written therefore in 1592–3.

Right Honourable, I know not how I shall offend in dedicating my unpolished lines to your lordship, nor how the world will censure me for choosing so strong a prop to support so weak a burden; only if your Honour seem but pleased, I account myself highly praised, and vow to take advantage of all idle hours till I have honoured you with some graver labour. But if the first heir of my invention prove deformed, I shall be sorry it had so noble a god-father, and never after ear so barren a land, for fear it yield me still so bad a harvest. I leave it to your honourable survey and your Honour to your heart's content, which I wish may always answer your own wish and the world's hopeful expectation. Your Honour's in all duty, William Shakespeare.

Notice the phrase 'in all duty': Southampton is the poet's patron; Shakespeare is his accepted poet, in Elizabethan terms, the Earl's servant — though not a household servant like John Florio, who was Southampton's Italian tutor. The difference of status is revealingly reflected in the different tone of Florio's dedication of his *World of Words* to Southampton. Shakespeare was independent as an actor, while his insistence on being regarded as a gentleman — which his bearing and conduct of himself well merited — gave him the status from which to talk to the young Earl on terms of an essential equality. Even today, when everything is falling all round us, we know that a gentleman talks to a peer on terms of social equality, for all the difference of external title.

These social subtleties are important to grasping the subtlety

C

of the relationship, as indeed a knowledge of Elizabethan society, social inflections and usages, is indispensable. If you do not have it, you do not know and cannot judge.

Many literary scholars have, however, observed the close parallel between the dedication of *Venus and Adonis* to Southampton and Sonnet 26, the envoi to the first section of the Sonnets persuading the young man to do his duty by his house, marry and carry on the line:

> Lord of my love, to whom in vassalage
> Thy merit hath my duty strongly knit,
> To thee I send this written ambassage
> To witness duty, not to show my wit,
> Duty so great . . .

Duty thrice emphasised, as in the dedications of *Venus and Adonis* and *The Rape of Lucrece*: the Sonnets were written for the obvious person, the young patron, as those poems were.

And indeed the element of duty in the Sonnets has been hitherto not appreciated, obvious enough as it is. This is the meaning of such Sonnets as 57, this is the situation, one element in the relationship:

> Being your slave, what should I do but tend
> Upon the hours and times of your desire?
> I have no precious time at all to spend,
> Nor services to do, till you require.
> Nor dare I chide the world-without-end hour
> Whilst I, my sovereign, watch the clock for you
> When you have bid your servant once adieu.

The situation is perfectly recognisable, to anyone with any social, or even human, perception. The situation of a dependent is made clearer still in the next Sonnet:

> That God forbid, that made me first your slave,
> I should in thought control your times of pleasure
> Or at your hand the account of hours to crave,
> Being your vassal, bound to stay your leisure.
> O let me suffer, being at your beck,
> The imprisoned absence of your liberty,
> And patience tame to sufferance, bide each check,
> Without accusing you of injury . . .

Have you never heard of being at someone else's 'beck and call'? It is a dependent relation, that of someone in some senses dependent on another.

It is generally agreed that the information going back to Sir William Davenant, who was in a position to know, that 'my lord Southampton at one time gave' Shakespeare a good sum 'to go through with a purchase which he had a mind to', refers to Shakespeare's being enabled to purchase a share in the Lord Chamberlain's company on its formation in 1594. That gave him financial security at last; thenceforward he never looked back. Come to Sonnet 117, towards the end of the Southampton sequence and we find:

> Accuse me thus — that I have scanted all
> Wherein I should your great deserts repay,
> Forgot upon your dearest love to call,
> Whereto all bonds do tie me day by day;
> That I have frequent been with unknown minds,
> And given to time your own dear-purchased right . . .

With the last sonnets in the sequence we find Shakespeare summing up the relationship.

> If my dear love were but the child of state,
> It might for fortune's bastard be unfathered
> As subject to time's love or to time's hate . . .
> No, it was builded far from accident . . .

Shakespeare is saying that his devotion to his young patron is not a matter of calculated policy, it does not depend on accident, varying with time and circumstance. In the next he says, summing up:

> Were't aught to me I bore the canopy,
> With my extern the outward honouring . . .?

Meaning, were it anything to me that I bore the canopy over you, with my exterior honouring the outward man? He goes on to say that there were plenty of others in such situations who were mere hangers-on.

> No, let me be obsequious in thy heart,
> And take thou my oblation, poor but free,
> Which is not mixed with seconds, knows no art
> But mutual render, only me for thee.

In the end Shakespeare asserts an inherent equality. Why assert it, if it were not for the obvious external difference of social status? — that difference, that 'separable spite' which had led Shakespeare at one point, when he felt that his name had been spotted, to say:

> I may not evermore acknowledge thee,
> Lest my bewailèd guilt should do thee shame,
> Nor thou with public kindness honour me,
> Unless thou take that honour from thy name.

After all, the young man was a peer, head of his house, bearer of a well-known name. Anyone of any judgment can see that the reference to bearing the canopy is figurative; but what it figures is that the young man was a person of state, as the young Earl was, no ordinary gentleman.

In the year 1594 Shakespeare dedicated to him his promised 'graver labour', *The Rape of Lucrece*, written therefore 1593-4.

The love I dedicate to your Lordship is without end: whereof this pamphlet without beginning is but a superfluous moiety. The warrant I have of your honourable disposition, not the worth of my untutored lines, makes it assured of acceptance. What I have done is yours, what I have to do is yours, being part in all I have, devoted yours.

[Recall the lines from the Sonnets:

> Since all alike my songs and praises be
> To one, of one, still such, and ever so.]

The dedication continues:

Were my worth greater my duty would show greater; meantime, as it is, it is bound to your Lordship: to whom I wish long life still lengthened with all happiness. Your Lordship's in all duty, William Shakespeare.

Most persons of sensibility have observed the increase of warmth and expressed affection between the dedication of *Venus and Adonis* in 1593 and that of *The Rape of Lucrece* in 1594. Sir Edmund Chambers declared himself unable to perceive it. I have been called over the coals for calling him 'the most massive, though not the most perceptive of Shakespearean scholars'. This carefully considered description is precisely right: Chambers was the most massive of Shakespearean scholars, and he was *not* the most perceptive. We all have the deepest reason to be grateful for the marvellous amount of work this great scholar accomplished in his life, all the more when we reflect that it was done in his spare time from his life-long occupation as a civil servant. But that is no reason for not getting him right.

The earlier Sonnets parallel *Venus and Adonis*, as the Sonnets about the dark woman parallel *The Rape of Lucrece*. The earlier have the sparkle, the vivacity, the dewy freshness, the sunny imagery of *Venus and Adonis*; the Sonnets about the mistress have the sombre, guilt-laden atmosphere, the psychological disturbance of the graver poem. The language, the images, the sensations are closely parallel. If some are impressed by the difference between the sonnets to the young man and those to the mistress, the contrast is no greater, is in fact less, than that between *Venus and Adonis* and *The Rape of Lucrece*. Within the Sonnets there is no greater spread, for some of the sonnets about the young friend are close in nature and expression to those about the mistress. It is all a question of decorum, of which Shakespeare was a master, of the difference proper to subject, and does not indicate any wide spread in dating. For the Sonnets belong all together to the same period, and tell their story coherently, consistently, intelligibly, as they are — as against the many otiose and absurd attempts to rearrange, disarrange and de-range them.

The dating of the Sonnets to 1592 and the following years, already clear from their close relationship to the two Southampton poems, is corroborated and consistently borne out by the historian's reading of the topical references they contain. As early as Sonnet 25 what do we find?

> Great princes' favourites their fair leaves spread
> But as the marigold at the sun's eye,
> And in themselves their pride lies burièd,
> For at a frown they in their glory die.
> The painful warrior famousèd for fight,
> After a thousand victories once foiled,
> Is from the book of honour razèd quite,
> And all the rest forgot for which he toiled.

This is a plain reference to the fall of Ralegh, which was the sensation of the summer of 1592. There are Ralegh's recognisable characteristics: the famous warrior who was no less well known for his industry — 'he can toil terribly', said Sir Robert Cecil of him; there is Ralegh's situation, almost in his own well-known phrase, 'once amiss hath bereaved me of all'. His seduction of, and secret marriage to, Elizabeth Throckmorton, one of the Queen's maids-of-honour, earned him his immediate loss of favour, imprisonment in the Tower, dismissal —

For at a frown they in their glory die.

Towards the end of the Southampton sequence, with Sonnet 107, we come to the most celebrated crux of all in dating the Sonnets:

The mortal moon hath her eclipsed endured,
And the sad augurs mock their own presage;
Incertainties now crown themselves assured,
And peace proclaims olives of endless age.

Notice that there are *two* references to contemporary events in those four lines. Those two references, converging upon one point, give certainty; they must coincide upon one date. To take the second — 'peace proclaims olives of endless age': this refers to the peace achieved in France, after the long religious wars, with the capitulation of Paris to Henri IV in March 1594; this gave hope of a lasting peace in France and the end of the war with Spain. 'The mortal moon' — all Elizabethan scholars of any judgment know that this phrase always refers to the Queen. (Samuel Butler thought that it referred to the Spanish Armada; but he was not an Elizabethan scholar of any judgment, but an original and eccentric writer, of great oddity, who thought that the *Odyssey* was written by a woman.) Elizabethan scholars know that the Queen is always the mortal moon, the terrene or terrestrial moon, Cynthia, goddess of the moon, a chaste deity. She has endured, i.e. come through and survived, a threat to her. In those months her personal physician, Dr. Lopez, was charged with being in correspondence with Spain with the intention of poisoning her. The Queen did not believe him guilty, but he could not establish his innocence, and

Southampton's admired leader, Essex, made the issue a personal one. Lopez was condemned to death on the last day of February 1594. We observe that these two topical references converge upon one date, and give us certainty. 'This most balmy time' is the spring of 1594.

This perfectly consistent dating is corroborated at the end of the Southampton sequence by Sonnet 124, with which Shakespeare sums up the relationship and the nature of his love: it does not fall

> Under the blow of thrallèd discontent
> Whereto the inviting time our fashion calls:
> If fears not policy, that heretic,
> Which works on leases of short-numbered hours,
> But all alone stand hugely politic . . .
> To this I witness call the fools of time,
> Which die for goodness who have lived for cime.

Anyone can see that the phrases of this sonnet are politico-religious; it refers to the government's campaign against the Jesuits and seminary priests, which reached a height at this time, 1594–5, with the executions of such noted Jesuits as Robert Southwell and Henry Walpole, or, among lesser known, Father John Cornelius, with whose case Ralegh was concerned. The position of the Catholics, in 'thrallèd discontent', was that these men were martyrs for religion; the government's was that they were traitors operating against the laws of the state in time of war. This is the meaning of the phrase,

> the fools of time,
> Which die for goodness who have lived for cime.

It is to be expected that Shakespeare, always a conformist, would share the point of view of the country in general in the matter. The date is 1594–5, and that is the terminus of the Southampton sequence, and of the Sonnets; for Sonnets 127–54, dealing mainly with the mistress, come within the Southampton sequence in point of time and belong, as we shall see, mainly to 1593–4. But there is no point in rearranging them: impossible in any case to insert them, and since they have a different subject and inflexion, they are best off where they are — intelligible there.

So now we have the dating for the Sonnets, a coherent dating, consistent at every point, yielding an intelligible story, borne out further by the plays of just this period.

What about the nature of the relationship with the young friend, of the poet's expressed love for him?

A number of people have entertained the idea that it was homosexual in character. Oscar Wilde, who might have been expected to hold this view, invented a William Hughes, who never existed — looking fatuously, as usual, for a Mr. W. H. as inspirer of the Sonnets — as the object of Shakespeare's affection. All this, like so much else on the subject, is mere rubbish. Everything shows that Shakespeare was, for an Englishman, more than normally interested in women. The Sonnets themselves reveal him as infatuated with his mistress: without any illusions about her, or himself, he cannot free himself from his fixation: it is a case of sheer sex-infatuation.

His feelings for the young man are quite different: they are not physical but ideal. If any one has any doubt in the matter, Shakespeare has taken the trouble to be quite specific about it, early on, in Sonnet 20. The young man is described as ambivalent, rather narcissistic, adolescent, not yet sexually directed: he is rather feminine to look at, with something of a woman's beauty, appealing to both sexes. (The Renaissance, unlike us, regarded this as doubly appealing: witness the French court-poetry directed to Henri III.)

> And for a woman wert thou first created,
> Till Nature, as she wrought thee, fell a-doting,
> And by addition me of thee defeated,
> By adding one thing to my purpose nothing.

It is perfectly clear what that means: the youth possesses something that Shakespeare is not interested in, and it is this that defeats him: if only the youth were a woman! Shakespeare was perfectly normal sexually, very much one for the women. If the situation still isn't clear to anybody, he makes it doubly so with his bawdy concluding couplet:

> But since she pricked thee out for women's pleasure,
> Mine by thy love, and thy love's use their treasure.

That is to say, they can use you, they can have you, provided I have your love—which, everything shows, was a platonic one.

What has given some intelligent people genuine difficulty is the warmth of Shakespeare's language, the flowery expression of his 'love', where we should say 'affection'. Two friends of mine, two of the cleverest men in England, disagreed with my view on this point; they felt that the Sonnets had a homosexual element in their feeling for the young man. I shouldn't in the least mind if it were so; but in fact it is not. Both these clever men are modernists, and were judging the issue as if the language of the Sonnets were that of today. But they were written four hundred years ago, under the Renaissance impulse, when people expressed themselves in very flowery language. My friends wouldn't know, for example, that the Court-language that surrounded Elizabeth I was the language of love — Ralegh himself, who wrote in it, afterwards protested that it went too far and went on too long. One has to have an historical sense, an acute sensitivity to time and place, to get these things right. My friends were wrong, and they have come round.

What adds subtlety to the matter is that the young friend was clearly ambivalent: he wouldn't have minded.

This is precisely the known personality of Shakespeare's patron, the young Earl. In 1592 he was eighteen, the head of his house and its only male representative: it was his duty to marry and carry on the line. His father had died at the age of eight:

> dear my love, you know
> You had a father: let your son say so.

This was precisely what the youth would not do. A great deal of pressure was put on him in these years by his guardian, the great Lord Burghley, who expected him to marry one of his granddaughters: but he would not and did not, and eventually was made to pay for it. A number of people were brought in to incline him to marriage, his grandfather, Lord Montagu, among others. His charming mother, the Countess, was very anxious to see him safely married:

> Thou art thy mother's glass, and she in thee
> Calls back the lovely April of her prime.

We must not exclude the possibility of the Countess herself encouraging the poet as part of her campaign to incline her son to marriage, for that is the theme of the first section of the Sonnets. When the youth becomes entangled with Shakespeare's mistress — the poet blames himself for having got his young lord to write to her on his behalf — Shakespeare reproaches him for wilfully enjoying what he refuses to undertake in lawful union:

> But yet be blamed, if thou this self deceivest
> By wilful taste of what thyself refusest.

This was probably his first experience of relations with a woman; I suspect that Shakespeare was unduly worried as to the effect on the youth, who was far less likely to succumb to an infatuation for the Dark Lady than the so susceptible poet, unable to help himself where women were concerned. With Southampton, naturally, not so — but there is an unmistakably tutorial element in the Sonnets towards the fatherless young peer, exposed as he was to every sort of temptation, now coming out into the world of the Court and society —

> Thou that art now the world's fresh ornament.

Southampton had two characteristic ambitions: he wanted to shine in action, to serve in the war though he was as yet too young, and to shine as patron of the arts. In the end he became the most frequently painted of all men of the age; there are more portraits of him that survive. He was very much of a target for patronage on the part of the needy writers of the time; many poems, many works altogether are dedicated to him. There is an aesthetic propriety in that he should have been the one and only acknowledged patron of Shakespeare. He was generous and affectionate, intelligent and well educated; he was courageous and loyal, ready to risk his life for his friend, Essex. He had a charming nature, came later on to be a much respected and trusted figure, and was always popular. Brought up a Catholic, his religion did not mean very much to him, any more than it did to Shakespeare; at James I's accession he conformed and prospered. Shakespeare was always one to conform.

This youth of eighteen to nineteen in 1592–3 is the 'rose-cheeked Adonis' of *Venus and Adonis* — the beautiful adolescent who will not yet respond to the love of a woman. Venus argues with the reluctant Adonis:

> Art thou a woman's son and canst not feel
> What 'tis to love, how want of love tormenteth?

As Shakespeare argues with his young patron in the Sonnets:

> And when a woman woos, what woman's son
> Will sourly leave her till he have prevailed?

This is the theme both of *Venus and Adonis* and of the earlier Sonnets — the Southampton theme. It is glanced at at the beginning of *A Midsummer Night's Dream* in 1594, since Southampton continued to refuse to marry:

> To live a barren sister all your life,
> Chanting faint hymns to the cold fruitless moon . . .
> But earthlier happy is the rose distilled,
> Than that which withering on the virgin thorn
> Grows, lives and dies in single blessedness.

The image of the flower distilling its essence to some purpose had been developed at greater length in Sonnet 5. The Southampton theme appears in another form as the point of departure of *Love's Labour's Lost*: the young courtiers who are led by their leader, Navarre, to abjure the society of women and give themselves up to books and study for some three years. This play offers a skit on the circle and its acquaintance by its poet, who found it a congenial subject to make fun of.

*A Midsummer Night's Dream, Love's Labour's Lost, Romeo and Juliet,* are all connected in their various ways with the Southampton circle, as the language of these plays, style, images, phrases and, in the case of *Love's Labour's Lost*, the prominence of the sonnet-form, connect them with the Sonnets.

*A Midsummer Night's Dream* was performed, we can now say, at the private marriage of the widowed Countess of Southampton with the elderly Sir Thomas Heneage on 2 May 1594. *Love's Labour's Lost* belongs to the same period, and that it had a personal significance for Southampton may be inferred from the fact that when he entertained James I at Southampton House in 1605 he chose to revive it for performance there — where no doubt it had been originally performed. The connection of *Romeo and Juliet* with Southampton is no less clear. His friends, the Danvers brothers — the younger, Sir Henry, was a particular friend — were involved in a feud with their Wiltshire neighbours, the Longs. This culminated on 6 October 1594 in the killing of Henry Long at Corsham by the Danverses. Southampton helped them to make their getaway to France; when the sheriff of Southampton was crossing Itchen Ferry to investigate the affair, he was threatened by Southampton's servants, one of them 'Signor Florio, an Italian'. How all these things come together! For his next play the dramatist of the circle, the Earl's poet, looked up a story placing the familiar theme of love in a new setting of family feud, duelling and death.

We must conclude that *everything* connects Shakespeare with his patron, Southampton, and with no other.

Then why have some people had such difficulty in recognising the obvious?

Simply because, not understanding Thorpe's dedication, they have been trying to find a Mr. W. H. as the inspirer of the Sonnets — a hopeless misconception. Let me repeat 'the only begetter' cannot mean 'the only inspirer', for there were *two* inspirers — the young patron and the Dark Lady, Shakespeare's mistress. We are now in a position to make clear Thorpe's dedication, which has been responsible for the misconception.

To the only begetter of
these ensuing sonnets
Mr W. H. all happiness
and that eternity
promised
by
our ever-living poet
wisheth
the well-wishing
adventurer in
setting
forth

T. T.

1. 'The only begetter.' The word 'beget' *could* be used in Elizabethan English for 'get', as in *Hamlet*: 'You must acquire and beget a temperance.' 'The only begetter' means the one

and only person who had got the manuscripts, instead of having to collect them from here, there and everywhere. They were evidently all together in one *cache*.

2. 'Mr W. H.' Mr is, of course, short for 'Master'. It was common form in the Elizabethan age to refer to a knight as Master; you could never refer to a lord as Master. The Countess of Southampton in her letters usually refers to her second husband, Sir Thomas Heneage, as Master Heneage: less pompous, more familiar, while still respectful.

3. The Countess married as her third husband a much younger man, Sir William Harvey. She died in 1607, leaving him all her household goods and chattels. In 1608 Sir William Harvey married a young wife: this is why Thorpe, in 1609, is wishing him 'all happiness and that eternity promised by our ever-living poet'. Notice that 'that eternity' is in apposition: Thorpe is wishing Harvey all happiness on his marriage and that eternity which Shakespeare had promised that other young man, years before, if only he would marry and carry on his line to perpetuity.

4. 'Wisheth the well-wishing adventurer in setting forth, T. T.' This refers to the immense enthusiasm in London in this year, 1609, for the colonisation of Virginia. It was the year of the second Charter, and almost everybody who was anybody was subscribing to the Virginia Company, i.e. becoming an adventurer in setting forth. You see that Thorpe's language is a little high-flown and inflated — one cause of the trouble. Southampton was one of the leading figures in the Virginia Company; it became one of his main interests in the later part of his life. Southampton hundred in Virginia was named after him.

We repeat: *everything* connects Shakespeare with his young and generous patron, Southampton, in the earlier, formative part of his career and work. There is nothing to connect him with the Herberts except a possible but shadowy connection with Pembroke's company before Southampton became his patron in 1592. The Pembroke who was the patron of that company was the second Earl, who died in 1601. It is his son, the third Earl, whom a minority of scholars have sought to

create the addressee of the Sonnets — under the double misconception that 'the only begetter' means inspirer, when there
were two inspirers, and that you could address a lord as 'Mr
W. H.'. You *could* address a knight as 'Mr.' — it was common
form; a lord would have had to be 'W. Lord H' or 'Lord W. H.'.

Young William, Lord Herbert, born in April 1580, was aged
twelve in 1592. Now one does not address sonnets like that to a
boy of twelve, urging him to marry at once and carry on the line.
To suppose so is absolute nonsense. And, for another thing: the
young man of the Sonnets was ambivalent, a rather feminine
youth, as Southampton was known to be. Young Herbert was
always a roaring heterosexual, very keen on the girls. Really,
besides sound scholarship, the professors need some knowledge
of the facts of life. It is no use trying to understand the goings-on
of Renaissance Court and aristocratic life from a background of
middle-class respectability.

When Heminges and Condell produced the First Folio in
1623, seven years after Shakespeare's death, they dedicated it,
most appropriately, to the third Earl of Pembroke and his
brother Philip, Earl of Montgomery. For Pembroke was the
Lord Chamberlain at the time, from 1615 to 1626, and as such
the person chiefly responsible for the conduct of the theatre, in a
special relationship to the King's men, who had been the
Chamberlain's men, among whom Shakespeare was a leading
actor and their dramatist from their formation in 1594. Philip,
Earl of Montgomery, succeeded his brother as Lord Chamberlain, 1626–41. Both brothers were devoted to the theatre and
were especially connected, later on in James's reign, with the
King's men.[1] It is not surprising that they appreciated Shakespeare's plays and 'prosecuted both them, and their author

[1] We know how devoted Pembroke was to Burbage, in particular, from his
letter shortly after Burbage's death on 20 May 1619, saying that after a grand
supper to the French ambassador the company had gone on to a play, 'which I, being
tender-hearted, could not endure to see so soon after the loss of my old acquaintance, Burbage'. (See E. K. Chambers, *The Elizabethan Stage*, ii. 308.) This disposes
of Miss C. V. Wedgwood's consideration in favour of the nonsensical identification
of Mr. W. H. with William Hatcliffe or Hatlive, Prince of Purpoole, etc., to the
effect that a poet could not be on such terms with a peer as Shakespeare was with
Southampton. If Burbage, who was doubtfully a gentleman, could be on such
terms with Pembroke *a fortiori* Shakespeare, who insisted on his gentility, could be
with Southampton. The social consideration was that a gentleman could be accepted
on some terms of social equality by a peer.

living, with so much favour'. But this was years later from the early 1590s and Shakespeare's formative association with Southampton.

There is no reason whatever for supposing that the Sonnets were written for anyone other than the obvious person, Shakespeare's young patron. In the realm of nonsense there are no comparatives, and nonsense is self-proliferating; it is also endless. It is no worse nonsense to say that the Sonnets were written for a William Hughes, who never existed, or a William Hatcliffe, or Hatlive, Prince of Purpoole, or William Hart the hatter, or the Mad Hatter, than to say that they were written for William, Lord Herbert. For all these superfluous suggestions are equally nonsense, when we know with as much certainty as we know most things, for whom the Sonnets were written. The fact that a great many people have made fools of themselves over this need not surprise, or detain, us; for that is but the normal condition of humanity, as Housman well knew, where anything to do with thinking is concerned.

### III

However, it is only fair to say that the great bulk of literary scholars have always held, sensibly, that the young man of the Sonnets was the obvious person, Shakespeare's patron. What I have been able to do is to make this absolutely certain by making firm the dating of the Sonnets, interpreting their topical references to contemporary events and showing how completely consistent and intelligible a story they tell as they are.

It is also fair to say that the bulk of literary scholars have held that the rival poet of the Sonnets could only have been Marlowe.

Here, too, the Sonnets yield a completely consistent and intelligible account: there is no mystery about it, and there need be no mystification. From the moment the rival poet makes his appearance he is always described, simply and directly, as a superior. He is one of the 'learnèd', by contrast with Shakespeare: this has the implication, against the Elizabethan background, that he is well educated, a university man. He is 'a worthier pen', 'a better spirit'; Shakespeare's 'saucy bark' is 'inferior far to his', which carries 'the proudest sail',

is 'of tall building and of goodly pride'. The rival poet is 'that
able spirit', but a rhetorical one, as opposed to Shakespeare's
naturalness and simple sincerity. When the rival poet is removed from the scene we immediately get, in the past tense —
it is the only one in the section dealing with the rival that is in
the past tense, naturally, for the rival has vanished, the rivalry
is over and is not mentioned again:

> Was it the proud full sail of his great verse . . .?

Marlowe's great achievement was to marry finest poetry to the
drama; before him the drama had exemplified but indifferent
verse. Not even Shakespeare ever wrote a play like *Tamburlaine*: ten Acts of it, all in blank verse of high quality. (All
Shakespeare's plays have some admixture of prose.) The phrase
for it of that exact critic, Ben Jonson, was 'Marlowe's mighty
line'. In summing up Shakespeare's work Ben Jonson insists,

> how far thou didst our Lyly outshine,
> Or sporting Kyd, or Marlowe's mighty line.

Now that precisely describes Shakespeare's early development:
the actor turning dramatist who modestly set himself Lyly as a
model, with *The Comedy of Errors* and *The Two Gentlemen of
Verona*, who followed in the steps of Kyd, with a gory revenge-
tragedy in *Titus Andronicus*, and then set himself to rival the
young master of them all, Marlowe.

The intimate connections between the work of Marlowe and
the early Shakespeare, the influence of one on the other, the
mutual influences, have not even yet been fully unravelled —
for there is now a great deal more to be said than my old
friend F. P. Wilson said in his admirable, *Marlowe and the Early
Shakespeare*. *Richard III* is the most Marlovian of Shakespeare's
plays; it follows Marlowe's usual specific of a play dominated
by a powerful character, a Machiavellian villain. Marlowe's
*The Jew of Malta* was the point of departure for *The Merchant of
Venice*. The excitement over the Lopez conspiracy led to the
revival of Marlowe's play in 1594: it was played at least fourteen times and brought in good money. Marlowe's Barabas suggested Shylock, with a touch of Dr. Lopez; Shakespeare set
himself to go beyond the dead master's *The Jew*, and we all
agree that he succeeded. Similarly, Shakespeare outshone

Marlowe's *Edward II* with his more sympathetic and touching *Richard II*; there is plenty of dramatic power in Marlowe's play, it is striking and sinister, but there is little sympathy in it and no charm. On the other hand, with *Edward II* Marlowe was taking a leaf out of his junior's notebook. For, with the *Henry VI* plays, the actor-poet was bringing something new to the stage: making chronicle-plays out of English history, with the dramatic interest distributed among a variety of characters, with a weak personality in the name-part. Marlowe took up the suggestion with *Edward II* in the last year of his life; it is a better constructed play than any of the *Henry VI* plays, though we can see in these that the actor, now turning dramatist, had a wider range and greater possibilities of development, especially in comedy. Marlowe could never have written *A Midsummer Night's Dream*; on the other hand, Shakespeare could never have written *Dr. Faustus*.

When Shakespeare came in at the formation of the Lord Chamberlain's company in 1594, he came not only as an actor but also already a dramatist; for three of his early plays, *Titus Andronicus*, *The Taming of the Shrew* and *3 Henry VI* are described on their publication as having been Pembroke plays. So, too, was Marlowe's *Edward II* — the only one of his that was: the rest of his plays belonged to the Lord Admiral's company. But here may have been some temporary association; something we should much like to know is lost here.

There is no doubt about the marked and tenacious influence of Marlowe on Shakespeare's mind — all the more striking when one considers how utterly different they were, what a contrast they afford in character, temperament and genius. Marlowe's unforgettable, obsessive phrases echo through Shakespeare's work, from the beginning to the end of his career. Just before the Rival Poet sonnets begin, in Sonnet 66 we have a tell-tale line that echoes a line from Marlowe's *Tamburlaine*:

> And captive good attending captain ill.

This is an echo of Marlowe's line,

> And all his captains bound in captive chains.[1]

[1] I am indebted to Professor Richard Hosley, of the University of Arizona, for this point.

D

It is just the kind of verbal clang that is so characteristic of
Shakespeare, the juxtaposition of words his ear infallibly picked
up. As at the beginning so at the end of his working life, in
*The Tempest*:

> Come unto these yellow sands,
>     And then take hands:
> Curtsied when you have and kissed,
>     The wild waves whist . . .

Shakespeare is remembering Marlowe's *Hero and Leander*, from
twenty years before; we shall see that he had special reason to
remember that poem:

> where all is whist and still,
> Save that the sea playing on yellow sand . . .

Marlowe was the only contemporary from whom Shakespeare
quoted a line, virtually by name:

> Dead shepherd, who knows not now thy saw of might,
> 'Who ever loved that loved not at first sight?'

'Dead shepherd' — there is pathos in the reference to his fellow
poet and dramatist, untimely dead. The play in which this occurs, *As You Like It*, has no less than three references to Marlowe,
including an extended reference to *Hero and Leander*; for in the
year in which Shakespeare was writing the play, 1598, Marlowe's poem was at last published, five years after his death.
This brought it back to mind: it is generally agreed that the
phrase, 'it strikes a man more dead than a great reckoning in a
little room' refers to the scene in the tavern at Deptford in
which Marlowe came by his end. After all, Shakespeare would
be in a position to know.

And we are in a position now to understand the Rival Poet
Sonnets, which run from 78 to 86 — some three-quarters of the
way on in the Southampton sequence, which ends in 1595 with
Sonnet 126. Just before they begin Shakespeare is asking, in
Sonnet 76:

> Why is my verse so barren of new pride,
> So far from variation or quick change? . . .
> Why write I still all one, ever the same,
> And keep invention in a noted weed,
> That every word doth almost tell my name,
> Showing their birth and where they did proceed?

His answer is,

> O, know, sweet love, I always write of you —

one more indication, if any were necessary, that Shakespeare's
poems were all intended for the same person, his young patron,
to whom in every sense they were owing.

Shakespeare himself tells us that the young man was 'fond on
praise', and we know that Southampton was anxious to shine as
a patron of letters. And thus he was willing to accept the service
of a more distinguished poet, though we know that he refused
to accept a dedication from young Thomas Nashe. Shakespeare
allows, with his usual courtesy,

> I grant, sweet love, thy lovely argument
> Deserves the travail of a worthier pen;

though he goes on to say for himself that his devotion is more
simple and sincere than the rhetoric of the newcomer, superior
spirit as he is, a recognisably grander figure:

> O, how I faint when I of you do write,
> Knowing a better spirit doth use your name . . .
> But since your worth, wide as the ocean is,
> The humble as the proudest sail doth hear,
> My saucy bark, inferior far to his,
> On your broad main doth wilfully appear.

The rivalry of this distinguished competitor is a serious matter
for Shakespeare; for in 1593, as in 1592, plague was again rife,
the theatres were closed practically the whole year. This, on top
of the discouragements of 1592, made it an urgent necessity to
acquire, or hold on to, a patron. How hard a time these years
were for the poets we can perceive from the fact that Thomas
Watson and Robert Greene died, the latter in want, in 1592:
they were only in their thirties; so too Kyd and Peele, who disappeared in 1594–5, while Marlowe was twenty-nine when he
was killed on 30 May 1593. After the disappearance of his rival
Shakespeare tells us, in Sonnet 92, how dire the necessity is, and
that his life may well depend upon his patron's support. No
wonder Shakespeare had such reason to be grateful to the
young patron.

And, anyhow, what was the rival poet rivalling him over? — nothing else but the patronage of a patron. That is to say, almost tautologously, that the Sonnets were written for the patron. Q.E.D.

The Rival Poet sonnets are few in number, which indicates that the rivalry covered a brief period, and they are, like the immense majority of the Sonnets, in the present tense: it is an experience continuing while the sonnets commenting on it are being written. Shakespeare modestly and courteously allows that it is natural for his young patron to welcome a new voice, to want now a change:

> So oft have I invoked thee for my muse . . .

> I grant thou wert not married to my muse . . .
> And therefore art enforced to seek anew
> Some fresher stamp of the time-bettering days.
> And do so, love; yet when they have devised
> What strainèd touches rhetoric can lend,
> Thou, truly fair, wert truly sympathised
> In true plain words by thy true-telling friend.

The rival is a rhetorician — true enough in both senses of the word: Marlowe was an academic poet, one of the 'learnèd', with seven years at Cambridge behind him, deeply trained in the discipline of rhetoric; and his style was essentially declamatory, where Shakespeare's was above all easy and natural. But Marlowe was a splendid poet, and Shakespeare leaves us in no doubt of his admiration:

> My tongue-tied Muse in manners holds her still,
> While comments of your praise, richly compiled,
> Reserve their character with golden quill
> And precious phrase by all the Muses filed.
> I think good thoughts, whilst other write good words,
> And like unlettered clerk still cry 'Amen'
> To every hymn that able spirit affords
> In polished form of well-refinèd pen.

No-one had closer reason to appreciate how polished a pen Marlowe wielded, how refined a style he had at command; but it was so like Shakespeare's 'open and free nature' to admit it candidly, and without jealousy.

With the next sonnet, Sonnet 86, the rivalry is at an end.

It is suddenly in the past tense; the rival is no more, he is not mentioned again. The whole episode is over; the sense of the sonnet is valedictory, summing up the rivalry, with its comments on the rival, that require elucidation:

> Was it the proud full sail of his great verse

—it is virtually but another way of proclaiming, as Ben Jonson was to do, 'Marlowe's mighty line' — was it this that had discouraged Shakespeare and struck him dumb?

> Was it his spirit, by spirits taught to write
> Above a mortal pitch, that struck me dead?
> No, neither he, nor his compeers by night
> Giving him aid, my verse astonishèd.
> He, nor that affable familiar ghost
> Which nightly gulls him with intelligence,
> As victors of my silence cannot boast.
> I was not sick of any fear from thence;
> But when your countenance filled up his line,
> Then lacked I matter: that enfeebled mine.

This says, as plainly as anything, that Shakespeare had been discouraged by the newcomer, with his strange and superior gifts, being received with favour by his patron. It tells us that the rival was taught by spirits to write above a mortal pitch. We know, from *Dr. Faustus*, that Marlowe, heterodox as he was about religion, was familiar with the spirit-world and the formulae for raising the spirits. The next four lines are obscure and have hitherto resisted interpretation. Nevertheless, Shakespeare did not intend obscurity: readers in his own time would recognise what he meant. 'His compeers by night giving him aid' — what does that mean? It refers back to the previous lines, to 'by spirits taught to write above a mortal pitch'. It is very characteristic of Shakespeare, especially in the Sonnets, to repeat the idea with a different phrasing. The *Oxford English Dictionary* informs us that the word 'compeer', which means a companion, also has the sense of a gossip or familiar. In the very next lines we have 'that affable, familiar ghost which nightly gulls him with intelligence'. We are here in the spirit-world: we do not have to look for any companion of Marlowe's n life. The fact that all this relates to the spirit-world is in itself a circumstance that corroborates that the rival-poet is dead. But he still walks the stage in the person of Dr. Faustus, his creation and — it is not too much to say — projection of himself. In this year 1593, in the brief interval when the theatres are open, *Dr. Faustus* is being played. Why should not 'that affable familiar ghost which nightly gulls him with intelligence' be Mephistophilis? — it is precisely the rôle he plays in relation to Faustus in the night-scenes of the play.

Yet Professor L. C. Knights has told us, out of his superior wisdom, that the suggestion 'has no value at all'. Another professor, Professor Terence Spencer, tells us that 'the argument that the rival poet must have been dead because Shakespeare uses the past tense of the verb at the beginning of Sonnet 86 is a mistaken interpretation of the syntax of the poem'. This portentous statement is visibly wrong. It is not merely that the sonnet begins in the past tense, it goes on to the end in the past tense. There are *nine* verbs in the past tense, and two past participles — can the professor not count? Something striking has happened: the rivalry is over. The sonnet stands out markedly, to anyone of any perception, among all the sonnets in the present tense before it and after it. There is one verb in a principal clause in the present tense, and one in a subordinate clause. These are perfectly right in their place, and do not contradict, but support, my suggested interpretation of the passage.

But this is not the end of the story.

When Marlowe died in May 1593, Shakespeare's poem *Venus and Adonis* was ready for publication; Marlowe's *Hero and Leander* was only half done. Though unfinished, it is superior as a work of art: more polished, more refined — to use Shakespeare's own words for his rival — more concise, more balanced and with greater aesthetic control, more perfection of workmanship and expression. It has always been recognised that these two poems bear a close relationship to each other. *Hero and Leander* begins with a charming salute to the rival theme: Hero wears

> wide sleeves green, and bordered with a grove,
> Where Venus in her naked glory strove
> To please the careless and disdainful eyes
> Of proud Adonis that before her lies.

'Rose-cheeked Adonis', Shakespeare begins; 'rose-cheeked Adonis', echoes Marlowe later on. There are the famous parallel descriptions of the restive horse breaking his reins and bit — as Shakespeare describes with glee, to go to the mare he has scented; as to this Marlowe is more reticent, less responsive to the theme. Each poem has a salute to Narcissus, Shakespeare's with his characteristic double reflexive:

> Narcissus so himself himself forsook,
> And died to kiss his shadow in the brook.

Marlowe no less characteristic:

> Those orient cheeks and lips, exceeding his
> That leaped into the water for a kiss
> Of his own shadow, and despising many,
> Died ere he could enjoy the love of any.

And there are other comparisons and parallel themes, that of use and usury, for example. Shakespeare writes,

> Foul cankering rust the hidden treasure frets,
> But gold that's put to use more gold begets.

Marlowe writes:

> What difference betwixt the richest mine
> And basest mould, but use? for both, not used,
> Are of like worth. Then treasure is abused
> When misers keep it: being put to loan
> In time it will return us two for one.

We are back with the theme of Shakespeare's Sonnets and the argument urged upon Southampton to breed and increase:

> That use is not forbidden usury
> Which happies those that pay the willing loan;
> That's for thyself to breed another thee,
> Or, ten times happier, be it ten for one.

One cannot resist the impression that each poem was well known to the other author, that they were written alongside of each other in friendly rivalry. And there is more similarity in situation than is generally appreciated. Adonis is not responsive

to the love of a woman. But even Leander needs arguing with
to put him up to it:

> Why art thou not in love, and loved of all?
> Though thou be fair, yet be not thine own thrall.

And even when Hero made it clear that she was willing,

> Like Aesop's cock this jewel he enjoyed,
> And as a brother with his sister toyed,
> Supposing nothing else was to be done,
> Now he her favour and good will had won.

But what sort of person was this Leander? When we look we
find that he is very close to the young man of the Sonnets. His
looks are ambivalent; his youthful charms are maidenly:

> Some swore he was a maid in man's attire,
> For in his looks were all that men desire,
> A pleasant smiling cheek, a speaking eye,
> A brow for love to banquet royally,
> And such as knew he was a man would say,
> Leander, thou art made for amorous play:
> Why art thou not in love — and loved of all?

It is the question that is asked again and again in the earlier
sonnets. And for Leander's appearance, his long, unshorn
tresses were his leading feature:

> His dangling tresses that were never shorn,
> Had they been cut and unto Colchos borne,
> Would have allured the vent'rous youth of Greece
> To hazard more than for the Golden Fleece.

There is a high rhetorical compliment to the possessor of those
long tresses. For these tresses were the characteristic feature of
Southampton by which all his portraits know him, right up to
and beyond his belated marriage and imprisonment in the
Tower. So, too, with the fairness of his skin and complexion.
Marlowe describes Leander in just such terms:

> His body was as straight as Circe's wand,
> Jove might have sipped out nectar from his hand.
> Even as delicious meat is to the taste,
> So was his neck in touching, and surpassed
> The white of Pelop's shoulder —

and more of the resounding rhetorical praise Shakespeare refers to in the Rival Poet sonnets. For, need we doubt any longer that Southampton provided the suggestion for Marlowe's Leander as for Shakespeare's Adonis; that the two poems were written in friendly rivalry by his two poets; and that Marlowe was the Rival Poet of the Sonnets?

John Bakeless, author of the standard two-volumed biography of Marlowe, writes me: 'I have always thought that Marlowe was the Rival Poet, but, until your dating of the Sonnets, it was impossible to be positive.'

Now we can be. In fact it is ridiculous to suggest anyone else. A number of reputable people have suggested Chapman. It is a perfectly superfluous suggestion with nothing to recommend it; Chapman does not begin to be heard of as a writer until several years later, in 1597–8, when all this is well over. Someone has had the absurdity — against this background! — to suggest Gervase Markham, the poet of farriery and horsemanship.

One suggestion is not much more silly than the other, for both are silly; one's comment on their proponents must be Shakespeare's:

> Lord, what fools these mortals be!

## IV

People who are so uncertain where we can be certain, i.e. with regard to both the young friend and the Rival Poet, are apt to be free with their foolish conjectures, where we can know nothing for certain at all, i.e. with regard to Shakespeare's mistress, the Dark Lady.

As a conscientious scholar, I should not be such a fool as to make any conjecture whatever in a region where we have no junction with the external world, and no external evidence. Any conjecture is utterly valueless.

All that we know of Shakespeare's mistress is internal to his work. It is not my purpose to depict the nature of the relationship, but simply to point out the indications Shakespeare gives us as to her character and status. It is fairly clear that she was a gentlewoman, of a superior social standing to the actor-dramatist. She was a loose woman, no better than she should be; but that does not mean that she was necessarily, a courtesan, as some have thought, or, as others have crudely put it, a prostitute. One must distinguish more subtly in these matters.

When we first meet her, in the sonnets mainly devoted to her, she is playing on the virginals — it would, in all probability, be a gentlewoman who would have that accomplishment in the Elizabethan age. The whole tone of the sonnets about her indicates that she is Shakespeare's social superior and that that is one of the elements in the trouble she gives him. She is not infatuated with him, as he is with her. She obviously looked down on him and expressed herself as such to others:

> O, though I love what others do abhor,
> With others thou shouldst not abhor my state.

But we have another portrait of the Dark Lady than that in the Sonnets: that of Rosaline in *Love's Labour's Lost*, whose appearance is described in precisely similar terms — naturally, since this was for public presentation, a favourable portrait. Sonnet 127 describes her striking, and unfashionably dark, eyes, hair, brows:

> In the old age black was not counted fair,
> Or if it were it bore not beauty's name;
> But now is black beauty's successive heir,
> And beauty slandered with a bastard shame:
> For since each hand hath put on nature's power,
> Fairing the foul with art's false borrowed face,
> Sweet beauty hath no name, no holy bower,
> But is profaned, if not lives in disgrace.
> Therefore my mistress' eyes are raven black,
> Her eyes so suited, and they mourners seem
> As such who, not born fair, no beauty lack,
> Slandering creation with a false esteem.

In *Love's Labour's Lost* Berowne, who represents Shakespeare and is a self-portrait in this skit on the Southampton circle by its poet, describes his lady in much the same words:

> O, if in black my lady's brows be decked,
> It mourns that painting and usurping hair
> Should ravish doters with a false aspect,
> And therefore is she born to make black fair.

The sonnets about the Dark Lady parallel *The Rape of Lucrece* of 1593–4 and *Love's Labour's Lost* of 1594. Words, style — in particular, the marked use of the sonnet-form within the play — theme and character, all cohere to make this clear. We may properly infer that the Dark Lady was a lady well known to the circle around young Southampton, and that is all that can usefully be said on the subject.

## V

My dating of the Sonnets, and consequent solution of the problems that can be solved, cannot be impugned at any point. People will go on fancying that these matters can still be disputed, but in fact these problems — always with the exception of the identity of the Dark Lady, which is not likely ever to be — are now cleared up once and for all. Nor will scholars be able to excuse themselves from accepting the position by claiming that there is not enough evidence for us to be sure. The position is at once more simple and more rigorous. With regard to the Dark Lady there is no point of junction with the external world, i.e. no evidence, whatever. With regard to the Young Man, the Rival Poet, and the dating of the Sonnets with their references to contemporary events, there is plenty of external evidence, as we have seen, completely at one with the internal story. As to historical evidence, the dating and chronology upon which the solution depends, the Elizabethan historian is in the best position to know. Where there is no evidence he makes no conjectures; where the evidence is sufficient and cannot be impugned he can at last give you certainty.

# THE SHAKESPEARE EXHIBITION

*For Charles Causley*

Now that the captains and the kings, or at least princes, have departed, the salutes and tributes from all over the world been received and forgotten — though it is a touching memory to think of the chancel of Stratford church wholly covered and banked up with flowers, one small sprig of flowering currant thrown over the communion-rail with the rest — what remains of it all, the ceremonies, the speeches and processions, in the mind?

Without any doubt, a work of creative art in itself, the Exhibition at Stratford.

I had no idea that it would be so. My New York friend — who would have no objection to being described as an intellectual — after a brief dash into it the day after the opening, put me off by calling it 'phoney'. I am easily discouraged, and to my shame never went to see it until months afterwards when with a Cornish friend, first of Cornish poets, I decided to go over from Oxford, without enthusiasm, without expectations.

There was the gay, light-hearted Exhibition building, with its curious little cupolas that light up like lanterns at night, in the meadow on the south bank of the river, opposite the Theatre, not far from Clopton's original, antique bridge, with clumps of valerian clinging in its crevices. We entered, a little gingerly, not prejudiced in its favour, open-minded without giving it the benefit of the doubt. We were unprepared, ignorant of what to expect; we had no idea of its creator's aim, to exhibit 'a new way of assailing the visitor's senses, using light, sound, changing scales and levels, smell and surprise: a technique elaborated and evolved by young artists on the other side of the Atlantic and given the name of "Happening"'. My New York friend should have recognised better than we that here was an American contribution to the Quatercentenary, and something very original.

A little lost in the prevailing darkness, nostrils assailed by the heavy exotic scent that already called to mind the back-stage of a theatre, we made our way to the more familiar company of Shakespeare's school-books. On the way I caught sight of, and was held by a glimpse of Elizabeth going by, halberdiers and pensioners around her coach, the imperious profile provokingly turned away — just as it might have been. At that moment, over the shoulder, rounding a corner in the dark street, the ear is seduced by 'Greensleeves' — for all its familiarity today the most nostalgic of Elizabethan tunes: it has all the poignant passion of the age in it. Birds sing from their cages in the narrow courts, the catches of the time follow us everywhere, past pillory and pulpit, 'Hey, Robin', 'In youth, when I did love', 'Hold thy peace', the catch that Sir Toby Belch and Andrew Aguecheek are caught caterwauling by Maria in *Twelfth Night*. At this point the dream begins: unknown to oneself, one has entered another world and lives in the age.

We stop to study the school textbooks, in the editions Shakespeare would have used at school — we both are interested, my friend being a school teacher in his spare time from writing poetry. Here is a horn-book, from which children learned their A B C, Alexander Nowell's Catechism and Lily's grammar, from which they all learned their Latin grammar. Shakespeare's plays are full of tags from Lily. Sir Toby again comes out with 'Not to be abed after midnight is to be up betimes, and *diluculo surgere*, thou know'st . . .' He was remembering his Latin grammar from schooldays: *Diluculo surgere saluberrimum est*, 'to arise betime in the morning is the most wholesome thing in the world'. Here one can watch the schoolboy's progress from early Aesop and Cato to Mantuan and Palingenius's *Zodiac of Life* — all leaving their traces in the early plays: 'Ah, good old Mantuan! . . . Old Mantuan, old Mantuan! who understandeth thee not, love thee not.' But what is Aphthonius doing here? — I wonder, till I recall that it was in this schoolbook that Ovid's story of Venus and Adonis was analysed as an example of the art of narration. And so to Shakespeare's favourite book, Ovid's *Metamorphoses*, whence he got so many of his classical stories, to Plautus, Terence and Seneca, the Renaissance models for comedy and tragedy.

The tendency of the best, most reliable recent Shakespeare scholarship — Professor Peter Alexander, for example — is to place the earliest of Shakespeare's work a year or two earlier than used to be thought, as early perhaps as 1588-9. I have become convinced that this is right. If I were writing my biography of him now I should bring out this new realisation of how immediately his earliest work stems from his school work: the earliest comedies, *The Comedy of Errors* and *The Two Gentlemen of Verona*, from Plautus, and *Titus Andronicus* from Seneca and Ovid.[1] This is also in keeping with the authentic early tradition that he was for a time a schoolmaster in the country. And I should place *Titus Andronicus* accordingly earlier than in my book: before the *First Part of King Henry VI*, not in 1593 but before 1590. Here the brilliant intuition of the creative artist who is the designer of the Exhibition has anticipated me. In the main he has followed Sir Edmund Chambers' conservative chronology of the plays; he has departed from it in the case of *Titus Andronicus*, 'so as to associate it closely with the blood and thunder of Marlowe and Senecan Kyd'. He is right to do so.

Then we are given a display of books to illustrate the London scene, once more the books known to have been read by Shakespeare and drawn upon in the plays. Many of them are familiar enough: Holinshed's *Chronicles*, in the second edition he used, which came out in 1587 ready to hand on the threshold of his career; Hall's *Union of the Two . . . Families of Lancaster and York*, much leaned upon for the plays about the Wars of the Roses; North's *Plutarch*, Hakluyt's *Principal Navigations*, the Bishops' Bible, Puttenham's *Art of English Poesy*, Lyly's *Euphues*, Sidney's *Arcadia*, Spenser's *Faery Queene*, Chaucer, Daniel, Ariosto, Florio's Montaigne. We have come to realise also how extensive and varied was Shakespeare's range of rapid reading — everything about him was rapid — mostly, and naturally, for the purpose of material for his plays. As Professor Nevill Coghill says, in his article on 'What Shakespeare Read': 'even the works he can be known to have used for professional purposes would make a fair-sized, miscellaneous library'. There would be, for example, a large number of contemporary plays, poems and romances, mostly in English, a few in Italian. For,

[1] I owe this point to the perceptiveness of Professor Andrew S. Cairncross.

in addition to a good working knowledge of Latin (no Greek), Shakespeare was fairly fluent in French — he was living in a French household at the time he was writing the French scenes of *Henry V* — and had a smattering of Italian (he was an intimate of Southampton's household along with Florio). It is not surprising that Coghill's essay is the best in the Guide to the Exhibition, as his book, *Shakespeare's Professional Skills* — no mere work of academic criticism, but illuminating at every point from a lifetime's experience of re-creating the plays on the stage — is one of the only two books called forth by the Quatercentenary that will last.

As one progresses one becomes acclimatised to the modernist idiom of the machines, sculptures, paintings and tableaux. They are completely of this age, restless, properly dramatic in their suddenness, sometimes shocking in their effect. Once or twice, when I haven't caught the intention, I am sure it is my own obtuseness. Not for want of responsiveness: I am overwhelmed by the drama of a scene from *A Midsummer Night's Dream* being presented before the Queen at Court. One glimpses it through the legs and around the hulking great bodies of the halberdiers: the whole effect heightened by cross-lighting, much of it in chiaroscuro, once more the poignant mask of the Court's deity. (She is the other Presence throughout the Exhibition, in counterpoint to Shakespeare.) Here I observe a mistake in the Guide: the play was not written 'possibly' for the marriage of Elizabeth Carey in 1595 but, we now know without shadow of doubt, for the private wedding of Southampton's mother, the Countess, to Sir Thomas Heneage on 2 May 1594.

Among the paintings the outstanding ones are contributions from Australia: Sidney Nolan's masks of love ('So true a fool is love that in your Will, Though you do any thing, he thinks no ill'): rich in colour, dramatic in effect, so powerful as to terrify, appropriate to the agonised infatuation for the Dark Lady; the Freudian project of Arthur Boyd for *Romeo and Juliet* — a womb-like world of blue, an ominous jewel. Love-songs accompany us now — but, then, so much of Elizabethan music as of poetry was about love: what a sexually-obsessed world they lived in — much more profoundly and more passionately than ours! Peter Pears sings Morley's 'Come Sorrow, Come', accompanied by the lute, and then 'It was a lover and his lass', that makes one think of walking through those fields of rye to Shottery. New York makes its contribution with madrigals and instrumental pieces performed by the New York Pro Musica ensemble.

Shakespeare's passionate response to music is outstanding among all others even in that age; oddly enough, the closest to him here among the dramatists was Ben Jonson, also a writer of exquisite, if less moving, songs. One of our best authorities, Dr. Sternfeld, tells us — another contribution from America — that 'there are over a hundred major cues for music scattered throughout Shakespeare's plays'; and that he used music in a more significant way dramatically than the others. He wove the music into the drama, and 'for this reason frequently employed echoes from the lyrics in the surrounding dialogue'. The melodies were generally those of popular songs, which were 'bound to be quickly recognised and to produce the desired dramatic associations'. As in the case of Desdemona's Willow Song, of which we are given the contemporary notation from the Lodge Book in the Folger Library at Washington. From an English source comes Queen Elizabeth's own cithern — a splendid Renaissance instrument with its great shell decoration and inlay — from Helmingham Hall in Suffolk.

Everywhere music accompanies us — airs, madrigals, lute-music, virginals, birdsong, catches, street-cries — as in the Elizabethan world. At length we find ourselves in the long gallery of a great house, hung, as the custom was, with the portraits of contemporaries. By a grand stroke of imagination this house is on the south bank of the Thames, so that through the latticed windows one sees the whole stretch of London, from the crowded houses on London Bridge, old St. Paul's and Paul's Wharf, with the mansions of the grandees — Essex House, Norfolk House, the Savoy, Cecil House, Durham House (occupied by Ralegh), York House (where Francis Bacon was born) — next to the Queen's Whitehall and the hulks of Westminster Hall and the Abbey. Historically right, too, since the Thames was the main artery of traffic in those days.

Looking round, one recognises all — or almost all — the grand figures of the age: here the historian is more at home. Gathered together on the panelled walls are these people who knew each other very well, loved or hated each other, were just friends, political or social acquaintances. Among the familiar portraits I concentrate on those unfamiliar or unknown to me. No portraits are better known to the English public than those of the Queen, Leicester, Essex, Burghley, Drake, Sir Walter Ralegh. But here is someone who fascinates me as a character, the reptilian Lord Henry Howard, whose features I had never seen before though very well up in his doings. I am surprised to find a good-looking man, under his tall crowned hat: fine intelligent eyes, good arched eyebrows, big sensual nose (he was one for smelling out things), sparse, close-trimmed, greying beard, trim moustache, with high ruff and blue ribbon of the Garter. James I made him Earl of Northampton; Elizabeth though his cousin, wouldn't make him anything: she knew what a snake he was.

I am glad to see my old friend Bess of Hardwick once more: red-gold hair, hazel-gold eyes, large downward nose under her countess's coronet — everything she touched turned to gold, ancestress of three dukedoms. This is the portrait I have before now worked under in the long gallery at Hardwick, turning over the pages of her household accounts under her eye. Looking along at Robert Cecil, I am reminded once more of the extraordinary delicacy, refinement and intelligence of the face. Not far away is Southampton, the portrait painted to commemorate his imprisonment in the Tower for his part in the Essex conspiracy, February 1601 to April 1603 — the period when Shakespeare was writing *Twelfth Night*, *Troilus and Cressida*, *All's Well that Ends Well*, with their autobiographical overtones of disenchantment, disillusion, sickness of heart. I am interested to see what Archbishop Bancroft looked like: furrowed brows — the Puritans gave him plenty of reason to knit his brows — fine blue eyes, grizzled hair, darkish skin and swarthy complexion (or is it the darkening of the canvas with time?) And there is a very curious portrait of Sir Christopher Hatton which I have never seen before: an astrological portrait depicting him within his horoscope, with the planets placed in position in the houses of the zodiac; in one corner the astrologer points to the sphere, in the other the painter is at his easel. Whoever can have painted this curiosity? — everything

E

underscores the fantasy of the age. Nothing perhaps more than the architecture: of all the fantasy-palaces that have vanished, royal Richmond and Nonsuch, Leicester's Wanstead and Burghley's Theobalds, the Marquis of Winchester's Basing House, I regret Hatton's immense Holdenby almost more than any.

One sees the same spirit of fantasy in the jewellery of the time. Here are two Renaissance pomanders from Burghley House — one of the fantasy-palaces to survive — that have come down in the senior line of Burghley's descent, the Exeter Cecils. One of them opens out into segments like an orange, with sliding lids upon which the perfume is inscribed Rosen, Sarah, Caunel — which makes me think it may be of German workmanship. From Burghley House, too, come a spoon and fork of agate and gold, and a splendid bookbinding such as were made for the Queen — Renaissance intellectual as she was — all of gold, with enamelled roses set with diamonds. This is of English workmanship — what can have been the little book so richly bound for her? Among the cameos and pendants the present Queen has lent the finest cameo-portrait of Elizabeth in profile, looking like a Roman Empress, carved from an oriental sardonyx. Then there are the splendid Renaissance medals struck in her honour — the 'Dangers Averted', after the Armada: 'No other diadem in the world more rich, not even dangers touch it'; and the Minerva of 1602, after the Essex rebellion: 'A thousand shall fall beside thee, and ten thousand at thy right hand, O Elizabeth, Queen.' What a cult they made of her! — but it was all part of the hieratic ritual of the Court, the quasi-religious, sacramental cult of monarchy, which goes back to far deeper anthropological roots and psychological needs than rationalist moderns can understand. Hence the astonishing impact and power of the theme of kingship all through Shakespeare's plays from the beginning to the end, all the way from early Henry VI to Prospero and Henry VIII, Elizabeth's father. The tradition is that Shakespeare himself played 'kingly parts'.

And so we move through the winding corridors and up chiaroscuro staircases out of the reign — noticing brilliant spurts of imagination everywhere we pass. Here is the tragic, skeletal figure of King John, reaching towards the brother's child, Arthur, whom he murdered. Then there are the grieving lines for a dead child that Shakespeare put into the play, at the time his own boy, Hamnet, died. The pedantic eye of the historian registers a small error — the boy was *eleven* when he died.

The transition from Elizabethan to Jacobean could not be more dramatically expressed: there is the towering steel framework of the dead Queen in her farthingale, the face of a skeleton, holding between her hands her own death-mask, the recognisable, beautiful Welsh oval, narrow forehead, high cheek-bones, claimed by death at last. At once we are in a new reign: here is clever, sad, shambling James, intelligent, disillusioned, kind eyes, with the boy-friends — the good-looking, stupid Carr and the beautiful, gracious Villiers. Here are the cronies who understood, and shared, James's tastes, Lord Chancellor Bacon, and the unspeakable Northampton. Here, too, are the Herbert brothers, Pembroke and Montgomery, to whom Heminges and Condell very properly dedicated the First Folio, since Pembroke as Lord Chamberlain was responsible for the King's men, the Globe company. Though Montgomery was a great favourite with James, both the Herberts were very heterosexual: not a chance that Pembroke could ever have been the ambivalent young man of the Sonnets — that many people supposed so only shows how utterly unperceptive they are. (One is consoled by the thought that most people do not qualify to hold an opinion on the matter, let alone express it.) The creator of the Exhibition, in his Introduction, though 'inclining' to the Southampton view, hedged it with the possibility that it might be Pembroke. There is no possibility whatever, as he now realises and accepts: the question has been settled for good and all — it should not be in the least surprising — by an historian of the age.

We grope, as if blindfolded — so completely are we captured by the imagination that has recreated the age for us, it could not be more powerfully — out of the world of James's Court into the Globe Theatre. What a stroke on the part of Richard Buckle — foremost of Britain's young exhibition-designers — to have withheld it to the last! We are back with Shakespeare's own words and characters and imaginings, expressed in the voices of the best actors and singers of our time on the empty stage of the Globe Theatre. We take our place on the benches; we are almost alone; the lights come and go over the so familiar stage, shifting and changing — now it is spring, now autumn, now it is early morning birdsong, now rich afternoon sunlight, now twilight. It is deeply disturbing to hear these voices — his multifarious voices coming from that empty stage:

> Take, O take those lips away
>   That so sweetly were foresworn;
> And those eyes, the break of day:
>   Lights that do mislead the morn . . .

> Tomorrow, and tomorrow, and tomorrow,
> Creeps in this petty pace from day to day
> To the last syllable of recorded time;
> And all our yesterdays have lighted fools
> The way to dusty death . . .

One is so moved one can hardly bear to hear these voices, *his* voice out of the grave:

> Fear no more the heat o' the sun
>   Nor the furious winter's rages;
> Thou thy worldly task hast done,
>   Home art gone and ta'en thy wages.

The performance is over, the play is done, the voices are silent. We have no word between us, no words for it all; we stumble out into the bright light of day; we are both in tears.

# IV

# QUEEN ELIZABETH I AND THE HISTORIANS

QUEEN ELIZABETH I has this in common with the Duke of Wellington — besides a hawk-nose — that she has been much exposed to authors. The most celebrated and the most scintillating figure among our sovereigns, how could it not be so? Though we can hardly say of her, as of the circulation of Macaulay's *History*, that it went up and down with the figures for the annual production of coal in the nineteenth century, still her reputation has waxed and waned with movements of political feeling, varied with party bias. It may be instructive to watch the ebb and flow of opinion about her, especially with the historians: it may tell us something about them as well as about her.

In the fifty years or so after her death we can already observe people's opinions forming according to their prejudices. We can hardly expect James I to have anything but an awkward attitude towards the disagreeable old lady who had given him so many scoldings in her time and kept him on tenterhooks about her inheritance. The correspondence of Elizabeth I and James VI makes a comic chapter in the relations of monarchs; in any case, sovereigns are apt to be sensitive on the subject of their immediate predecessors. But after some grudging expressions at the beginning, James recovered himself in time to pay a tribute in his first Parliament to 'one who in wisdom and felicity of government surpassed all the princes since the days of Augustus'. There speaks the don in him; but it was a generous tribute, and it was as well. It set the standard for such a reference as that familiar to us from the Preface to the Authorised Version — 'upon the setting of that bright Occidental star, Queen Elizabeth of most happy memory'. Certainly Elizabeth had set such a high standard as a ruler that she made it all the more difficult for her successors, the Stuarts.

Some sense of this peeps through the priggish words of Lucy

Hutchinson: 'the felicity of her reign was the effect of her sub-mission to her masculine and wise councillors; but wherever male princes are so effeminate as to suffer women of foreign birth and different religions to intermeddle with the affairs of state, it is always found to produce sad desolations'. From which we see that Lucy was a good patriot, and no feminist. Cromwell himself, in the days of the Republic, did not hesitate to cite Elizabeth's name before Parliament, 'Queen Elizabeth of famous memory — we need not be ashamed to call her so'; and he went on to refer in terms almost of gallantry, for a Puritan, to the 'assassination designed upon that lady, that great Queen'.

But the detestable Civil War divided England, and we find a different view suggested by Clarendon. He quotes an axiom of hers with a wry, dry comment: 'the popular axiom of Queen Elizabeth that as her greatest treasure was in the hearts of her people so she had rather her money should be in their purses than in her own Exchequer (which she never said but at the closing of some Parliament when she had gotten all she could from them)'. And against the glories of the age, he sets 'the charge, trouble and anxiety of a long continued war (how prosperous and successful soever) even during the Queen's whole reign; and (besides some domestic ruptures into rebellion, frequently into treason, and besides the blemish of an unparal-leled act of blood upon the life of a crowned neighbour, queen and ally) the fear and apprehension of what was to come (which is one of the most unpleasant kinds of melancholy) from an un-known, at least an unacknowledged successor to the crown: clouded much of that prosperity then which now shines with so much splendour before our eyes in chronicle'.

There you have a rather demeaning picture of the reign from the pen of a Stuart partisan, who happens to be the first of our great historians. Prejudice speaks in the insinuations of the Lord Chancellor's majestic parentheses. Prejudice betrays itself in the historical error as to the duration of the war: which occu-pied not the whole reign, but the last twenty years of its forty-five. And within the country people had reason to remember the reign as a long period of internal peace: that is the theme of the famous speech Shakespeare put into the mouth of Cranmer in *Henry VIII*: like Shakespeare's whole attitude on such matters it was representative, not exceptional.

Note, too, the partisan statement of Mary Stuart's case, whom Elizabeth protected for years against the indignation of Parliament. Then there is the quite unjust innuendo as to Elizabeth's attitude towards taxation. Her concern to protect the pocket of the citizen was perfectly genuine. She thought the subject's money was best in his own purse and most profitably employed by himself. A very benighted and out-of-date attitude, of course: we know better: we have changed all that.

It is interesting to see in this — in Cromwell's admiration and Clarendon's dislike — the formation of the tradition: Queen Elizabeth as the heroine of Parliament, the Protestant, the Whig Queen; Mary Stuart, the martyr in the eyes of the Tories and Jacobites, the heroine of the long Stuart romance.

Actually, how ironical it is! Elizabeth conducted a lifelong struggle with her Parliaments, on one issue after another. Her 'affection to govern princely' was disapproved by her own Archbishop; in other words, her views of her prerogative might be described as very much anti-Whig and high Tory.

We prefer the *naïveté* — the innocence of such matters — of Pepys: 'I confess I have sucked in so much of the sad story of Queen Elizabeth from my cradle that I was ready to weep for her sometimes.' This was *à propos* of a revival of Heywood's play, *If You Know Not Me, You Know Nobody*, which deals with her story. Pepys found the play 'the most ridiculous that sure ever came upon the stage'; but he consoled himself with the pleasure of seeing the beautiful Knipp dance among the milk-maids 'in her nightgown with no locks on, but her bare face and hair tied up in a knot behind, which is the comeliest dress that ever I saw her in to her advantage'. Pepys is an exception: it is always the human appeal that touches his feelings. And people's feelings are usually better than their silly opinions.

In the middle of the eighteenth century the issue was brought into the open with the controversy aroused by Hume's *History of England* and Robertson's *History of Scotland*. For a Scot who professed not to care very much for England and the English, Hume did us proud in his remarkable *History*. (But what a Scot! — the most fertilising, the most universal philosopher the island has produced.) Hume discovers a real enthusiasm for the English Queen, unwonted in one who prided himself on the cool and even temper of his judgments. 'Her vigour, her constancy, her magnanimity, her penetration, vigilance, address are allowed to merit the highest praises and appear not to have been surpassed by any person who ever filled a throne. . . . By the force of her mind, she controlled all her more active and stronger qualities and prevented them from running into excess. . . . Her singular talents for government were founded equally on her temper and on her capacity. Endowed with a great command over herself, she soon obtained an uncontrolled ascendant over her people; and while she merited all their esteem by her real virtues, she also engaged their affections by her pretended ones. Few sovereigns of England succeeded to the throne in more difficult circumstances; and none ever conducted the government with such uniform success and felicity. Though unacquainted with the practice of toleration, the true secret for managing religious factions, she preserved her people, by her superior prudence, from those confusions in which theological controversy had involved all the neighbouring nations.'

Perhaps this is the core of her achievement: at a time when other nations were divided from top to bottom by ideological conflict and civil war — France, the Netherlands, Scotland, Germany — she kept her country united so that it could forge ahead, where other countries were held back for decades or even centuries. No conception of this among her critics. I suppose that is because most people are more capable of appreciating the private and family virtues, rather than those essential in public and political life. But a Tudor queen has to be estimated as a statesman, not as a cosy helpmate in the stress of suburban life. Elizabeth I was certainly not a cosy character. What won her Hume's intellectual sympathy was that she was a Laodicean, a moderate, a trimmer: all that made the uncompromising Knox call her 'neither good Protestant nor yet resolute Papist'. Like the most intelligent people of her time — or of any time — she was a *politique*, not a fanatic engaged in making life intolerable for sensible people.

Then, too, Hume as a Scot, and a very frugal one, understood the wisdom of her financial prudence. 'The natural frugality of her temper, so far from disqualifying her for . . . great enterprises, only enabled her to execute them with greater certainty and success; and all the world saw in her conduct the happy effects of a vigorous perseverance in judicious and well conducted projects.' In truth, finance was the clue to the success of her rule: when other powers — including her greatest adversary, who had all the treasure of America at his disposal — went bankrupt, she was not held up in the course thought best in the interests of the country, her policies were never thus frustrated. In our time we are in an all too instructive position for appreciating how economic circumstances set limits to what we can do in the world.

Hume, who understood everything, understood this very well; where 'middling historians', as he calls them, are apt not to. Robertson, who — in spite of the fact that he was a best-seller — was more than a middling historian, appreciated this too. (It was left to the Victorians to attack Elizabeth on the grounds of parsimony.) Robertson has a strong tribute to Elizabeth as a great queen. But he was writing the history of Scotland; and 'whosoever undertakes to write the history of Scotland finds himself obliged, frequently, to view her in a very different and in a less amiable light'. He concludes that the hand Elizabeth took in the contending Scots factions of the time effected, 'what the valour of her ancestors could not accomplish', the reduction of 'that Kingdom to a state of dependence on England'. But must an Englishman regret that she was successful in this? From an English point of view, she was engaged in rendering Scotland, so often dangerous, innocuous. From a wider point of view, she was engaged in preparing the eventual union of the island. Who can say that she was wrong to do so? She was pursuing an obviously right and sensible policy from both points of view.

But it is when he touches Mary Stuart that the Presbyterian reveals himself a gallant. 'No apology can be offered for her [Elizabeth's] behaviour to Queen Mary; a scene of dissimulation, without necessity, and of severity beyond example. In almost all her other actions, Elizabeth is the object of our highest admiration: in this we must allow that she not only laid aside the magnanimity which became a queen, but the feelings natural to a woman.' Feelings natural to a man, perhaps — a better knowledge of psychology would suggest. For Mary certainly had a way of appealing to the soft side of menfolk. The utmost that the Doctor can bring himself to utter against her is — 'To say that she was always unfortunate will not account for that long and uninterrupted succession of calamities which befel her; we must likewise add that she was often imprudent.' As for her passion for Bothwell and the murder of her husband, 'Humanity will draw a veil over this part of her character which it cannot approve and may, perhaps, prompt some to impute some of her actions to her situation more than to her dispositions', etc.

But this was not enough for William Tytler, Writer to the Signet, who in 1760 produced *An historical and critical Enquiry into the evidence produced by the Earls of Murray and Morton against Mary, Queen of Scots; with an Examination of the Rev. Dr. Robertson's Dissertion and Mr. Hume's History with respect to that evidence*. I fear the lawyer proved himself neither historical nor critical. I have read his work and it is worthless — though it made a stir in its day. Nothing would suit him but the assertion of Mary's purity and innocence. There is nothing more boring than such *parti-pris*. One studies history to discover what the truth is; this lawyer to make a case.

It is a poor one. Nothing is said of Mary's aggressive step in laying claim to the English succession when Dauphiness in France or the danger she made herself to Elizabeth, or of her long run of follies, mistakes, crimes, conspiracies. As for Elizabeth's attitude, it was temporising; she did not want to have to let down the common front of crowned and anointed heads; she would have given Mary support at various critical junctures if Mary had genuinely wished to co-operate. What was fatal about Mary was that with very weak cards she insisted on gambling. She would have come through perfectly all right if she had played the game by, and with, Elizabeth. (Was that too much to ask?) Elizabeth was under constant pressure from Parliament to execute Mary after her plots. Not unnaturally Elizabeth wished to be rid of such a torment, going on year after year: enough to give anyone a complex. In the end, she certainly wished her made away with. Mary not only wished as much for Elizabeth, but attempted it — ineffectively as usual. Such became the mutual feelings of these two ladies, cousins, for each other.

Tytler allows that Elizabeth was a 'great Queen (for such, according to the ordinary sense of the word she was)'. But 'the hand of time has now pulled off the mask from this imperious and arbitrary Queen. . . . The humane will drop a tear to the memory of an unfortunate princess, the most amiable and accomplished of her sex who, by the unrelenting cruelty of a jealous rival, through a series of bitter persecutions, was at last brought to the grave!' One recognises the *clichés* of the eighteenth-century epitaph in this third-rate writer. But he succeeded in impressing Dr. Johnson, who was already convinced, and in annoying Hume, which was not so easy.

Johnson, who was brought up a Jacobite, wrote: 'It has now been fashionable, for near half a century, to defame and vilify the house of Stuart, and to exalt and magnify the reign of Elizabeth: the Stuarts have found few apologists, for the dead cannot pay for praise; and who will, without reward, oppose the tide of popularity?' In fact, the Stuarts will never want defenders: one-half the English aristocracy are descended from them. Wherever one goes in great English houses — such as have not put up the shutters for good and all — one finds romantic defenders of Mary Stuart. Among them it is Elizabeth, who left no progeny, who wants defenders and has little sympathy. Perhaps her personality is apt to alienate it, since she was one of those persons very capable of looking after themselves — and people somehow find that unattractive. Yet why should they? Must we always find the weak and the feckless, the foolish and the failed, appealing? (There is too much of a cult of all that in contemporary literature: our unappetising substitute for the heroic and the brave.) Yet ought that fact to prevent people from yielding their sympathy to her? There was a certain heroism about the woman who for forty-five years of strain and stress bore the responsibility for the well-being of her people; and in the end, was alone with herself. She once said, 'To be a king and wear a crown is more glorious to them that see it, than it is pleasure to them that bear it.'

It is a more adult thing to understand the strain of

Elizabeth's life, the unending demands upon her courage and
will-power, the sacrifice she made of her womanhood for it all.
This Mary Stuart never was capable of. She has her reward:
Dr. Johnson's 'Such a Queen as every man of any gallantry of
spirit would have sacrificed his life for'. Unfortunately for them,
only too many did. However, the Doctor did allow that
Queen Elizabeth 'had learning enough to have given dignity
to a bishop'. That was no more than the truth.

But Hume, who was Tytler's real target, was very much
annoyed. He did not reply, since he had made a sensible resolution at the beginning of his literary life not to reply to anybody.
But he wrote round to mutual friends protesting at being misrepresented. 'That trick is so frequently practised by thieves,
pickpockets and controversial writers (gentlemen whose morality is pretty much upon a footing) that all the world has ceased
to wonder and wise men are tired of complaining at it.' Wise
man that he was, he did complain: his correspondence has
some very unphilosophical expressions about Tytler: from
which we see that the great philosopher was just as touchy as
the rest of us at being attacked. We may wonder why *le bon
David*, who was hardly ever annoyed by anything, should have
been so vexed by this insignificant lawyer. It may be that
nothing infuriates a clever man like being misrepresented by a
stupid one: there is somehow an indignity about it.

Walter Scott, whom we must regard as an historian as well
as historical novelist and everything else, has, in spite of his
Stuart sympathies, a just portrait of Elizabeth in *Kenilworth*.
'Elizabeth united the occasional caprice of her sex with that
sense and sound policy in which neither man nor woman ever
excelled her.' And there comes that memorable image: 'the
mind of England's Elizabeth . . . was of that firm and decided
character which soon recovers its natural tone. It was like one
of those ancient druidical monuments called rocking stones.
The finger of Cupid, boy as he is painted, could put her feelings
in motion, but the power of Hercules could not have destroyed
their equilibrium.' (It is amusing to note that this and other
things in the book like the character Tresillian, come from
Scott's reading of Cornish lore at this time.)

The nineteenth century presents us with a continuation of

these themes, with a much wider spread and greater variety. There is Queen Victoria's well-known dislike of her predecessor: 'so unkind to my ancestress, the Queen of Scots'. It is with something of a shock that we realise that Queen Victoria was a descendant of Mary Stuart — whose domestic life was so very unlike that of the dear Queen. We are apt to think of her much more as a successor of — and in some sense a parallel to — Elizabeth. Her disapprobation was part of her romantic *schwärmerei* for the Stuarts; but might there not also be in it a little feminine jealousy of so famous a precursor? It went back very early: at her accession a motion was proposed in Parliament that she should take the title of Elizabeth II. The young woman of nineteen was determined that she would do no such thing: she would stick to her own name Victoria and make something of that.

We open up with the heavy howitzers of the Whig historians. Hallam has a just appreciation of Elizabeth. 'Her own remarkable talents, her masculine intrepidity, her readiness of wit and royal deportment, which the bravest men unaffectedly dreaded, her temper of mind, above all, at once fiery and inscrutably dissembling, would in any circumstances have ensured her more real sovereignty than weak monarchs, however nominally absolute, can ever enjoy or retain.' This, if a trifle wooden — like everything about that estimable man — is at any rate sensible. What dogs him is his moralism, which leads him, oddly enough, to praise Essex — he cannot have known what sort of man Essex really was; and to condemn Leicester, as everyone does — much too easily, in my opinion: 'that bold, bad man, whose favour is the great reproach of Elizabeth's reign'. Whatever Leicester was, he was not a bold man; and though he was not a nice man, he was not exactly a bad one. He was a sly customer, out for his own ends, like everybody else. But Elizabeth made of him a lifelong servant of hers and of the state, in difficult and sometimes humiliating circumstances.

When we come to the young Macaulay, to the famous essay on Burghley in which he trounced the unfortunate Dr. Nares with such terrific spirits, all the flags are out, all the drums beating. We are first given a very sombre picture of an England without the delights of a free press. The Queen 'often spoke to her parliaments in language as haughty and imperious as that which the Great Turk would use to his divan. She punished with great severity members of the House of Commons who, in her opinion, carried the freedom of debate too far. She assumed the power of legislating by means of proclamations. She imprisoned her subjects without bringing them to a legal trial.' And so on. Then comes the other pan of the scales, bumping down heavily with a celebrated tribute. 'Such was this government. Yet we know that it was loved by the great body of those who lived under it. We know that during the fierce contests of the sixteenth century,[1] both the hostile parties spoke of the time of Elizabeth as of a golden age. That great queen has now been lying two hundred and thirty years in Henry VII's chapel. Yet her memory is still dear to the hearts of a free people.'

The saxophone note of Victorian moralising is now heard. 'We are far from saying that the English of that generation were irreligious.' Would it not have been better if they had been — or, at least, less religious? They would have had the less excuse for killing each other. 'That which is the great stain on the character of Burghley is also the great stain on the character of Elizabeth. Being herself an Adiaphorist, having no scruple about conforming to the Romish church when conformity was necessary to her own safety, retaining to the last moment of her life a fondness for much of the doctrine and much of the ceremonial of that church, she yet subjected that church to a persecution even more odious than the persecution with which her sister had harassed the Protestants. We say more odious. For Mary had at least the plea of fanaticism. She did nothing for her religion which she was not prepared to suffer for it. If she burned the bodies of her subjects, it was in order to rescue their souls. Elizabeth had no such pretext.'

There is no difficulty in perceiving what nonsense all this is, besides the inaccuracy of its conception of Burghley and Elizabeth's attitudes towards religion. Both may justly be described as Anglican, Burghley more Protestant, Elizabeth less so; in fact, as with Palmerston's choice for bishops, one Low Church, one High Church. The fact that Mary believed the nonsense

---

[1] No-one seems to have observed that Macaulay must have meant seventeenth century here, or to have corrected the slip.

for which she burned, is no plea to my mind: it only reveals her as a fool. Elizabeth at least had the plea of self-defence, a course regrettably forced upon her by necessity. The young Macaulay has the brashness to reproach Elizabeth with the ease with which she 'might have united all conflicting sects under the shelter of the same impartial laws and the same paternal throne, and thus have placed the nation in the same situation, as far as the rights of conscience are concerned, in which we at last stand, after all the heart-burnings, the persecutions, the conspiracies, the seditions, the revolutions, the judicial murders, the civil wars of ten generations'.

'After'! — the twentieth century has had something to say to all that. What incomprehension it reveals of the illimitable depths of human folly! Intelligent people in the sixteenth century, like Burghley and Elizabeth, Erasmus and Montaigne, had a better understanding of them. They realised that a moderate middle way was the only chance of any peace from these idiocies, and that external conformity was the necessary condition for the maximum freedom of which humans were capable. 'I desire to open a window into no man's conscience,' said Elizabeth; and that was saying a lot in the sixteenth century.

'This is the dark side of her character,' says Macaulay. 'Yet she surely was a great woman. Of all the sovereigns who exercised a power which was seemingly absolute, but which in fact depended for support on the love and confidence of their subjects, she was by far the most illustrious.' I dislike the antithetical rhetoric of the Victorians — so unsubtle, and so untrue. If the Queen were so great a woman, is it likely that she was so wrong about the matter of the preceding paragraph, that she could have achieved a toleration at all, let alone with any ease? Catherine de Medici, who tried it by bringing the two sides together into conference at Poissy, found that it only gave them the excuse to get at each other's throat; France lapsed into civil war over religious doctrine; society was split from top to bottom. No: Elizabeth, with the spectacle of the world around her, was right: in the circumstances of the sixteenth century, it could not be done.

Let us leave Macaulay: he had not the advantage of our melancholy experience of the twentieth century.

The leading Catholic historian of England, Lingard, expresses a more balanced view — even if he states it somewhat equivocally as that generally held, rather than necessarily held by him. No doubt a useful course in casuistry had formed part of his clerical training. Observe — 'in the judgment of her contemporaries — and that judgment has been ratified by the consent of posterity — Elizabeth was numbered among the greatest and most fortunate of princes. The tranquillity which, during a reign of nearly half a century, she maintained within her dominions, while the neighbouring nations were convulsed with intestine dissensions, was taken as a proof of the wisdom or the vigour of her government; and her successful resistance against the Spanish monarch, the severe injuries which she inflicted on that lord of so many kingdoms, and the spirit displayed by her fleets and armies . . . served to give to the world an exalted notion of her military and naval power. When she came to the throne, England ranked only among the secondary kingdoms; before her death, it had risen to a level with the first nations of Europe.'

This stately pronouncement by the distinguished historian who was a cardinal *in petto*, even if uttered with a personal caveat, puts in its proper place the nonsense written about Elizabeth by his co-religionists in our time — Belloc and others who do not care whether what they say is true or not: the ultimate sin for an historian.

But when the priest can say a derogatory word for himself as to Elizabeth's private character, he does. 'The woman who despises the safeguards, must be content to forfeit the reputation of chastity.' He proceeds to insinuate that Leicester and others were her lovers. There is no evidence whatever that this was so; and a knowledge of psychology would suggest the contrary: Elizabeth had all the symptoms of the disappointed spinster: she displayed an unattractive, if understandable, jealousy of the young couples around her who were free to enjoy each other, when she was not. The very archness and freedom of her behaviour in public to Leicester and others is in itself an indication of the sad truth, of the sacrifice of her woman's life for the queen's.

The most interesting case is that of Froude, and the most

important; for the second half of his *History* — a work of brilliance, imagination and literary power, the one possible rival in
the century to Macaulay — is devoted to Elizabeth's reign up
to the Armada, with which he ended. He started with a prejudice in her favour, as the daughter of Henry VIII — the
hero of the first half of his *History* — and as the continuer of
Henry's policy. In Volume I we read: 'In her vital convictions
she represented the free proud spirit of the educated laity, who
would endure no dictation from priests of either persuasion, and
so far as lay in them, would permit no clergy any more to fetter
the thoughts and paralyse the energies of England.' Perhaps
we see here Froude getting his own back on those clergymen,
his father, his brother and the Oxford Movement. But of Elizabeth, it is true. In Volume III his judgment is: 'A middle course
was therefore chosen — a course which at the time pleased no-
one but the Queen and the half-dozen or dozen intelligent
persons who surrounded her; but it was the same which her
father had marked out before her, and its eventual success may
be allowed to prove that it was wise.' He could even state her
admirable Laodiceanism justly: the Queen told the Huguenot
leader, Cardinal Chatillon, that 'whatever he and his party
might think of the abomination of going to mass, she would
herself sooner have heard a thousand than have caused the
least of the million villainies (*méchancetés*) which had been committed on account of it'.

As the years went on and his successive volumes came out,
Froude grew more and more out of sympathy, until in the end
he became incapable of doing her justice. In the concluding
pages of his *History*, in his summing up of her character, we
read: 'To Elizabeth the speculations of so-called divines were
but as ropes of sand and sea-slime leading to the moon, and the
doctrines for which they were rending each other to pieces a
dream of fools or enthusiasts.' (Well, weren't they, very largely?)
'Unfortunately her keenness of insight was not combined with
any profound concern for serious things.' (Her profoundest
concern as Queen of England was the well-being of her country
and peace at home and abroad. What more could anyone want
or expect of her?) 'She saw through the emptiness of the forms
in which religion presented itself to the world. She had none

F

the more any larger or deeper conviction of her own.' (Suppose there is none?) 'She was without the intellectual emotions which give human character its consistency and power.' (I should have thought that consistency and power were precisely what her character showed, and her intellectual emotions were sufficient to provide the driving force for them. Indeed, unflagging energy of mind was her most marked characteristic.)

We are told that 'her entire nature was saturated with artifice. Except when speaking some round untruth Elizabeth never could be simple. She was unnatural even in her prayers, and she carried her affectations into the presence of the Almighty. . . . Obligations of honour were not only occasionally forgotten by her, but she did not seem to understand what honour meant.' Well, she was a woman, and honour is a masculine concept; for a woman, Elizabeth was exceptionally responsive to considerations of honour, more particularly of her honour as a queen. Froude concludes: 'Vain as she was of her own sagacity, she never modified a course recommended to her by Burghley without injury both to the realm and herself. . . . The great results of her reign were the fruits of a policy which was not her own, and which she starved and mutilated when energy and completeness were most needed.'

This is wholly unjust and quite untrue. Yet it is a charge that has often been repeated: we owe its reverberations, especially among naval historians, mainly to the impression made by Froude's *History*, read — like Macaulay — by thousands. The charge that Elizabeth starved her navy of resources has been completely disproved in our time by historians who today understand better the difficulties that condition the action of all government. In fact, the Queen struggled all her life to keep the government of her country financially sound; when her hand was removed we see the difficulties the Stuarts got into at once. I do not propose to say any more on the subject: it has been dealt with once and for all in the work of Sir John Neale.

Froude is a fascinating case. To some extent his repugnance may be due to the growing distaste of the researcher living for too many years with his subject. He wrote of Burghley to a friend: 'He, it is more and more clear to me, was the solitary author of Elizabeth's and England's greatness. . . . The private

letters which passed between him and Walsingham about Elizabeth have destroyed finally the prejudice that still clung to me
that, notwithstanding her many faults, she was a woman of
ability. Evidently in their opinion she had no ability at all
worth calling by the name.' That does not at all represent the
opinion of this very exclusive men's club. Both Burghley and
Walsingham had much to put up with: above all, the Queen's
determination that they, not she, should bear the responsibility
of necessarily unpopular measures. But that was all in the game:
the popularity and prestige of the Crown must be preserved at
all costs. Unfair, but quite right: they understood the terms of
the game, and — bemoaning their lot to each other when it
became too intolerable — accepted it. Burghley in fact never
ceased to admire, and came to stand in awe of her: there is his
political testament to his clever son and successor Robert to
witness: alway to present the true facts of the case to the Queen,
but never to press her beyond her better judgment, her knowledge of men and her experience were such and so great.

Froude's judgments are emotional and go back to an element of instability in his personality. There was an ambivalence
in his make-up, which gives him an uncertainty of focus — by
contrast with the too great clarity of Macaulay. The child of
the Oxford Movement who had lost his faith had been rescued
by Carlyle and given a harsh injection of Calvinism of a kind;
the boy who had been bullied by his brother, the inquisitorial
Hurrell, and beaten so badly at school as to have been ruptured,
grew out of his early weakness to admire force and understand,
better than any other Victorian, the rôle of violence in history.
Froude was all his life under attack for what he understood
about human beings; to my mind he is more vulnerable where
he conformed to the nonsense they thought. The muscular
Victorianism that was indoctrinated upon him, as with the cult
of the manly virtues that was inculcated by his brother-in-law,
Charles Kingsley — both were over-compensations for something they felt lacking in themselves, for both bore the stigmata
of genius.

Hence Froude's harping on Elizabeth's feminine tortuousness, her unfathomable guile, her lack of candour, the insin-
cerities of her prolonged marriage negotiations. All this was

politics as well understood by others in the game. Froude's
Victorian manliness was disgusted. Things were too simple for
him. The only time he made an incursion into politics himself
— in South African affairs — he put his foot in it, and, though
right on the main issue, made a frightful hash by his candour.
We may not be able to accept the necessary disingenuousnesses
of politics in practice; but as historians we should at least
understand them. That practical politician, Catherine the
Great, well understood the silly superiority of the armchair
doctrinaire, who supposes that in great affairs things happen
'comme sur le papier, qui souffre tout'. So did Elizabeth: her
tortuousness served England well: she never slipped up.

This was what Creighton appreciated better than anyone:
he was a bishop, and no mean *politique* himself. Of Elizabeth's
personal character he writes: 'Self-mastery and self-restraint
had been forced upon her. Bitter experience had taught her
how little she could satisfy her own desires, how little she could
confide in the wisdom or discretion of others.' Of course, self-
control is the indispensable condition to control of others; and
that was her magnificent, life-long job. She had this advantage
— unthinkable for either Mary Tudor or Mary Stuart — that
'she was both intellectually and emotionally cold. In politics
and in private life alike she cared little for decorum, because
she knew that she could stop short whenever prudence made it
needful.'

It is the prime virtue of Creighton's biography that he understood completely the inner significance of Elizabeth's political
rôle; that in a world torn in two, like ours, by ideological conflict, she could not afford to be too clear: she must wait and go
on waiting with complete self-restraint — in a way that no man
could have done, except possibly her grandfather, Henry VII
— until the success of her rule over the years vindicated her.
'The one thing she strove to avoid was an outburst of strong
feeling, or aught that would divide England into opposite
camps.' The identification of the Queen with her country and
her country's long-term interests was Creighton's theme; to
appreciate that, one has to have a long-term perspective. 'She
represented England as no other ruler ever did. . . . By avoiding
risky undertakings, by keeping down public expense, she was

not merely indulging her tendency to parsimony; she was warding off from her people demands which they were unequal at that time to sustain. . . . But when it came to decisive action she fell back upon her instinctive perception of what England wanted. As she could not explain this, she was driven to all sorts of devices to gain time. She could not, on the other hand, fully take her people into her confidence. It was the unconscious tendency of their capacities which she interpreted, not their actual demands' — in other words, their long-term interests, of which the people themselves are not usually the best judges. In short, 'Elizabeth's imperishable claim to greatness lies in her instinctive sympathy with her people.' They have rewarded her, and time — always her friend — has vindicated her: the best-remembered of all the figures in the long pageant of those who have occupied the English throne.

It is pleasant to think that the man who would have been Archbishop of Canterbury, if he had lived, understood her best. His is by far the most perceptive and true judgment of Elizabeth of any of the great historians. Creighton was by nature a states-man; his special bent as an historian was for high politics and statesmanship. Not for nothing he had served his apprentice-ship and trained his eye on the Popes of the Renaissance. His short biography came out at the end of the nineteenth century; his judgment stands unlikely ever to be reversed.

So we do not have to bother with the captiousness of lesser Victorians — the puerile antitheses of the egregious Freeman, for example, who made it a regular habit to attack a better man than himself, in Froude, whenever he saw a chance. One needs no very deep knowledge of psychology to understand the motive. Gardiner, though an Irvingite, was more just, and in his own way may be taken to answer Macaulay on the question of the religious settlement. 'In taking her stand, as she did, against the abolition of Episcopacy, Elizabeth was on the whole acting on behalf of the liberty of her subjects.'

It is curious to note what a fuss the Victorians made about the adulation, the language of devotion in which Elizabeth was addressed in her own time: Macaulay, Froude, Freeman, Dean Church — they all were shocked and protested at what they called gross flattery. 'The gross, shameless, lying flattery paid to the Queen,' writes mild Dean Church; 'there is really nothing like it in history. . . . It was no worship of a secluded and distant object of loyalty: the men who thus flattered knew perfectly well, often by painful experience, what Elizabeth was: able, indeed, high-spirited, successful, but ungrateful to her servants, unjust, and in her old age, ugly.' Ungallant Dean! Inaccurate Dean! We may well apply to him the words she used to a tactless bishop who referred to her advancing years in preaching before her — 'Now I see that the greatest clerks are not the wisest men.' It is surely anachronistic to condemn the language in which the sixteenth century thought it proper to address such a lady, such a Queen. I find it has a charm — so revealing of the fantasy, the romantic mirror of the Renaissance world in which they lived. And was it so unexampled with the Victorians? What about the language in which Tennyson addressed his Queen? Or the demonstration Disraeli was making of how effective such language could be in sweetening the relations between a Victorian Sovereign and her Prime Minister?

The besetting sin of the Victorians, in regard to Elizabeth, as in so much else, was their moralism. It made it almost impossible for them to do a Renaissance woman justice. Even Creighton, according to the dragon, Mrs. Creighton, regarded the age as 'more and more demoralised the better he understood it; those whom Froude had called "wanderers on the Spanish main" or "pioneers in the tangled path of discovery" he saw to have been men who deserved no better name than buccaneer or pirate; while with an increasing appreciation of the extraordinary ability of Elizabeth, he had a constantly diminishing opinion of her morals'.

*Morals!* There you have the incessant, grinding concern of the Victorians. It is as if everything — politics, literature, philosophy, economics, but especially aesthetics — had to be translated into morals before it could be understood or discussed. I prefer to take my subjects clean. And the censoriousness! — how they indulged themselves: the greatest pleasure, it would seem, of the high-minded.

We live in a world, like the sixteenth century, too distracted, too dangerous, for such facile condemnations. We know how difficult it is even to keep society together, how easy to plunge it into the abyss, how thin is the ice of civilised conduct covering what black waters beneath. The standards of the Victorians were the product of an epoch of exceptional security in human history: never again shall we see such another. We are back in the recognisable main stream of history once more. With the irreversible verdict of Creighton, on the threshold of the twentieth century, we may take leave of a woman who in her time did what she could to hold up the avalanche, and strove, with greater success than is given to most, to build some fabric of sense and sanity, of moderation and internal peace, within this fortunate island amid the storms outside.

V

# SIR WINSTON CHURCHILL AS AN HISTORIAN

It is an honour to be invited to give the Founder's Day Address at this famous institution; but it is also an opportunity to pay tribute to the creative foresight of the Founder, and the care with which successive trustees have carried out the intentions of his trust. Napoleon claimed, 'J'avais le goût de la fondation, et non de la propriété'; which I may translate freely as 'I had a taste for founding things, rather than for property as such.' In these days of Welfare States I do not underrate the values, and uses, of property: did not Arthur Young say, 'the magic of property turns sand into gold?' But, nowadays, if you want your name to go on for good, then found something good. Mr. Henry E. Huntington's beneficent shade has reason to be well pleased: his foundation presents not only static objects of beauty to the view, its essential character is that it is creative. What excuse have we grateful scholars for not being creative, working in such a library, art gallery at hand, in the environment of a beautiful garden, placed between the San Gabriel mountains and the sea?

The subject I have been encouraged to take is that of Sir Winston Churchill considered as an historian. I am not to consider his place in history, his contribution as a maker of history but — rather more austerely — as a writer. Will you forgive me if I make it occasionally a little personal? — the books are there for us all to read; but some touches of personal contact may illuminate a point here and there, and make a useful addition to the record.

We may begin with the conclusion of an English authority on American history, Professor H. C. Allen, that when we consider the total bulk of the historical work, 'judged as an historian alone, and setting aside all his other manifold and in some cases greater achievements, Sir Winston Churchill's fame would

78

be secure'.[1] It is extraordinary to think that in a lifetime of such activities, as soldier, journalist, politician, painter, traveller, statesman — who has held nearly all the highest offices of state as President of the Board of Trade, Home Secretary, First Lord of the Admiralty (twice), Minister of Munitions, Colonial Secretary, Secretary of State for War, and for Air, Chancellor of the Exchequer, Prime Minister — he should have found time to write two historical masterpieces, each in four volumes. Any reasonably eminent historian might consider himself fortunate to achieve one. Sir Winston has written two: The *Life and Times of John Churchill, Duke of Marlborough* and *A History of the English Speaking Peoples*.

I propose to devote myself mainly to these two, though he has made other important contributions. There are two bulky works of Memoirs: those of the First World War, in which he played his part, *The World Crisis* in six volumes, and those called *The Second World War*, in which he played a far greater rôle, also in six volumes. Sir Winston is so conscientious a practitioner of the art that he does not describe his war-books as history, 'for that belongs to another generation. But I claim with confidence that it is a contribution to history which will be of service to the future.'[2] These volumes are historical memoirs, surveying the scene from the point of view of an individual participant in the action: they are in fact an indispensable contribution to history, in addition to being classic examples of the art of the historical Memoir.

Besides this, there are other works of his that come into the category of history, and some that lie on the frontiers of it. His big two-volumed life of his father, Lord Randolph Churchill, was hailed by Lord Rosebery, with perhaps pardonable exaggeration, as 'among the first dozen, perhaps the first half-dozen, biographies in our language'. If this is putting it too high, it may well be nearer the mark if we restrict the term to what Lord Rosebery probably had in mind — political biographies. Here the young Churchill, not yet thirty, had the advantage of having all his father's private papers; but many an historian twice his age has not known how to put manuscript material to such

---

[1] *English Historical Review* (1959), 311.
[2] W. S. Churchill, *The Second World War* (Cassell, 1948–54), I. vii.

good use. The book is masterly: firm in structure, which is a prime necessity for a book; with a political grasp of period and subject; warm, living, vivid. What more could one ask? Too often a political biography is a cold mausoleum, 'This Way to the Tomb.'

Already, when only twenty-five, he had written *The River War*, a two-volumed account of the war in the Sudan, which showed a mastery unusual at such an age. For it is not only a dependable and vivid account of the operations, it begins, according to proper historical method, with a history of the Mahdi's fanatical movement — written with remarkable sympathy — and a survey of the geographical lay-out of the country, the conditioning environment of the campaign. Other books of his trench on history, too: notably his *Great Contemporaries*, incisive portraits, though generous and just, of the leading figures of his time. And what about *My Early Life*? — his own self-portrait up to the first stage of his career in office. Autobiography can be a contribution to history — Clarendon's is a classic example — especially when the story is that of someone who has played a significant part in his time.

Perhaps we may now concentrate on his two masterpieces, and first for his *Marlborough*.

The motive for undertaking this work was to vindicate his ancestor — first of English soldiers and an outstanding figure in history — from the aspersions of Macaulay. Macaulay depicted this great soldier and servant of the state as a mean villain, not far removed from a traitor. Macaulay's genius as a writer blackened Marlborough's reputation, and fixed this picture of him in the history-books and in our tradition — such was the power of a brilliant pen. Now rectifying this was not only a question of family piety with his descendant but also a case of putting right a grave historical injustice.

We can all agree that Churchill completely accomplished this task with his big book. We may now conclude, quite simply, that Churchill is right and Macaulay was wrong. But how did Macaulay go *so* wrong? Well, historians are very far from infallible; Macaulay had a cocksure, Victorian certainty, which was profoundly antipathetic to the ambivalence, the moral velleities, the capacity for trimming sail, of the ambitious men of the late seventeenth century. Marlborough lived in revolutionary times: he was never a candid man, and his course was often a devious one. But in time of revolution it is unwise to be too candid, and it is sometimes necessary to be devious in order to survive. This is not necessarily to be a bad man — and Sir Winston has described Macaulay to me as 'a liar': he rightly felt strongly about this denigration of a great, if not morally great, man.

Macaulay's great-nephew, George Macaulay Trevelyan, has in conversation given me an excuse for Macaulay's conduct, and I think it is just. Macaulay's manner was that of a Parliamentarian speaking in rhetorical antithesis sharpened for effect. He underlined the not very heroic first half of Marlborough's career, with its shady passages, in order to bring out the more strikingly the heroic achievements of the second half, the genius of Queen Anne's war against the French, who more than anyone else ended Louis XIV's ascendancy in Europe. Then Macaulay died before he got to Queen Anne's reign. It was very unfair of him: it left his vilification of Marlborough standing uncorrected, unanswered, with the other side of the picture for ever missing.

Or, at any rate, effectively missing until the 1930s, when Sir Winston was kept out of office by Baldwin and Chamberlain and was free to dedicate his main energies to historical writing. That dedicated task turned out to be not without practical effect upon the man; a former colleague of his gave it to me as his opinion that it was in the course of writing that work that Churchill matured as a statesman. It turned out an incomparable apprenticeship for the task that would befall him in the war. For, during these years he was studying in Marlborough, who was the military and diplomatic linch-pin of the Grand Alliance against Louis XIV, all the problems of conducting such a war and how to keep the alliance together. By the time he had reached the third volume in the 1930s he had learned to put up with what he would find in action in the 1940s: 'the history of all coalitions is a tale of the reciprocal complaints of allies'.[1]

[1] W. S. Churchill, *The Life and Times of John Churchill, Duke of Marlborough* (1933–8), iii. 246.

But we must here confine ourselves to historical writing. The book is not only the Life of Marlborough, it is his Times. It is a splendid canvas of the whole life of the age, painted in strong and glowing colours, full of vivid portraits, scenes — especially battlefields, descriptions — especially of political and court life, presented with generosity of judgment, immense gusto and intellectual energy. Two things are obvious: that he had enjoyed it all, when with some historians one would think writing was worse than having a tooth extracted; the other thing, which we are apt to ignore, is that Churchill is a man of a powerful and original intellect. Nor is he afraid to add humour to the category of the historian's gifts. It is a thing to be careful about; but some of the best historians have had the gift: certainly Gibbon and Hume and Clarendon, and even the erring Macaulay, who wrote, 'there is a vile phrase of which bad historians are exceedingly fond, "the dignity of history" '.

After this, we need not be surprised at Churchill describing a meddling Dutch deputy, Goslinga, who seems aptly named, as a 'militarily-minded civilian, fascinated (without any professional knowledge) by the art of war, who would have liked to command the army himself. He combined the valour of ignorance with a mind fertile in plans of action. His military judgment was almost childishly defective; his energy was overflowing.'[1] Nor need we be surprised, after this downright judgment, at Sir Winston's phrase for inhibited historians who are so impersonal as to be unreadable: 'the reserve of modern assertions — in which the fear of being contradicted leads the writer to strip himself of almost all sense and meaning'.

Churchill's strong personality is present in all that he writes — the man expresses himself in every inflexion of his style. Personality cannot be excluded from the writing of history; impersonality eviscerates, and in any case one cannot jump out of one's own skin. What one wants is justice of mind, that certainly does not mean not judging wicked men, or failing to condemn the bad record of some peoples in the interest of a frightened neutralism of mind. Justice means holding the scales fairly; it does not mean no condemnation, where it is due.

[1] W. S. Churchill, *The Life and Times of John Churchill, Duke of Marlborough* (1933–8), iii. 38.

How has Churchill done his writing?

Well, he writes, or rather dictates, every word himself: every word bears his personal stamp. It is true that he uses the aid of research assistants to delve in the archives for him and to look out, under his direction, the large masses of material he likes to deploy. But, very much of an artist, he organises and shapes up the material himself, gives it his own structure and character down to the last button. Then, when the volume is in draft, he has it vetted by a recognised authority on the period or subject, and, with his artistic conscience, he considers and acts on the suggestions made, the corrections and emendations proposed — as I can testify from reading for him the Tudor section of his *History of the English-Speaking Peoples*.

The result is to be seen in a remarkable degree of accuracy in one who has written so much. Sir Richard Lodge, an eminent authority on the eighteenth century — as unexciting a writer as any academic could wish — paid tribute to this feature of Churchill's *Marlborough*, vol. i: 'few academic historians, dealing with a period of fifty years, have made so few blunders in matters of fact, though many readers may differ from him in matters of opinion'.[1] One need not be deterred by that: with Churchill's long experience of politics his opinions must be taken into account. In this first volume too much space is given up to Churchill's controversy with Macaulay — as Sir Winston has admitted to me; but he felt he had to do it, to rebut Macaulay's accusations point by point, and he has done it once and for all. One of Macaulay's habits he has followed to good purpose — which other historians might practice to advantage: namely, of going to see the places one is writing about, describing them as they lie under one's eye. Hence, in part, the visual vividness of his books. He has told me how he followed Marlborough's route across Germany to Blenheim and studied all his battlefields on the spot — as he has a good many of the American Civil War battlefields. He has had the advantage of his early training as a soldier, and of a passionate interest in every aspect of war, strategy, tactics, new methods and weapons, at sea as on land, and latterly in the air. The importance of this was not appreciated in the slack, pacifistic atmosphere

---

[1] *English Historical Review* (1934), 716.

of the 1930s, in which his was a solitary voice speaking out against the well-meaning illusions of the democracies. The factor of power, after all, is the first consideration, though it may not be the last, in human affairs. Some reflection of his irritation with our fondness for illusions appears in his summing up of Marlborough's achievement at half-time: 'one man and three battles had transformed all. Let men bleat — *War settles nothing*'.[1] The sad truth is that sometimes only a war will settle something: the evil of Nazi Germany, for example, or Napoleon's tyranny over Europe. Or what about the American Revolutionary War or the Civil War?

The rôle of force in history is rather comically appreciated at the beginning of his *History of the English-Speaking Peoples* with his graphic description of the transitions from the flint age to the bronze, and from bronze to iron. Neolithic man had discovered the utility of flint-heads for arrows: 'already man had found out that a flint was better than a fist'.[2] Then how to make bronze was discovered: 'other things being equal, the men with bronze could beat the men with flints. The discovery was hailed, and the Bronze Age began.' Next iron was forged: 'men armed with iron entered Britain from the Continent and killed the men of bronze. At this point we can plainly recognize across the vanished milleniums a fellow-being. A biped capable of slaying another with iron is evidently to modern eyes a man and a brother. It cannot be doubted that for smashing skulls, whether long-headed or round, iron is best.' And so, forward to the age of guided missiles.

The miserable decade of the 1930s in Britain, which kept Churchill out of office and enabled him to finish *Marlborough*, also gave him time to write the first draft of his *History of the English-Speaking Peoples*. Let him tell the story of this book in his own words penned at New Year, 1956. 'It is nearly twenty years that I made the arrangements which resulted in this book. At the outbreak of the war about half a million words were duly delivered. Of course there was still much to be done in proof-reading when I went to the Admiralty on 3 September 1939. All this was set aside. During nearly six years of war, and an even longer period in which I was occupied with my war memoirs, the book slumbered peacefully. It is only now when things have quieted down that I present to the public *A History of the English-Speaking Peoples*. If there was need for it before, that has certainly not passed away. For the second time in the present century the British Empire and the United States have stood together facing the perils of war . . . and we have become more conscious of our common duty to the human race. Language, law, and the processes by which we have come into being, already afforded a unique foundation for drawing together and portraying a concerted task. I thought when I began that such a unity might well notably influence the destiny of the world. Certainly I do not feel that the need for this has diminished in any way in the twenty years that have passed.'[1]

There was the motive — the prophetic motive — of the book.

Once more Churchill had undertaken an immense task, a narrative history on a large scale such as professional historians nowadays are apt to shrink from. There was much professional curiosity as to how he would acquit himself. We need not have feared: it turned out a masterpiece, though he had not finished his work upon it — in his usual conscientious manner, rewriting, correcting, inserting, shaping up — until his eighty-third year. One thing we academic historians may take some pride in: the reception of the book was all that one could wish — no narrow, carping spirit, not much niggling over details, but a proper recognition of the greatness of the achievement and the special qualities this historian had to offer.

Even the historical technicians saw the point that Churchill's immense political experience, his proved long-sighted vision into affairs, his practical grasp of statesmanship, gave extra value to his judgment of affairs in the past which is the staple of history. 'History is past politics' is a restricted definition of the subject, but it serves for Churchill. Men have the defects of their qualities, but also the qualities of their defects. He has never been much interested in economic matters — a surprising omission in a former Chancellor of the Exchequer. (He once said *à propos* of the Gold Standard, 'are we to be at the mercy of a lot of negro women scrabbling with their toes in the

[1] W. S. Churchill, *A History of the English Speaking Peoples* (1956–8), i. vii.

mud of the Zambesi?' — this, it was true, after a good dinner.)
His real concern as an historian has been with the state as such,
its government and institutions, its power expressed in its armed
forces, diplomacy and the art of war — which is, alas, one
aspect of the relations of the powers. This is the central thread
of history to him: what governs, not what wells up from below.

The first volume, *The Birth of Britain*, goes from prehistoric
times to the end of the Middle Ages. It is at its best on Roman
Britain, perhaps too favourable to the imperial idea at the
expense of the native Celts; though when he comes to a doughty
fighter among them — Cassivellaunus, who delayed the Roman conquest — he is ready with a salute: 'little is known of
Cassivellaunus, and we can only hope that later defenders of
the Island will be equally successful and that their measures
will be as well suited to the time'.[1] This, with an eye on what
was to come at the end of that decade. The fact that little is
known of these early figures Sir Winston did not find unduly
daunting. We know little enough of the great Offa, King of
Mercia, except his Dyke along the Welsh frontier and his coins:
he paid Peter's Pence to Rome, 'part of it unwittingly paid in
these same infidel coins which proclaimed an opposite creed.
In studying Offa we are like geologists who, instead of finding a
fossil, find only the hollow shape in which a creature of unusual
strength and size undoubtedly resided.'

He is equally good about those tough fighting folk, the
Vikings and the Normans, about the Wars of the Roses, and
also on the development of the Common Law and the growth
of Parliament — as a good Parliamentarian should be. On the
payment of Danegeld to the Vikings by the too easy-going
Anglo-Saxons he has a good comment: 'the pious English had
accepted far too literally the idea of the absolution of sins as
the consequence of monetary payment to the Church. Their
sins were many, their repentances frequent, and the Church
had thrived. Here were easy prizes for sharp swords to win.'[2]
We notice another trait: he always likes to be generous in his
estimate of kings; it is a good fault, but he is sometimes too
much so. Richard Cœur-de-Lion — naturally he would fall

---

[1] W. S. Churchill, *A History of the English-Speaking Peoples* (1956–58), i. 14, 67.
[2] Ibid., i. 77, 189.

for him: 'worthy by the consent of all men to sit with King Arthur and Roland and other heroes of martial romance at some Eternal Round Table which we trust the Creator of the Universe, in his comprehension, will not have forgotten to provide'. Now the truth is that Richard I utterly neglected his country, and drained it of resources in order to go careering off on a crusade. He was a bad king of England. There is little about social growth, literature and the arts, and hardly anything about the economic development of the country — he has always regarded economics as the dismal science. Himself a product of the Victorian age, he has been careful to incorporate the corrections subsequently made upon Victorian and Whig scholarship, with regard to the development of our early institutions, for example, and a too exclusively Anglo-Saxon view of our racial origins. After all, we Celts were in the islands before they were — and are still there.

Remote as our medieval history may seem, it comes alive in his robust imagination and breezy humour — sometimes the two are combined. There is Richard III, the murderer of the two princes, his nephews, in the Tower. On Richard's first coup against his nephew's maternal relatives and defenders, 'Edward V took the only positive action recorded of his reign. He wept. Well he might.'[1] For, what happened next? — the murder of the young king and his brother. In modern times there have been people ready to stake their word, though not perhaps their fortune, that this was not so; as others have been ready to stake their word, for what it was worth, that Shakespeare's plays were written by Francis Bacon, or the Earl of Oxford, or Derby, or (for all I know) Queen Elizabeth — anybody rather than that he should have written them himself. Sir Winston's common sense says the last word on one of those harmless lunacies: 'Richard III held the authority of government. He told his story with what facilities were available, and he was spontaneously and almost universally disbelieved. . . . It will take many ingenious books to raise this issue to the dignity of a historical controversy.' Nothing more need be said.

The next volume, on the Tudor and Stuart period, the sixteenth and seventeenth centuries, shows no falling off in

[1] W. S. Churchill, *A History of the English-Speaking Peoples* (1956–58), i. 383–4.

G

quality. As a general criticism, I find he makes personal factors over-important; as against this, everyone appreciated the splendid gallery of portraits of personages. Again he is too generous to some kings, in especial to Charles I, who, a fine connoisseur of the arts, was hopeless as a ruler. Once, in conversation with Sir Winston, he made a plea for this unhappy monarch. We have to remember, he said, that in his time rulers had to see to everything for themselves, there were no specialised departments to help them; where nowadays everything was prepared and came up from the civil service for political leaders to make their decisions upon — things were more difficult for Charles I than for us. It was an interesting point, which I duly registered; registering also that it did not excuse Charles for his incompetence as a ruler. Of James II Sir Winston says, 'his sacrifice for religion gained for him the lasting respect of the Catholic Church, and he carried with him into lifelong exile an air of royalty and honour'.[1] This is much too handsome for a crowned nincompoop: Madame de Sévigné's judgment of him on his arrival in France, after three years of fatuity as king, was more to the point. Or, for that matter, the unspoken judgment of Churchill's ancestor, Marlborough, whose career James had made; in the hour of his need Marlborough deserted him: it was the only thing to do with such a man, not only in Marlborough's interest but the country's.

However, it must be very agreeable to be able to regard, and to write about, these passages of English history as all in the family.

My own criticism of this volume and the next is that there should have been much more about the development of the colonies in the seventeenth and eighteenth centuries, their characteristic idiosyncracies, their culture, the remarkable growth of their trade and maritime interests which have left beautiful memorials in such unspoiled towns as Newcastle, Maryland or Salem and Newburyport, Massachusetts, the settlements on Narragansett Bay with their prosperous eighteenth-century houses, not to mention the grand houses of tidewater Virginia and in and around Philadelphia. Nevertheless, our most austere eighteenth-century historian, Richard Pares,

[1] W. S. Churchill, *A History of the English-Speaking Peoples* (1956–58), ii. 325.

paid tribute to 'the splendour and variety of Sir Winston Churchill's second volume, with its broad stream of narrative, its interesting and often convincing political analyses, and its full-length delineation of personal destiny and personal character'.[1] Even in volume iii Pares finds that the political portraits are 'almost uniformly just, even to national enemies, to failures and characters of a type with which he can have little personal sympathy'.

There is general agreement that volume iii, dealing with the eighteenth century — the Revolution of 1688, the quarrel with America, the struggle with Napoleon — is the weakest. The constitutional achievements of 1688 are not gone into; Pares says, 'the fact is that Sir Winston, like William III himself, has scrambled over these matters as quickly as possible in order to get to the wars'. These, with the descriptions of campaigns, are 'admirably effective and vivid, as we should expect from this great master'. But there is too much of them, and not enough, next to nothing, about the Industrial and Agrarian Revolutions which were the foundation of modern Britain. Hardly a thing about the Wesleyan and Evangelical Revivals, which had such far-reaching consequences for society; for these we could have sacrificed several battles. What is so curious for a painter is that the great age of English painting, from about 1760 to 1830 — which the Huntington Gallery so splendidly exemplifies — is not even mentioned; nor is the greatest age of English architecture, the Georgian — very odd for someone born in Blenheim Palace. Yet, after these criticisms, Pares concludes, 'the work is a noble work'.

When we come to volume iv, which attempts to cover Britain, the Empire and the United States in the nineteenth century, we begin to wonder whether the enterprise is at all possible. And the truth is that this volume becomes a parallel history of Britain and the United States, rather than a history of the English-speaking peoples: that would require a fifth volume. Still, this volume is more varied and entertaining than any; the good humour is at a high level and is often politically perceptive. On the professional historians' controversy over the nature

---

[1] *English Historical Review* (1958), 497 ff.

of political party in eighteenth-century Britain, which reached absurd disproportion under the banner of Namier, the professional politician has something salutary and sensible to say: 'if caution must be the hall-mark of history, all that may be said is that the men in power were vigorously opposed by the men who were out, while in between stood large numbers of neutral-minded gentlemen placidly prepared to support whichever group held office. It is not much of a conclusion to come to about a great age of Parliamentary debate. The ins and outs might as well have names, and why not employ the names of Whig and Tory which their supporters cast at one another?'[1] Or there was the fiasco that overwhelmed the revolutionary threat of Chartism in 1848 in a downpour of rain. 'As Wellington remarked — still an imperturbable Commander-in-Chief at the age of seventy-eight — the English are "a very quiet people". This is especially so when it is raining. More spectators than Chartists assembled on that wet spring day at Kennington. When the police forbade the proposed march the demonstrators quietly dispersed. Their petition was conveyed to the Commons in three cabs. Such was the measure of revolutionary feeling in London in 1848.'

With his treatment of American history, it is generally agreed that he gives disproportionate space to the Civil War — that is, if it is possible to give disproportionate space to the Civil War. My chief criticism of this volume is that it omits the western migration across the prairies that conquered a whole continent, and is one of the decisive folk-movements of history: the grand epic of nineteenth-century America. So far as the Civil War is concerned he gives us, as we should expect, a most vivid account of the campaigns and the battles, set in a generous perspective: 'Thus ended the great American Civil War, which must upon the whole be considered the noblest and least avoidable of all the great mass-conflicts of which till then there was record.'[2] He sums up the losses, and the historic gain. As an old soldier his sympathies are with the soldiers on both sides, rather than with the politicians: 'if these two Presidents had let McClellan and Lee fight the quarrel out between them as they thought

[1] W. S. Churchill, *A History of the English-Speaking Peoples*, iv. 169, 174, 202.
[2] Ibid., iv. 207.

best, the end would have been the same; but the war would have been less muddled, much shorter, and less bloody'. As you would expect, his soldier's admiration goes to Lee, but he has a fine tribute to Lincoln: 'Lincoln's political foes, gazing upon him, did not know vigour when they saw it.' And his own war-time experience shows in the knowledgeable comment: 'it is sometimes necessary at the summit of authority to bear with the intrigues of disloyal colleagues, to remain calm when others panic, and to withstand misguided popular outcries. All this Lincoln did.'[1] At the same time there is perhaps too generous an estimate of Jefferson Davis: we need not be surprised, for generosity, magnanimity are the life-blood of this historian.

Here is the most powerful criticism of the book — that the real history of the English-speaking peoples proceeds and finds a living unity 'on levels of the historical process with which Sir Winston does not concern himself at all'.[2] English-speaking ties in the nineteenth century were above all economic and social, demographic and popular. There was the fundamental inter-change of British manufacturers for American raw materials and food; the contribution of British shipping and capital invest-ment, especially in railways, in opening up the new continent. 'British emigration was supremely significant as a unifying factor among the English-speaking peoples; this is understood clearly in the case of Australia, New Zealand and Canada, but less clearly in that of the United States. . . . The movement of populations was as much an economic as a social phenomenon. Here, then, is a moving central theme, the great transmission in the nine-teenth century of English language, ideas, customs and wealth throughout the four quarters of the globe.'

And there is the reverse process: the immense impact of America on Britain in this period, the constant influence of American writers from Fenimore Cooper onwards — some-times their fame was first made in Britain; of American political and social ideas in the extension of democracy and equality; of American religious and revivalistic movements; of folklore and popular music and entertainment of every kind from Negro spirituals to circuses; not to mention the humbler inventions

[1] W. S. Churchill, *A History of the English-Speaking Peoples*, iv. 169.
[2] H. C. Allen, *English Historical Review* (1959), 308.

that lightened millions of working class homes with paraffin lamps, sewing machines, harmoniums, at length electricity.

If justice were to be done to this dual process of action and reaction at every level it would need another volume. But it is not Churchill's subject, and he has done enough for one lifetime.

Perhaps we may sum up.

What are his qualities as a writer of history? They are allied to those of the maker of it, the man of action. The combination of powerful common sense with imagination is always a stronger one for an historian than any amount of ethical uplift — more in keeping with the facts of life, the subject-matter of history. There is no humbug in Churchill, not a trace: it has been one of his disadvantages as a politician. Nor is he in any way religious: he is at the opposite pole from any sort of mysticism — though he has *pietas*, like an ancient Roman. His lifelong inspiration has been patriotism, an out-of-date virtue today. He is philosophically a rationalist, who sees life in terms of struggle; his intellectual outlook was much shaped by his reading of Darwin when young. What are his values? — courage, resource, to do one's duty by one's country and by mankind, for no-one is more human, who values achievement of all kinds and enjoys fulfilment in all spheres of action, physical and mental.

All this appears in the historian: such a sense of life, such a way of re-creating the past; the choice of subjects of significance combined with the presentation of new material, marshalled like troops on a battlefield; vitality, perception, political understanding, and the style to express it: without these no historical writer can properly be regarded as a great historian, however good he may be as an historical technician.

Of course, Churchill has had a double dose of vitality, a double inheritance. I have said that his chief inspiration has been patriotism, which he has come to broaden out to apply to the English-speaking peoples as a whole. In this, too, he has had the two-fold advantage that in him the British and American strains are equally strong. He sees, prophetically, that our separate histories are tending to merge into one stream: his last words to us on his last page are, 'nor should we now seek to define precisely the exact terms of ultimate union'.

# VI

# ERASMUS AND ENGLAND

## I

It is fitting that we should commemorate the quatercentenary of Erasmus (he died on 11 July 1536), since so much of his life and work was bound up with England. He owed to it some of his closest and most fruitful friendships, he derived from it an essential impulse to his life's work and in the end contributed something of his own spirit to the solution which the English found for their religious difficulties in the sixteenth century and to the tradition which has been continuous since that time. Erasmus has always been best understood and treated with most sympathy in Anglo-Saxon countries: they appreciate best his humanitarianism, his love of peace and liberty, his lifelong service to international ideals, his spirit of moderation and tolerance in religion. Of this greatest of Europeans, it might almost be claimed that he was half an Englishman. He first came to England, along with the young peer, Mountjoy, who was his pupil in Paris, in the early summer of 1499. Already his reputation as the most brilliant of the younger scholars there had preceded him. Colet and the young More had, for example, heard of him. Colet, but recently returned from Italy, was at Oxford delivering that famous course of lectures on St. Paul's Epistles which, in breaking through the crusted accretions of commentary which the Middle Ages had collected and going straight to the meaning of the text, had an immense influence in inaugurating the movement for reform in the Church. Indeed, Colet's ardent spirit had a profound influence upon Erasmus at this decisive turning in his life. Less clever than Erasmus intellectually, Colet had that strong ethical passion which could give the more brilliant, more sensitive man a sense of direction. As the distinguished Dutch historian, Huizinga, says:

It was Colet's word and example that first changed Erasmus's desultory occupation with theological studies into a firm and lasting resolve to make their pursuit the object of his life.

Hardly less important than this sense of purpose communicated to his life, were the friendships that Erasmus made here, which lasted to the end. For all the extreme sensitiveness and the thin skin of the man of genius, Erasmus had a genuine gift for friendship. So, too, had Thomas More, the most delightful companion ever to become a saint, whom Erasmus was wont to call, in the language of the time, his 'darling'. Then too there was Colet, eager and inspiring: we recall the famous disputation that arose at dinner in an Oxford college, Colet presiding. Prior Charnock on his right and Erasmus on his left; how vividly Erasmus describes it all in the *Letters*, so that we see them all clear as in a portrait after the lapse of centuries. They were a charming circle, those Oxford humanists, drawn together by their common love of scholarship and by the ties of friendship. Their life has been described for us, with sympathy and insight, by older English writers, by Seebohm in his *Oxford Reformers* and by Froude in his *Life and Letters of Erasmus*. But Erasmus himself has described the happiness he found among those friends in early years:

'How do you like our England? you will ask' (he wrote to Robert Fisher). 'Believe me, dear Robert, when I answer that I never liked anything so much before. I have met with so much kindness and so much learning, both Latin and Greek, that but for the curiosity of seeing it, I do not now so much care for Italy. When I hear my Colet, I seem to be listening to Plato himself. In Grocyn, who does not marvel at such perfection of learning? What can be more acute, profound and delicate than the judgment of Linacre? What has nature ever created more sweet, more endearing, more happy than the genius of Thomas More?'

Fortunately for him, he could have no idea of the wreckage that was to be made of the group of friends by the storms of the Reformation.

He was here again in the autumn of 1505, extending his acquaintance in the Church, to include the kindly, generous Warham, Archbishop of Canterbury, Fisher, Bishop of Rochester, Fox, Bishop of Winchester, the gentle, scholarly Tunstall. And for the greater part of the years 1509–14 he lived in England, partly in London with Mountjoy and More, partly at

Cambridge. Of these fruitful, laborious years, certain abiding achievements remain. He wrote his brilliant work, *The Praise of Folly*, in More's house in Bucklersbury. Much of his work on Jerome and for his great edition of the New Testament was done in London and at Cambridge. In the comparative freedom of England he wrote, though he never dared to acknowledge, the scathing tract *Julius Exclusus*, his exposure of the bellicose Pope, Julius II. Then there are the innumerable pictures of English life contained in his *Letters* and *Colloquies*: the insanitariness of the houses, Dame Alice, More's shrew of a wife, the gaunt and saintly Fisher in his draughty palace at Rochester.

Perhaps, in the end, England was something of a disappointment to him, as all countries were to the fastidious soul of the idealist with the gift of irony, bent upon his own inner dream of perfection and reason. He had had a shock upon his first visit, when the money he had collected for his journey to Italy was confiscated by the Customs at Dover under a Statute of Edward III prohibiting the export of coin: it meant five years' more drudgery in Paris before he was free at last to go. Then, too, the sanguine hopes that were offered by his English friends on the accession of Henry VIII, which induced him to leave Italy, were disappointed. But Warham was generous, and presented him to the benefice of Aldington in Kent, from which he drew a pension of twenty pounds for the rest of his life. With the outbreak of Henry's French War he was no longer at ease, and complained that it had 'altered the spirit of this island'. As soon as peace was signed he left the country, though with a graceful tribute upon his lips; for when an Italian envoy tried to persuade him to go to Rome, where he might enjoy the first place instead of living alone among a barbarous nation, he replied that England contained such a number of excellent scholars among whom he would be content to occupy the humblest place.

One recalls that when he describes the things upon which various nations pride themselves, the Scots their nobility and logical sense, the French their breeding, he says of the English that they 'particularly challenge to themselves Beauty, Music and Feasting'. What a change of values from the England of the Renaissance to the nation of shopkeepers!

In the great struggle over the Reformation which divided Europe into two camps, Erasmus was all for moderation and the appeal to reason — in vain. His last writing on Concord in the Church, his constant deploring of over-much definition of belief as likely to lead to only worse conflicts of dogma, is closest in spirit to the Anglican compromise that later developed. It was sad that his last years should have been filled with the sufferings of his English friends, More and Fisher; nor could he know to what extent his own influence was to bear fruit in the *via media* of the Elizabethan Church. If the Church of England had a process of canonisation, Erasmus should certainly be among its saints.

## II. The Erasmus Exhibition at the Bodleian

The uncertainties of this extraordinarily inclement spring threaten, lift off, then descend upon the Library. A thunder-cloud lours over the Radcliffe Square outside, bringing out and making vivid and distinct the inherent colours of objects, the black and gold of the Camera, the white rim to the sky, the green of weather vanes. Rain patters against the panes of the long Exhibition Room; wind and rain stir together among the trees of Exeter garden, bringing to mind the phrases of Arnold, of another, earlier spring, 'the vext garden-trees . . . the volleying rain'. The shower over, a burst of sun comes in from the garden, the silver birch shivering and gleaming with wetness, the chestnut flowers now gone from the ancient tree in the corner, that sends the noise of innumerable leaves into the still and faded room. An unexpected finger of light lies along the cases pointing to the Froben edition of Chrysostom, sumptuously bound for Henry VIII with the royal arms engraved upon it, lighting up the gilt roses and the leopards.

The Bodleian authorities have followed up their More and Fisher Exhibitions with this to commemorate the quatercentenary of Erasmus, no less informative if a trifle less intimate than that. Anything to do with Thomas More has a charm and intimacy all its own. The personality of Erasmus has a less obvious appeal; there are no jokes that survive by which we remember him; his talk and his writing were alike in the Latin of the Renaissance which comes between us and the realisation of a singularly vivid, sensitive being, a character that should have an especial appeal for us of the modern world. He was much in England, a well-known figure in that day, four hundred years ago. His life, more than any other, was the thread that drew together the Renaissance in Northern Europe — Germany, the Low Countries, France, England. He resided here at Oxford, 1499–1500; at Cambridge and in London for the greater part of the years 1509–14. He was a formative influence in the revival of learning in England: an indebtedness appropriately repaid by the fact that the leading Erasmus scholar of our time was an Oxford man, P. S. Allen.

Most of the cases are taken up by a representative collection of early editions of his works. Altogether they give a fair picture of his life, since so much of his life was in his books, from that early commendatory letter with which he was asked to fill up the blank page at the end of Gaguin's *De Origine et Gestis Francorum* — the Latinity of which was so much more elegant than that of the book itself that it called attention to himself, a newcomer then to the literary world of Paris, rather than to Gaguin. This was Erasmus's first appearance in print, in 1495; here is the third edition of the work in which the superior merit of the preface was recognised by placing it at the beginning of the book, as it always has been subsequently. It was by this that his name was first noised abroad among the world of scholars and by which Colet, when studying in Paris, first heard of him. Next to it is a tiny volume of poems, *De casa natalitia Jesu et paupere puerperio dive virginis Mariè Carmen noviter emendatum*, which appeared in the same year, his first separate work. These are very early works, products of the lean years in Paris, the plain living and arduous study at the Collège de Montaigu from which so much of the later work sprang, but of which he could never afterwards think without a shudder. It was not until some time after his visit to England that the full stream of his works began to appear from the presses of the time. His sensational literary career was in a sense the creation of the printing press; he saw the splendid opportunity opened up by it, leaped to it with both hands, living with the press and by it.

It was by the *Adages* and the *Enchiridion Militis Christiani* that he gained a wider audience for himself; here is an early edition (Antwerp, 1509) of the *Lucubrationes aliquot*, among which the *Enchiridion* first came out, though it was subsequently published separately, the first among his best known works. The first English version of it appeared in 1518; here is a copy of the second translation, said to be by Tyndale, the translator of the Bible. Others of his English connections are brought to mind by the first edition (Paris, 1506) of the translation into Latin of several of the dialogues of Lucian, so popular an author with the Renaissance, a work in which Erasmus collaborated with More; it is dedicated to Fox, Bishop of Winchester. Similarly, the beautiful Aldine edition of the *Adages* (Venice, 1508), a product of the visit to Italy in 1506–9, is dedicated to Mountjoy. The number of items — proverbs and phrases with their explanations and expansions, sometimes into whole essays on important subjects like the famous one on war, *Dulce bellum inexpertis* — amounted in this edition to some three thousand, having increased from eight hundred in the first collection. Next to it is the 1536 Froben edition of the *Adages*, no less beautiful than the Aldine; it was the last to be issued in Erasmus' lifetime, and by then the number of pieces had increased to over five thousand.

And so to a whole case devoted to various editions of *The Praise of Folly*, in various European languages, from the year it was published to the present day. Among them are editions of 1511 and 1521 (Basel), and the first English translation by Sir Thomas Challoner, with a Renaissance title-page decorated with caryatids and flowers and fruit, published in 1549. I suppose that this is the best known of all Erasmus's works: the most famous example of the remarkable literature of Folly during the Renaissance, a form of literary expression even more suitable to our own time and circumstance. The big items here are the fine Froben editions of the New Testament, the first and the last in his lifetime, Basel, 1516 and 1535: both splendid pieces of craftsmanship, though the latter has a more crowded text because of the increasing Annotations that the years brought: Erasmus' chief contribution to scholarship. There follow fine examples of the Froben texts of the Fathers, Cyprian, Chrysostom (Henry VIII's copy), and Ambrose in whom Erasmus had been interested from his earliest years: the original edition of his work on Free Will, against Luther, *De libero arbitrio* (Froben, 1524), with Luther's reply, and the rejoinder which Erasmus put together in ten days in time for the Frankfurt Fair in September 1526.

What is of most interest to us are the two cases containing a number of his last letters, written in his own hand, and now belonging to the Bodleian, together with some relics of his English friends. A large Greek book which once belonged to Grocyn has his name inscribed upon it; a little account-book which once belonged to Linacre, opens at the page which gives, 'Md. for my costs when I went to maydstone for ye greke boke'. There are the charges for barge hire from Gravesend, and so to Halling and Maidstone and back again; 'for carynge of ye hamper from ye colege to ye water syde id.; for karyage of ye sayd hamper to London vid.; for caryage from ye water to yor howse iid'. Trifling in themselves, these personal details bring back to us these men, Linacre, Grocyn, Colet, Erasmus, More, all bound together by friendship and their devotion to the new learning. The storms of the Reformation — that age so like our own — swept down upon them, scattering the friends, breaking the lives of some of them, ruining all their hopes like ours. These last letters of Erasmus, which the Bodleian was so fortunate to obtain just before the war of 1914, are full of the disasters of the time, particularly of the ruin in England. He writes in June 1535 to his confidant Erasmus Schets, of the imprisonment of More and Fisher, that the latter has lost his sight, while he fears More will lose his head. 'I wonder whither this savagery of the King will lead,' he writes. Henry's accession in his golden youth had seemed to offer such hopes to them all. Mountjoy had died, but of a natural death, he says; it is a sufficient comment upon the drift of the time. Next year, in June again — it is his last letter — he scribbles a brief note to Schets: '*Prodigiosa scribis de Anglia*. Would that these things had stopped before the death of those good men.' (More and Fisher had been brought to death upon the block the year before.) Erasmus subscribes himself, for the last time, '*aegra manu*'. A month more, and he too was dead, working in the house at Basel right up to the end.

There are a few portraits of no particular consequence, yet appropriately brought together; a copy of a Holbein portrait of Erasmus, a book open before him (his life was books); a late copy of a portrait of the printer Froben, an honest, ugly face, blunt and deeply lined. Higher up on the wall hangs a portrait of the man who played such a part in the revolution that scattered them all: Thomas Cromwell.

### III. THE PERSONALITY OF ERASMUS

Erasmus is one of the great names of Europe; but it is doubtful whether he is much more than a name to us today. There upon the library shelves stand the dozen or more tall folios of the Louvain edition of his works; there are the ten volumes of his *Letters*; in addition, his texts of the Fathers, Chrysostom, Cyprian, Jerome, Ambrose, Augustine, together with his life's crowning glory, the edition of the New Testament. Is it any wonder that the man should be buried under such a mountain of Latin and Greek?

In spite of all this, he comes through to us as a singularly modern personality: a sensitive, queasy, thin-skinned, human being, self-conscious and self-aware like a modern man, no medieval. His problems were very much ours; he was agonised by similar issues, extraordinarily contemporary in character; living as he did in that sickening period when the Renaissance passed over into the Reformation and the Wars of Religion, he was caught at a dangerous turning of the ways in Europe. It is fitting that we should call him to mind: he was the first of modern writers, and his life holds a special significance for our age.

Let us begin by calling up his physical appearance. He was so famous in his lifetime and so much painted, that his features at least are familiar to us. We see him as so often depicted, seated at a desk, for ever writing, writing, writing. There are usually books in the background, an open book before him. The face is deeply expressive: sensibility, refinement, self-awareness in every line of it. It is the face of a very clever man, who is also a valetudinarian; something of an invalid, perpetually overworking, nervous, alert; querulousness in the brow, no satisfaction in the tight repressed lips. It all bespeaks the life of incessant worrying labour this man lived; beneath the surface appearances, the sparse greying hair, the thin worn cheeks, the mobile hands heavy with rings, there is yet unmistakable determination, tenacity of purpose, the eager, anxious spirit. The expression of the face has something ambivalent about it: at once grave, yet on the verge of a smile; half tender, half querulous: evidently a personality with a sharp edge to it, the more fascinating to study because of the touchiness, the one skin too few, the combination of extreme sensibility with nervous tenacity.

All this mirrors the man we know him to have been. He was first and foremost the scholar, prince among the scholars of the Renaissance. He won this position after an apprenticeship over years, at school at Gouda and Deventer, at the Augustinian monastery of Steyn of which he was a canon, in Paris teaching himself Greek, at Oxford where Colet inspired him with a sense of his vocation, at Cambridge where he lectured and taught and studied. It was not until he was a man of thirty that he began to reap the rewards of his industry in a growing fame. In addition to his scholarship he was a brilliant original writer. Few had handled the Latin language as he since the Dark Ages closed down upon Europe, a resuscitation of the classical Latin of Cicero. If less of a living language than medieval Latin, at least it was living to Erasmus, who took pains not to speak his native Dutch and as far as possible to converse in Latin only, so as not to spoil his natural style.

No-one had more arresting things to say: he was a preternaturally sharp observer of events and persons, an acute commentator upon opinions, essentially moralist and critic, with a biting wit. He belongs to the small, well-defined class of writers to which Voltaire and Swift belong. But not even Voltaire's European reputation equalled Erasmus' recognised position in his lifetime. He was the admired of scholars, churchmen and princes, sought after by Charles V, Francis I, Henry VIII and successive Popes, the friend of Sir Thomas More and Fisher, since promoted saints; different countries competed for the honour of his presence, their leading men loaded him with presents and kindnesses.

Of the works that went to justify this immense reputation, we cannot here deal with those of pure scholarship; let us take his own original writings. I suppose the *Moriae Encomium* (*The Praise of Folly*) to be his most characteristic work, that one which best speaks for the man. The idea of the book occurred to him while journeying over the mountains from Italy to Northern Europe, on his way to England in 1509; arrived in London, he wrote it in the space of a few days in More's house in Bucklersbury — a characteristic play upon More's name gives it its title. The subject of the book is the foolery of mankind, the tragic condition that lies at the root of human nature. Why is it that man, the one animal gifted with reason, should choose the irrational, the foolish, the obviously absurd course? One sees that the book belongs to the same class as *Gulliver's Travels*, Voltaire's *Candide*, and Grimmelshausen's *Simplicissimus*. Why the Renaissance should have been so much concerned with the subject of human folly is an interesting, and perhaps profitable, speculation; there is a large Fool-literature of the time, of which the *Ship of Fools* and Rabelais's works are examples. The perfect expression of all that literature is, however, Erasmus's *Praise of Folly*.

The treatment of the subject is appropriately ironical, and indeed at times one can hardly distinguish between what is seriously and what is frivolously intended. There is scarcely any form of human folly that is not touched upon, sometimes with a mock serious approval, sometimes with open castigation. The latter is employed for the abuses of the Church, the attention to forms instead of to things of the spirit, the concern with property and pomp instead of preaching the gospel, the character of secular priests who justify their name by being so much better acquainted with the affairs of this world than of the next. Let us take an example from the book:

To work miracles is old and antiquated, and not in fashion now; to instruct the people, troublesome; to interpret the Scripture, pedantic; to pray, a sign one has little else to do; to shed tears, silly and womanish; to be poor, base; to be defeated, dishonourable and little becoming him that scarce admits even kings to kiss his slipper [*i.e.* the Pope]; and lastly, to die, uncouth; and to be stretched on a Cross, infamous.

The desire for practical reform is constantly in evidence, but more philosophical, or even anthropological, is such a thought as this:

In a word, this Folly is that that laid the foundation of Cities; and by it, Empire, Authority, Religion, Policy and public Actions are preserved: neither is there any thing in Human Life that is not a kind of pastime of Folly.

Nothing could be more far-reaching than the scepticism implied by that: human folly is the foundation of all politics, and provides the necessity for authority, religion, the state: if only men were reasonable there would be no need for empires, states, authority. These two tendencies in Erasmus, the reforming and evangelistic ardour, and a profound scepticism regarding life and men, were held together in a delicate equipoise which gives the whole character to his mind. The equipoise was broken by the irruption of Luther into the European scene. The conflict between these two sides to Erasmus' nature was tragically revealed in the conflict with Luther over the Reformation.

Up to 1518–19 all had gone well with Erasmus: he stood at the apex of his European reputation. As both humanist and reformer, he appeared at the head of the movement for Reform within the Church; all men looked to him as such, yet he retained the favour of kings, Emperor and Pope. The revolutionary upheaval which Luther set in train destroyed all this. The confident Victorian age considered that Luther showed up Erasmus' weakness as but a Laodicean, as certainly he confessed that he was not the stuff that martyrs are made of. But the tragedy went deeper: it was that the sensible, moderate course of reasonable reform, within the framework of the universal Church, became impossible in the mad onrush of events with men's passions unleashed, their hatreds aroused.

The essential point of Erasmus' position was that he was a rationalist, he wanted men to be guided by reason. He had been not unsympathetic to Luther in the beginnings of his movement for reform; but he foresaw as Luther went farther and farther in his challenge to the Church, that new dogmas were being set up against the old and that this would lead to

H

disastrous conflicts and wars, leaving the world in a worse state than before, Europe riven in two. Erasmus was right, but could do nothing; his own views about the folly of men were being only too precisely justified in the destruction they were bringing on themselves and in the ruin of all his hopes of agreed reform in a spirit of moderation and forbearance. Erasmus was caught by the whirlwind out of the interior depths of barbaric Germany, in much the same way as the Girondins were caught by the French Revolution, or the Mensheviks by the Russian. The contemporary parallel is obvious. It is regrettable that human beings are unable to bring about obvious and necessary reforms without pulling the house down about their ears. There is a discerning phrase of Froude's in his book on Erasmus, to the effect that two centuries of religious wars were to vindicate the rightness of his judgment.

Similarly with his views on internationalism and peace. He had a horror of war and killing which went with his shrinking, unmasculine temperament and civilised preferences. A modern German scholar has called him 'the first of pacifists'; and some of his finest writings are denunciations of war and war-mongers. The fiercest exposure of all, the *Julius Exclusus*, is reserved for the most eminent offender, the war-like Pope Julius II, author of a general European war, whom Erasmus had seen entering Bologna in triumph and never forgot the spectacle. He is depicted clamouring for admission at the gate of Heaven: to be rejected.

Erasmus was a citizen of Europe, equally at home in the Netherlands, France, Italy, Germany or England, in Paris or London, Antwerp, Venice or Basel. Perhaps in the end equally homeless, for the city of the mind in which he dwelt was that Europe of which he was such a good citizen, but which has not even yet come to be.

# VII

## THE TUDOR CHARACTER

It is an agreeable occupation to reflect, in walking through a portrait gallery, how different historical periods produce their corresponding types of face and appearance. There is, for example, the earlier Tudor type of the Court of Henry VIII, clean-shaven and heavy-jowled, which the genius of Holbein has made familiar to us upon the walls of the picture galleries of Europe, though nowhere more richly than at Windsor. Or, again, more familiar, more intimate, is the Stuart type: there is none so charming as this, with its vein of mingled melancholy and refinement. The eighteenth century produced a dominant type altogether more placid and contented, as well it might: it was a good world for them, and it was not the meek who inherited it. As the century went on they became even more at ease in Zion; the type loosens, becomes more florid and well-liking, until it moves into the romantic *bravura* of the Regency.

Something of these changes of type and appearance may be put down to fashion; with the men to different styles in the cut of the beard, from the full spade-beard fashionable in the later years of Elizabeth to the small pointed beard of Charles I's time or to the imperial of the mid-nineteenth century. These changes in external appearance may also reflect differences in type and character. Character must be in part a function of social environment, since it is built up so largely out of responses to its surroundings. If this is so, it should be particularly evident in the leading figures of an age, who are more conspicuously in contact with the main currents of thought and action in their time than any others. It is thus that we may usefully take such a figure, a Thomas Cromwell or an Oliver, a Strafford or a Ralegh, and to illuminate the age through the currents that flow through him.

The earliest years of the Tudor period, the reign of Henry VII, have something of the impersonality of the Middle Ages about them still; so that we do not know much about Cardinal

Morton or Fox, or even Henry himself, as men. We cannot easily penetrate beneath the mask, beyond that silence. With the accession of a young prince of such promise as Henry VIII there came a release; those were joyous years; Erasmus called it 'a golden age indeed'. Youth and merry-making were to the fore; in the background, though by no means in obscurity, was the charmed circle around More's family, Colet and Linacre, and Erasmus coming and going. The foreground was taken up by heartier and lustier characters: the young King — we recall Giustiniani's description of him coming from tennis, or the atmosphere of enjoyment in many of Skelton's and Wyatt's Court poems. There was Wolsey with his moods and emotions, his feasts and his tears, his gluttony for work and play — a genial type, when all is said; or the Duke of Norfolk, who thought that 'England was merry England, before all this New Learning came in', and the Marquis of Exeter, Henry's companion from boyhood — but with them the shadows begin to fall.

The men who were thrown up in the upheaval of the Reformation, or who survived it, were a different type again; since the times were dangerous, full of pitfalls, they look out of their portraits wary, steely, hand on hilt. In thinking of them one is reminded of Keynes's description of the Parliament of 1918: 'hard-faced men who looked as if they had done well out of the War.' Since it was a time of social and religious revolution, those who survived were necessarily tenacious and adaptable; and perhaps it was better to be adaptable than tenacious, for the mortality in those scuffling front ranks was very high. One has only to think of that little area within the communion rails of the chapel of St. Peter-ad-Vincula within the Tower — Macaulay's 'saddest spot in Christendom'. Those came off best with whom principle sat more lightly, who moved and conformed with the times: the Russells, for instance, whose loyalty to the existing order (whatever it was) and to their own fortunes deserved the success they obtained. Catholic in doctrine under Henry, they yet more devoutly upheld the Royal supremacy; Protestant under Edward VI, they found no difficulty in accepting the Mass again under Mary. Sir William Cecil at the same time received a priest into his household 'for the better direction of his spiritual affairs'. Or there was the old Marquis of Winchester who held office in all four reigns, under Henry VIII, Edward, Mary and Elizabeth, and was Lord Treasurer from about 1550 until well on into Elizabeth's reign, when he died near ninety, in 1572. It was said of him that he was made of the bending willow, not out of oak.

The constraint, the watchfulness, the latent savagery of the time are depicted for all to see in the portrait that Holbein painted of Cromwell — the immense capacity of the face, the cunning, clever eyes, the fat hands — no less than in the tell-tale note among his Remembrances, 'This day the Abbot of Glaston to be tried and condemned', or in his last piteous letter to Henry crying for mercy. But with the country's emergence from the years of internal crisis, the scene is less dominated by the harsher, more foxy types — it is significant how frequently particular statesmen in the literature of the time are compared to the fox: 'the foxy Gardiner', 'Bonner the fox', 'the old fox Burghley'. We move from these, and from others like them, Northumberland, Walsingham, to the more settled assurance of Elizabeth's later years and to a new type, the young men, more brilliant and dashing, unrestrained by the fears of their fathers, more gallant and adventurous, even quixotic, sometimes no less unfortunate. Of these Ralegh and Essex were the types, to many of them rival inspirations.

Magnificence was the foible of this later generation; not only in the externals of life, in their dress and appointments — Cromwell was magnificent enough in this respect, a great collector of Venetian glass, of carpets, tapestries and books — but in their behaviour and bearing, in the way they thought of themselves. It was this last that gave a certain unreality in their judgment of the external world, that led some of them, Essex and Ralegh notably, to their undoing. No one expressed this spirit better — that of power and possessions, pride of knowledge — than Marlowe: the first is the real subject of *Tamburlaine the Great* as the second is of *Faustus*:

> How am I glutted with conceit of this!
> Shall I make spirits fetch me what I please,
> Resolve me of all ambiguities,
> Perform what desperate enterprise I will?

> I'll have them fly to India for gold,
> Ransack the ocean for orient pearl,
> And search all corners of the new-found world
> For pleasant fruits and princely delicates.

The men of action and the politicians fell hardly at all behind the words of the poets. The cautious Cecils built sumptuously. The elder had his houses at Wimbledon and Theobalds and the palace that remains at Burghley; the younger built Cecil House in the Strand; he filled it full with rare and precious things, of which the inventories remain, and then went on to provide himself with a more splendid palace at Hatfield. With this magnificence there ran a spirit of bravado, a braggart emphasis, which is the quality least congenial to us in the Elizabethans. But the gesture was often inspired, and remembered to enrich succeeding centuries with the memory: Drake before the Armada promising the Queen to send the Duke of Medina Sidonia back to 'St. Mary Port, among his orange-trees'; Essex, throwing his hat into the sea before the assault on Cadiz; Philip Sidney wounded, forgoing his drink of water to a dying soldier. With Ralegh the gesture was apt to have contemptuous overtones, a corrosive edge:

> Say to the Court it glows
>     And shines like rotten wood,
> Say to the Church it shows
>     What's good, and doth no good.
> If Church and Court reply,
>     Then give them both the lie. . . .
>
> Tell zeal it wants devotion,
>     Tell love it is but lust,
> Tell time it meets but motion,
>     Tell flesh it is but dust,
> And wish them not reply
>     For thou must give them the lie.

Magnificence, with a man of such gifts as Ralegh, went with intellectual pride: that, even more than ambition, which was but one expression of it, was the root of his being. We recall Poe's phrase, 'the mad pride of intellectuality'; it was the element that chiefly made Ralegh impossible as a practical politician — that and his self-will and recklessness. It was a characteristic frequent enough among the Elizabethans — Essex had much the same failing; Northumberland and Cobham were ruined by it; among the poets, it was the mainspring of Marlowe's genius. In our time public men take more pains to disguise any blemish of intellectuality behind a decent exterior of commonplaceness than the Elizabethans took to display their brilliance. But, then, this is a democratic age, as the Elizabethan was not; it was essentially aristocratic, if at the same time showy, theatrical, exhibitionist. However, its *arrivisme* can be exaggerated: people did not rise, under Elizabeth, from the bottom of the social scale. Sir Robert Naunton observed, 'It is a certain note of the times, that the Queen in her choice, never took into her favour a meer new man, or a Mechanick,' and he says of her attitude to the Howards, 'it was part of her naturall propension, to grace and support ancient Nobility, where it did not intrench, neither invade her interest'. Ralegh — for all his being regarded as an upstart, and in spite of the insulting references to his origins by those indubitable aristocrats, the Earls of Oxford and Essex with their Norman descent — came from an old medieval family of the West Country.

Ralegh's practical career was fragmentary, baffled and in the end shattered. But was his life, as is so frequently said, a failure? To have been so fine a poet, so philosophical an intelligence, so fertile in expedients for colonising and planting, in setting on foot voyages of exploration and discovery, in the art of chemistry, in the sciences of navigation and war; to have founded Virginia, to have risen from 'poor beginnings' by his wits to a leading place among the constellation of talents that Elizabeth drew around her, to have written the *History of the World* — is failure the word to describe so rich, so creative a life? No: his career rather lights up the fortuitousness, the hazards of the time, the chances that were there to be taken. As Naunton wrote of him:

Sir Walter Rawleigh was one that (it seems) Fortune had pickt out of purpose, of whom to make an example, or to use as her Tennis-Ball, thereby to shew what she could doe; for she tost him up of nothing, and too and fro to greatnesse, and from thence down to little more than to that wherein she found him (a bare Gentleman).

Or, as Shakespeare wrote with him clearly in mind at the
time of his fall:

> Great Princes' favorites their faire leaves spread,
> But as the Marygold at the suns eye,
> And in themselves their pride lies buried,
> For at a frowne they in their glory die.

His career may stand as an example of a tragic fortuitousness, rather than of failure. The one implies that though the
man suffered, the work remained; the other that both alike
went down to common oblivion and fruitlessness. But not so,
for consider what remains. There are the poems — and he is
one of the outstanding, most idiosyncratic of Elizabethan poets.
There is the prose — and after Bacon he is perhaps the finest
of that age of native prose-writers. Even so perceptive a writer
as Virginia Woolf speaks of 'the lumbering Elizabethan prose'.
That comes from too much regarding a few artificial flowers of
literary composition, Sidney's *Arcadia*, or Lyly's *Euphues*. If one
reads their letters — Essex wrote letters as fine as Ralegh's,
while Drake and Howard of Effingham and Robert Cecil are
no less eloquent and expressive — or if one reads the reports of
the seamen, the voyages of discovery gathered together in
Hakluyt or Purchas, one sees how natural and vigorous people's
writing mostly was in that age. Then, too, Ralegh made himself the leader of the group which carried out the most persistent
attack upon the decisive question for England's future — her
share in the opening-up of the New World. To have played the
part he did in making North America English can hardly be
regarded as the work of one whose career was a failure.

'The proud fantastic community known as the Court formed
the matrix of Elizabethan society,' it has been said. Sir Edward
Dyer, like Ralegh, was essentially a courtier, in his time a
scintillating one, though now remembered only as the name
attached to the poem often anthologised:

> My mynde to me a kyngdome is,
> Suche perfect joy therin I fynde,
> That it excells all other blisse
> That worlde afords or growes by kynde:
>> Though muche I wante which moste would have,
>> Yet still my mynde forbides to crave. . . .

I laugh not at an others loss,
I grudge not at an others gaine:
No worldly waves my mynde can toss,
My state at one dothe still remayne:
   I feare no foe, I fawne no freende,
   I lothe not lyfe, nor dread no ende.

That gives something of the man's temper, the undertone of melancholy which so many Elizabethans had (none more than Ralegh) by way of reaction perhaps from so much pushing and striving for place and power. In addition, there is a certain detachment of mind, which not all of them possessed, a spirit of independence, which may in part have accounted for Dyer's lack of success in life. For he was, though his biographer does not insist upon it, a failure. It was not, at first, for lack of trying. Born in the same class as Ralegh, the lesser gentry who had done well out of the spoils of the Church — the Dyers obtained several of the Somersetshire manors of Glastonbury Abbey — he began early at Court, lost the Queen's favour by some youthful prank, recovered it again by a skilfully devised entertainment at Woodstock such as Elizabeth loved, and spent the rest of his life at Court and with it all his patrimony and fortune. He belonged to the generation before Ralegh: this was his importance poetically, as a link between Wyatt and Surrey and the full blossoming towards the end of the reign. He was educated, like Ralegh, at Oxford, where, according to Anthony Wood, 'his natural inclination to poetry and other polite learning, as also his excellency in bewailing and bemoaning the perplexities of love, were observed by his contemporaries'. He had a good singing voice and sang his own songs to the lute.

At Court he became an especial friend of Philip Sidney's, accompanied him to Penshurst, where they versified together, and was a leading mourner at his funeral. This was the friendship of his life, and afterwards he made no other, though Essex was attached to him and sought his advice with respect, while Cecil too had a friendly regard for him. We find him engaged in the ordinary pursuits of the Court, giving and receiving splendid presents from the Queen, overspending himself, tilting at tournaments, subscribing to Frobisher's voyages, being used on a few unimportant diplomatic missions, where he acquitted himself well. At one time talked of as Secretary of State, he was in the end promoted to be Chancellor of the Order of the Garter, a post more honorific than important. His name was chiefly known, outside the Court circle, to poets, particularly to those of the next generation, who looked up to him as a father in the art. Certainly his poetry is technically skilled, while in adhering to the native accented measures in spite of his quantitative experiments with Sidney, he showed his instinctive sense of the language. Some of his writing seems to have been lost: with these courtiers it was a point of honour not to set much store by their verse, or to make any effort to preserve it.

One thing reveals this little-known courtier and poet in a stranger and more searching light than anything that remains of him — his passionate interest in the semi-scientific, arts of semi-magical Dr. Dee and his associate, the unsavoury medium Kelly. Dyer journeyed twice across Europe to the Court of the Emperor Rudolph II at Prague, once to find out for himself if Kelly really had found the way to transmute into gold, and once (in vain) to bring him home at Burghley's orders. It is this queer fascination — for the rest of his life seems unimpassioned enough — that brings him close to the restless and various imagination of Ralegh. They were both types, in this time, of 'the searching unsatisfied spirits of the English'.

# VIII

# AN ELIZABETHAN EXHIBITION

IT is sad to think how little of Elizabethan London, or even of the London that Elizabethans knew, is left to us. The age was not a time of much significant building in the capital — though there was an immense growth of ramshackle tenements in the vacant spaces of the dissolved monasteries, Austin Friars, Blackfriars, St. Bartholomew's, Smithfield, Whitefriars and Charterhouse. That much of London which we have in common with them, buildings which an Elizabethan would know if he were to return to a strangely unrecognisable city, has mostly come down from a time earlier than theirs. And these are but a few fragments; in the west, the Abbey, Westminster Hall and St. James's; in the east, the Tower and some remains of older churches — St. Bartholomew's and St. Saviour's, Southwark; with connecting links in some of the Inns of Court, the Temple church and the splendid hall of Middle Temple, for example, and in a few old houses in Holborn. Only the river remains the same — yet hardly the same. For London has become historically Georgian, but dominantly a Victorian city in its chief aspects: all the best of it the creation of the eighteenth and nineteenth centuries.

And yet, on a smaller scale, there are innumerable relics — pictures, books, armour, tapestry, furniture, jewels, ornaments — out of which it is not difficult to construct something of that earlier age. Indeed, the Elizabethan Exhibition succeeds in creating within a few rooms the illusion of the bristling life of the time. What a singular thing it is that here are these men and women, vanished from the earth three hundred years and more, whose bodies are but dust, and yet whose little cherished objects — a ring, a crucifix that Mary Queen of Scots wore to her execution, an ivory walking-stick made for the hand of Elizabeth — remain to tell something of the lives and hearts of their owners, when everything else has gone.

The Exhibition naturally centres upon the figure of the

Queen. There are half a dozen portraits of her, besides minia-
tures; from the time when she was a young woman of twenty,
in the Tower, and gave this portrait of herself to Sir John
Harington, a fellow prisoner with her, to the time when she
was already a figure of legend. These portraits from private
possession hardly rival the famous ones in the National Gallery:
especially those two so familiar, one with a pearl-spangled
veil and holding up a flower in her hand, the other with a
string of pearls twisted on one side, a feather-fan held in
front.

It is clear how difficult the Queen made it to render the
woman, there was so little chance given of getting at the person
behind such a barrage of ornament, at the human being behind
the mask of sovereignty. The public was conditioned to a
definite image of her — she laid down precisely how she was
to be painted, with never a shadow falling upon her face. This
was the image she was determined to print upon her people and
upon posterity. Hence the impenetrability behind the so familiar features, the paradox of impersonality in so personal a
vision: nothing is given away. She had a clear idea of herself,
and of what was due to her; her life was one magnificent piece
of acting the part. Hence the pageantry kept up around her,
the inordinate wardrobe, the inscrutable behaviour, the in-
comprehensible style of writing in which she enveloped what
she wished to say. It was all a defence against the world — and
at the same time a way of imposing herself upon it.

But there was a pathetic side to it all, to anyone who has the
clue. The place of honour is given to the Rainbow portrait from
Hatfield: there is the Queen, with an elaborate head-dress, the
arch of a rainbow in her hand, with the motto *Non sine sole Iris*.
Next to her hangs the splendid Leicester, painted rather late in
life when beard and hair were grey; but his black cap is set at a
rakish angle, and he is still handsome and swashbuckling as
ever. He was the love of her life; and of all the flatterers that
surrounded her, he had a genuine feeling for her in his heart.
But their love had no consummation. Elizabeth, unlike Mary
Queen of Scots, sacrificed her private happiness for the sake
of politics, that she might be a great ruler, unique and sole,
and leave an immortal name behind her. Leicester died, worn

out in her service, just after the defeat of the Armada, fourteen years before she finished her course. Now here at last they hang beside each other, with a bowl of spring tulips between them.

The simplest and most impressive portrait of the Queen is the lead head from Westminster Abbey, by Maximilian Colt, based on a death-mask: hence its convincing veracity. It is so simple and sculptural in its lines — doubtless the medium dictated that — that it brings out better than any picture the fine structure of the head, the Welsh forehead; the bony oval with high cheek-bones, the hawk-nose, downward-pointing; the eyes slightly slanted, the small regular mouth, with the tight lips so impossible to extract any secrets either of life or State from. There she lies, pillowed in the high ruff, a string of pearls with a pendant at her throat, and long pearl drops at her ears. The leaden effigy, resplendent upon its purple velvet, recalls the scene at her funeral:

The city of Westminster surcharged with multitudes of all sorts of people in their streets, houses, windows, leads, and gutters, that came to see the obsequy; and when they beheld her statue or picture lying upon the coffin set forth in royal robes, having a crown upon the head thereof, and a ball and sceptre in either hand, there was such a general sighing, groaning, and weeping, as the like had not been seen or known in the memory of man, neither doth any history mention any people, time, or State, to make like lamentation for the death of their Sovereign.

A more usual vision of the Queen — though indifferent from a pictorial point of view — is that recalling her many processions by water up and down the Thames, and garnished with the sort of quaint conceit that the age loved and Elizabeth fed on:

The Queen was bro't by water to Whitehall
At ev'ry stroke the oars did Tears let fall;
More clung about ye Barge, Fish under water
Wept out their eyes of pearl and swome blind a'ter.
I think ye Bargeman might with easier sighs
Have rowed her thither in her people's eyes
For, howsoe'er my thoughts have ever scann'd
Sh'ad come by water had she come by land.

In the next place of honour come the Cecils, the brains of the régime. The *Rainbow* portrait of the Queen has Leicester on one side, but on the other, the right hand, it has Burghley: on one side her affections, on the other her political judgment. It is the well-known picture of Burghley as Lord Treasurer, holding the white staff in his hand, and wearing the large black cap with ear-flaps that lend a slightly comic touch to an otherwise sedate and grave countenance. Why should the Cecils look so melancholy in their portraits? The weight of affairs of State? But they had pretty much their own way in politics; and if they hadn't positively the last word — Elizabeth always had that — they had the next to the last word. The Queen would never settle on any course of action or policy without waiting for Burghley's opinion. Up the staircase there is a double portrait of them, the old Lord Treasurer and his favourite son Robert together, that throws some light on the question. There is a common look of delicacy in the pale, watchful faces with the candid brows. Robert Cecil's is that of an invalid — he was diminutive — with long sunken cheeks and deep shadows under the eyes; but the eyes themselves very wide open and coldly taking everything in. That was like his character; what Lytton Strachey says of him is true.

'A discerning eye might have detected melancholy and resignation in that patient face. The spectacle of the world's ineptitude and brutality made him, not cynical — he was not aloof enough for that — but sad — was he not a creature of the world himself?'

There he is; a finished speaker, the most astute political intelligence of all the younger generation. Yet this omits something of him. As a young man, he was like Pitt in his youth — before the responsibilities of office grew thick upon them and made them both older than their years — high spirited and gay. In an age of excellent letter-writing, he was among the best; in a court full of wits and merry-makers, he was not the least witty or the least gamesome.

In close propinquity to these hang Essex and Southampton: the tragic Essex, the secret of whose immense appeal to the age is now somewhat difficult to appreciate; and Southampton, who in spite of youth and beauty, makes an unhappy impression. The portrait of him here shows him as a prisoner in the Tower for his part in the Essex Conspiracy; he is surrounded with all the trappings of melancholy, dressed in black as if in mourning, with long auburn hair falling below his shoulders. However, the picture affords some evidence of the comfort obtained in the Tower. From what we can see, Southampton has a pleasant room, with a window open behind him, and a comfortable oak window-seat; he has his book and he has his cat, a black-and-white one looking very knowing out of the canvas.

Around these grand figures, there is a crowd of lesser ones who decorated the Court or Elizabeth's service. There is Hunsdon, her cousin, her only near relative surviving in her latter years, of whom she was fond. 'My Harry,' she would write to him and sign herself, 'Your loving kinswoman, Elizabeth R.' How well one remembers his signature in old age, the large clear fist all of a quaver, as if he drank too much or suffered from ague. Then there is the young Edward de Vere, Earl of Oxford, whom the age thought not much of; and Sir Edward Hoby at the age of eighteen, a foppish-looking youth with a tall Charles IX hat and a white slashed tunic; he looks anaemic and puffy about the eyes, his head propped up by an intricate lace ruff — but he survived to go on the Cadiz expedition with Essex and well into the reign of James I. All around are the fine young men who filled Elizabeth's Court. There is Sir John Pakington, whom she called 'Lusty Pakington' for his feats of strength and athletic skill. He once laid a wager with three other courtiers to swim from Westminster to London Bridge, but for some reason the Queen would not allow the match. Here he is, long-limbed and athletic-looking, a gawky rough; yet he has the long fine hands of an artist. The ladies of the Court are much less in evidence; one remembers only the Lady Catherine Howard, an old-fashioned dame with a complicated head-gear, and her eyes wide open with surprise, as if in alarm at finding herself here. And so we come to the two Somerset brothers, very much of a type, both of them extremely handsome; Sir George in a glittering suit of armour with an arabesque pattern; and his brother Sir Charles, Captain of the Rysebank at Calais, in the famous black-and-gold armour now in the Tower. In the former, an arrogant pose goes curiously with a shifty look in the eyes; but the latter, painted in 1566 when he was thirty, needs no qualifying. It is a portrait of the handsomest Elizabethan type; a swarthy complexion, long beard and high forehead, with wide-apart dark eyes and beautifully curved brows.

Let us pass into the room given up to the men who in the end brought more glory to the reign than all these: the seamen. Here is Drake to the life, down to the wart on his nose; the small slanting head compact with furious energy stands out from the canvas darkened with age. On a table by him is a globe, with the map of the world, at his belt the large pendant jewel the Queen gave him. Near him are the maps his voyages produced, contemporary accounts of them, written and published, and the astrolabe that Humphrey Cole made for his aid in navigation. He seems so alive, in spite of the years, that looking at the flesh-coloured cheeks of the seamen, I am reminded of the force of the man, as revealed in his letters to Elizabeth when keeping watch in the Channel for the Armada. 'The Lord of all strengths is with you,' he writes to her; and then, 'I surely think there was never any force so strong as there is now ready and making ready against your Majesty but that the Lord of all strengths is stronger.'

Sir Humphrey Gilbert's picture reveals a similar slant head to Drake's; only where Drake had a fresh colour, blue eyes and brown hair, Gilbert was sallow and dark like a Spaniard. He too, has the same bravado, this time expressed in a motto, *Quid Non*: what not, indeed! What would they not do, these explorers of unknown seas; what dangers were they not prepared to face, what deaths to invite? The end with Gilbert is inscribed upon the canvas, 'Drowned in the discovery of Virginia, *anno* 1584.' We all know the story of the little 10-ton bark, the *Squirrel*, in which he foundered, the dark night, the light at her mast which suddenly disappeared and was seen no more; how when his companion ship last saw him, Gilbert was sitting in the stern with a book in his hand, and refused to change ships, calling out, 'We are as near to heaven by sea as by land.'

Last of them comes the Lord Admiral, Howard of Effingham, painted on a large scale, life-size or more, in his robes as a peer, red velvet and grey-tawny satin. His face is an old man's, with grizzled beard and large nose, a turban close-fitting on his head; it reveals all that he was — a grand public figure, of obvious integrity. The painter, with the romantic touch of the Flemish school, has painted in a seascape beyond the rich hangings, with dim shapes of ships tossing on the grey waves. He is recalling for us the stormy summer of 1588, when the fleet lay heaving in Plymouth Sound, and the Lord Admiral was writing to Walsingham: 'Myself and my ships do continually tarry and lie aboard in all the storm, where we may compare that we have danced as lustily as the gallantest dancers in the Court.' Meanwhile provision was running short, 'and if it do not come', he wrote, 'yet assure yourself we will not lose any opportunity nor we will not lack, there is good fishing in the seas'.

So, passing hurriedly through the remaining rooms, we make for a quieter, more peaceful, side of the reign. In passing, an engaging picture catches one's eye, of an Elizabethan captain, looking very young and rather frightened, but all the same looking out of his frame as if he were alive. The date is 1587, the year before the Armada; it has a typical inscription, just the kind of sentiment that would commend itself:

> Only · death · makes ·
> Captains · quayle ·
> And lusti · souldiers
> for · to · fayle ·

How many such young captains must have left their bones on the plains of the Netherlands, fighting under Norris or Leicester against Don John, or the redoubtable Parma? Sir Nicholas Parker, whose portrait comes from the royal collection, served as a captain in the Low Countries and in France; but he came home again to marry into a Cornish family and live to a hale old age as Governor of Pendennis Castle. He appears in gorget and black tunic, a lean narrow-faced man with narrow temples and steel-grey eyes; while he brandishes above his head a heavy broadsword, with the inscription *Pro Fide et Patria*.

One does not think of Sir Philip Sidney as a warrior, he seems to belong to that earlier time before the storm descended. Half the pathos of his end lies in that — that the most chivalrous man of his time, the pattern of courtesy, one of those men like Lord Falkland who saw beyond the fighting, should have

I

come upon his death in battle. He was mortally wounded outside Zutphen — not far from Arnhem, of heroic memory to us in our time — lingered a while and died. When he died, his contemporaries felt that something had finished in them, that spring had gone out of the morning. There is here a famous print of his funeral procession, with his friends about him carrying the pall and bearing his standards: Fulke Greville, Edmund Pakenham, Henry Sidney, Edmund Walsingham, Will Sidney, Edward Wootton, Edward Dyer; and not far away there is a curious momento — one of the mourning hoods worn by the heralds.

The portraits of him show him bright and happy in his young years; one of them is taken with his brother Robert, two boys arm-in-arm in white doublets and stockings and plum-coloured breeches; the other shows him as a young man, with fair hair and light hazel eyes. On the other side is his sister the Countess of Pembroke, for whom he wove the long dream-like tale of the *Arcadia* in the groves of Wilton. Wilton was their Arcadia; and the thought of Sir Philip Sidney and his sister seems ever to be associated — in the picture she is holding a lute — with music and gardens.

It was Bacon who wrote, 'God Almighty first planted a garden'; and Bacon himself, in philosophic rivalry, was a gardener; he made the garden at Gray's Inn, and spent years over the gardens of Gorhambury. When one thinks of how Elizabeth spent her time, one has the impression of much walking and talking in gardens; as often as not, her conversations with foreign envoys, no less than with her courtiers, took place while walking up and down the gardens of her palaces. From a tapestry in the Exhibition, one may gather something of how they conceived of a garden; it is of a romantic character with an Eastern potentate reclining in a corner, a large attendance crowded among the formal walks, the box-hedges and the roses. In the background there is a carriage going by, a gaily-curtained affair on springless wheels, drawn by two small ponies. This is realistic enough: it reminds one of the way in which Elizabeth and the Court were always trundling from Richmond to Whitehall, from Nonsuch to Oatlands and Greenwich and then back again.

English music reached a height of achievement in Elizabeth's reign which it has never since attained; William Byrd was to Elizabethan music what Spenser was to poetry. There are all too few relics of him here, a manuscript of some songs and a signature on a document — not much to suggest the depth and range of his genius. There is a pleasant portrait of the libidinous Dr. Bull, organist of the Chapel Royal and virtuoso performer: in black satin, very clear in texture like a Hals, with white ruff and wristbands by way of contrast, his spruce moustaches waxed out to a fine point. Various other relics exhibit the musical skill of the time: there is a viola da gamba, of exquisite workmanship, made by John Rose in the old palace of Bridewell, a viriginal of 1570 still in good playing condition and several pieces of music, the funeral Psalms of Mr. Henry Noel, with music by John Dowland, and Thomas Morley's *Plain and Easy Introduction to Music*.

There is a much fuller and more representative collection of documents in the section devoted to literature. Among many first editions of Spenser and Sidney, Peele and Kyd and Dekker (no Marlowe, however), there is a first quarto of *A Midsummer Night's Dream* 'as it hath been sundry times publicly acted by the Right Honourable, the Lord Chamberlaine his servants'; and John Lyly's *Sappho and Phao*, 'Played before the Queenes Majestie on Shrove Tuesday by her Majesties' children and the boyes of Paules'. One recalls the jollifications at Court at Shrove-tide, the payments to the players that regularly appear in Elizabeth's Household accounts. Throwing no less light on the minds of men then is the translation of a book published in 1572: *Of ghostes and spirites walking by nyght and of strange noyces, cracks and sundry fore-warnyngs, whiche commonly happen before the death of menne, great slaughters and alterations of kyng-domes*. We recall:

> And yesterday the bird of night did sit
> Even at noon-day upon the market-place,
> Hooting and shrieking. When these prodigies
> Do so conjointly meet, let not men say,
> 'These are their reasons — they are natural';
> For I believe they are portentous things
> Unto the climate that they point upon.

Much to our loss, very few portraits of the poets and dramatists have come down to us — perhaps not many were even
painted. Spenser is represented to us in Thomas Wilson's copy
of a contemporary portrait now vanished. It is much what one
would expect, a massive though delicate head, a notably high
forehead and an air of melancholy dignity; the eyes are large,
blue and heavy-lidded — the whole impression dreamy and a
little weak.

Among the other documents nearly all the well-known signa-
tures appear; the crabbed spidery crawl of Burghley, the fluent
Italian hands of the young men at Court, Robert Cecil, Essex,
Bacon. There are letters of Mary Queen of Scots, and a number,
as there are a few portraits, of the French Court, Catherine de
Medici, Charles IX and Henry III. Last, there is Elizabeth
herself, from the self-conscious, self-confident, elaborate signature of the early years of the reign, to the loose scrawl of her
last years, in which one sees reflected all the storms that have
passed over her in the years between. 'Je prieray,' she writes
to the young Charles IX on the eve of the Massacre of St.
Bartholomew. 'Je prieray le Seigneur Dieu vous garder de tout
mall et vous donner bonne vie et longue.'

One might specify a conspicuous gap here: the virtual absence
of Ralegh from the Exhibition. True, we are given his pipe, and
a formidable object it is; but it is not as the populariser of
smoking that the Elizabethans chiefly knew him. Perhaps,
owing to the ill-fortune that overtook him and wrecked his
family, few relics of him remain in private hands. And more
space might have been given to the Opposition — the Catholic
circles which would not accept the new régime. Their view of
things is expressed in scarlet needlework on a nightdress of
Mary Queen of Scots: *Camisia sanctissimae martyris Mariae
Scotorum Reginae quae passa est sub Elizabetha Regina Angliae 1587
Feb. 18.* There are a number of families, the Norfolks, the
Arundells of Wardour, the Eastons, Welds, Bedingfields, whose
treasures it would have been a privilege to see — such things,
for instance, as the fine portraits of the Venerable Philip, Earl
of Arundel, in the possession of the Jerninghams, or a relic of
Cardinal Allen's.

But perhaps these things would have struck a discordant note amid the unanimity of glory. There is a sufficiently curious reminder in the shrivelled hand of Sir John Heydon, cut off in a duel in 1600, yet still in perfect preservation to the nails, of the more gruesome side of the Elizabethans: the dangers that attended life on all sides, the executions, the rackings, the heads on the gateways of towns, the gibbets at cross-roads.

In spite of the recognisably English characteristics of the age, there seems something alien to us in its spirit, some combination of magnificence and cruelty, a streak of the Italian, of the Italy of Machiavelli. One seems to see it looking out of the face of Elizabeth herself, and her environment was no less marked by Italian refinements; when half the musicians at Court were Italian, when Italian was the fashionable language, spoken by the Queen herself, when translations from Italian were all the vogue with the dramatists and poets. It is the Renaissance in full blow on English soil, though a little late, that explains it: the common spirit giving common form to these innumerable diverse objects here brought together. Look at this great chimney-piece from Madingley, with its noble proportions: with half-shut eyes, one can appreciate the classical structure as pure as the purest Georgian, yet here it is bulging with caryatids and figures and fruits. The same is true of all these things, the full-blown suits of armour, the flagons and silver bowls, the capacious chairs and flowing gowns, no less than of the humbler vessels of green glaze or earthenware.

One comes to see a common spirit in the inflated, pantaloon-like breeches of the men, the farthingales of the women and the bulbous legs of the tables — an expansiveness, a generosity of line, a vulgarity unrestrained by the taste of a more sophisticated age. They were children; they rioted in extremes of opulence, ardour, joy; they must even have derived pleasure from their exaggerated griefs. The sedate Lord Burghley, when he could not persuade the Queen to what he wanted, gave way to tears. A sober statesman overeats at a feast, and having to take physic, has to absent himself from important affairs of State for days or weeks. The same unrestraint, the same bravado that led a sea-captain to sail his ship up the Thames with sails of damask, that led Ralegh when there was a rumour of his disgrace to show himself to the people who hated him, clad in silver from top to toe, inspired the ladies to their fantastic ruffs, the joiners to their over-emphatic efforts and the dramatists to pile the stage with corpses in their final acts. In a word, the Elizabethans were unrestrained, because creative, and put the whole of themselves into the act, with conscious or unconscious rhetoric.

# IX

# ELIZABETH AT RYCOTE

Now it is afternoon over the rolling Oxfordshire country between Shotover and Brill and Thame — much of it part of the
old Royal Forest of Shotover. We have come by Waterperry
and Waterstock and round by Shabbington, where in front of
'The Old Fisherman' a duck-board conducts the villagers along
the low-lying road, so liable to be flooded by the sudden and
uncertain Thame, and from there across the fields to Rycote.
Having scrambled down and up the narrow moat and through
the little nineteenth-century plantation gone wild, full of lilacs
and rhododendrons among the bushes and small sycamores,
we now sit by the lakeside, tired with our long walk. I turn
back to see the chestnuts holding their candelabras low down
upon the water, their heavy flowers reflected as in a mirror.
It is the sleepy hour of the afternoon, but the angry rooks are
restless and disturbed above the treetops, cawing for minutes
together and then falling silent. Everything leans towards quiet
and sleep-in-the-sun; the cry of a moorhen out on the water,
a lonely 'qurr', only deepens the silence.

Looking up the lake, between the trees, I first catch sight of
the house and remember Elizabeth. Here, then, she was happy
once with Leicester; here she came often enough to see the
Norrises, coming from Woodstock or from Oxford over Shotover, or in earlier, more difficult days, from Brentford, being
conducted to the half retirement, half confinement of Woodstock
while Mary reigned. Not much of the house remains as it was
then; only a wing, and the chapel in the grounds. In the orchard
below the house there is a detached octagonal turret of the
Elizabethan house still standing, of diapered red brick, upon
the line of the old front; and behind the walled garden, in the
open field there are humps which indicate a ruined gate-house
or outbuildings. And all around in the fields are scattered oaks
and beeches, a few of the oldest oaks the remains of the medieval
forest: one of them standing not far from the house, very old

and wide and dying at the top, may even have seen Elizabeth. It is chastening to think that some natural or inanimate object, a house, a tree, has looked upon Elizabeth, or all the Henrys and Edwards before her, that long procession of time which, a human being, one can never know: some reminder to abash one, of the shortness, the fragile uncertainty which is our lot in comparison.

What remains of the house is still satisfying, with its pleached and patterned brick, the end-wall rising to a Flemish gable, stepped and parapeted, as was then the fashion, a sunken flower-garden below the balustrade of the terrace. One can almost see those formal figures, the pleated farthingales, the ruffs, the heads held high, moving stiffly, so many figures on a chess-board, among the vanished box-hedges and trimmed yews. One great yew still stands that outdoes them all, even those shadows, in time, standing sentinel by the tower of the chapel among the graves. The tree, this little stone building with its western niche for the saint, remember days, years, centuries before Elizabeth and Leicester came here; the chapel of St. Michael and All Angels founded in the year 1449 by Richard Quatremaine and Sybilla his wife, the yew going back perhaps to Edward III's order to plant yews in the churchyard of every parish, in the time of the French wars.

To this pleasant house in a fold of the hill, looking to the east and the south, Elizabeth came first in 1554 on her way to Woodstock, when Mary was Queen. Here she was entertained by Lord Williams of Thame, to whom Henry Norris, her kindly keeper at Woodstock, succeeded in the first year of her reign. Her time at Woodstock must have been not unpleasant: it ministered to wounded pride to nag even at Bedingfield; perhaps it was all a game to her, practising the part of injured innocence that was so useful in later years, sharpening her talons upon an old, blunt, fanatic knight. At any rate, Norris was all kindness, and she grew to like him and his dark wife, her 'black crow' she called her, having names for everybody. When she came to be Queen, she remembered them as she remembered all who had been kind to her and to the mother she never spoke of: Norris was made Ambassador to France, became Lord Norris of Rycote, and later was several times graced by the Queen herself coming to visit him.

She came again, this time with Leicester, in 1566, after the festivities of her reception at Oxford, the interminable orations in Latin and Greek, the disputations in the Schools, the sermons, the verses, the plays in Christ Church Hall — one of them in English, Richard Edwards' *Palaemon and Arcyte*, a sprig from which grew the mighty tree of the Elizabethan drama; another in Latin, called *Progne*, by a Canon of Christ Church — 'but it did not take half so well as the much-admired play of Palaemon and Arcyte'. All which over, she rode away to Shotover, the Masters and Scholars of the University accompanying her; and turning back to the city, said farewell: 'Farewell the worthy University of Oxford; farewell my good subjects there; farewell my dear scholars, and may God prosper your studies: farewell — farewell.' 'And so she rode that night to Rycote, to Mr. Norris's house, eight miles from Oxford.'

It was early September — Leicester was with her — and the height of their intimacy: she a woman now in her early thirties; he handsome, rakish, well educated. He too had been a prisoner in the Tower when she was there: one among the many memories, of shared danger and pleasure, that held them together.

The years passed on and over; she was here again in 1568, and in 1570, always at the same time of year, late August, early September. Then for many years she did not come at all. The Norris children, six fine strapping lads, grew up about these fields. In 1582 it was rumoured that she was coming; but the Norrises could not have been so pleased when Leicester, magnificent deputy, arrived instead. However, his Lordship found them 'a hearty noble couple as ever I saw towards her highness'.

The storms of war were gathering, and Elizabeth did not move far into the country. Then at the end of August 1588, that memorable month, Leicester was here once more, straight from the camp at Tilbury. It was the time when he and Elizabeth had been there together, the high, late summer; now the remnants of the King of Spain's fleet were labouring their way through the northern seas around Scotland homeward. Remembering the earlier years, he took up pen and wrote to her, inquiring after her health, 'the chiefest thing in this world I pray for'; and then, dated his letter, 'From your old lodging at Rycote'. There was constancy in that and true affection. Five days later he was dead. When the news came, Elizabeth took the letter and, writing upon it in her own hand 'His last letter', folded it up and put it away.

Four years later, at the end of September 1592, she came here for the last time, on her way from Oxford. There were the usual jubilations, the usual speeches. But somehow it did not go with a swing as of old; there was no Leicester there; perhaps there were too many ghosts. On Thursday, 28 September,

Her Highness departed from the University this day, about eleven of the clock in the forenoon, in hir open and princely carriadge. And heard, lastly, a long tedious oration made unto hir by the Junior Proctor of the University, about a mile from the city, in the very edge of their bounds or liberties towards Shotover.

Arrived at Rycote, she was received with a ceremonial set-piece such as the time delighted in: 'an olde gentleman, some-time a souldier' delivered a speech:

'I meane not to recount my service' (he said) 'but to tell your Majesty that I am past al service, save only devotion. My horse, mine armour, my shielde, my sworde, the riches of a young souldier, and an olde souldier's reliques, I should here offer to your Highnesse; but my foure boies have stollen them from me, vowing themselves to armes, and leaving mee to my prayers. This is their resolution, and my desire, that their lives maye be imployed wholy in your service, and their deathes bee their vowes sacrifice. Their deathes, the rumour of which hath so often affrighted the Crowe my wife, that her hart hath bene as blacke as her feathers. I know not whether it be affection or fondness, but the Crowe thinketh her owne birds the fairest, because to her they are dearest, and although nothing be more unfit to lodge your Majestye than a Crowes neste, yet shall it be most happy to us, that it is by your Highnesse made a Phoenix neste.'

It was Norris, protesting his devotion and his sons' serving abroad for the Queen. Twenty years had gone by since Elizabeth was here last, and the six lads were grown into stalwart men, two of them, John and Henry, among the celebrated soldiers of their time. The wars now continuing, and to continue for the rest of her life, they were serving in Ireland (where one of them,

William, had already died: no wonder the Crow was so fearful for her brood), in the Netherlands, in Brittany, the various theatres of the war. On the Sunday, 'her Majesty going to the garden, was received with sweete Musicke of sundry sorts'. There letters were brought to her from different directions; one delivered by an Irish lackey, in which was enclosed a dart of gold, set with diamonds, with this motto in Irish, 'I flye onely for my Soveraigne'. A second brought a skipper from Flanders, with a key of gold, and a truncheon set with diamonds, and with mottoes in French and Spanish. These last were from the brothers waiting to take shipping into Brittany: 'the same time that I received letters that her Majesty would be at Ricot, the winde served for Britaigne: I was overjoyed with both; yet stoode in a mammering whether I should take the opportunity of the winde, which I long expected; or ride poste to do my duetie, which I most desired'. The letters read and the presents delivered, in this little garden scene, 'the olde man kneeling downe, ended thus': 'That my sonnes have remembered their dueties, it is my harts comfort; that your Majestie accepteth them, their harts heaven. . . .' This being done, 'there was sweete musicke and two sonnets; which ended, her Majesty went in'. Next day she took horse and left, never to come again.

A few more years and the shadows thicken round the faithful house. The pigeons wheel in and out and around the dovecote; the yew darkens by the chapel tower; the house grows emptier than it was; old age steals perceptibly on and there are youthful images that linger in the dark corners of the rooms, or where a turning comes in the passages or in the garden walks on late summer evenings, in August or early September. One day in 1593, word comes that Maximilian the youngest had been killed in Brittany, fighting under his famous brother, Sir John. Then another day, in 1597, John died, worn out with service and war wounds, in Ireland. The Queen, grown old now, called her secretary, and wrote by him a letter of proud consolation to the Lady Norris:

Althoughe wee have deferred long to represent unto you our grieved thoughts, because we liked full ill to yielde you the first reflection of misfortune, whom we have always sought to cherrishe and comfort, yet, knowing now that necessitie must bring it to yo$^r$ eares, and nature consequently must move both griefe and passions in your harte, we resolved no longer to smother either our care for yo$^r$ sorrowe, or the sympathy of our griefe for his love, whearin, yf it be true that society in sorrowe workes diminution, wee doe assure you, by this true messenger of our minde, that nature can have stirred no more dolorous affection in you as a mother for a deare son, than gratefulness and memory of his services past hath wrought in us his Soveraigne aprehension of our misse of so worthy a servant.

It was the Queen that spoke, in her royal style, words of majestic consolation. Then the woman in her was moved, and taking up the pen, she wrote a few words in her own scrawling hand — the hand that had been so neat and beautiful once — now witnessing in itself what storms had passed over her, what stresses of state: 'Myne owne Crowe, harme not thyselfe for booteles healpe; but shewe a good example, to comfort yo$^r$ dolorous yokefellow.'

Not long now, and Norris and his Crow were dead and buried in the vault beneath the altar of the little chapel, the stately monument to them both, supported by their six sons, rising in the Abbey at Westminster.

So remembering, we go over the hill, the house sinking below its shoulder. The sun comes out over Brill and Muswell Hill; the sky that was grey is now blue; a cuckoo flutes across the fields. There is a silvery quality in the tufts of grass in this field, I notice; my feet find a ridge-way running through it: under the turf, between two banks is the old carriage-way going due west to Shotover. A haze of memories surrounds that house below the hill; I see an old triumphant woman in her carriage coming this way from the west. What, I wonder, was the reason for her constancy, her fidelity to this house? That memory of Leicester; her affection for her Crow? And then I remember yet another shadow, a man she never knew — her father's young companion, victor of so many tournaments, the man who died for being her mother's lover: poor ghosts whose innocence she chose to vindicate so, keeping silence through all the years. For Norris was his son.

# X

# THE SPANISH COLLEGE AT BOLOGNA

I WENT, in memory of Edward Armstrong whose historical writing I admire, to see the Spanish College at Bologna: he wrote a delightful sketch of its history. So many English people who spend a day or two in the town contrive to go away without ever seeing one of its most interesting sights, certainly its rarest, for it must be the only survival of a medieval college on the Oxford and Cambridge model remaining on the Continent. Perhaps it is due to its being tucked away down a side street on the edge of the town; or still more to the fact that Baedeker hardly mentions the existence of the College, devotes no more than a sentence to it.

The College occupies an island site towards the south-west corner of the town, between the Via del Collegio di Spagna and the Via Urbana with its tram-lines. Along the former runs the irregular line of its red-brick buildings, and along the latter a high parapeted wall with overhanging creeper, above which appear the cedars of the garden within. A very attractive place it is, all built of the pleasant baked brick of Bologna, and though the foundation dates from the fourteenth century, the buildings have the appearance of the sixteenth. The point of the triangle at the junction of the two streets is occupied by a patch of grass with a few trees; the entrance gate is at the side. On entering there is the porter's lodge with a quadrangle behind, the chapel opposite, and the rooms of the students grouped around: a familiar arrangement to a wandering Oxford man on the Continent. But, this being Italy, the sets of rooms give not directly upon the court but upon a loggia that runs round the four sides. Armstrong called it 'a small English college translated into Italian', and described its character, not quite correctly, as 'in a manner the All Souls of Bologna'.

It was founded by the great Cardinal Albornoz, Legate of the Holy See in these parts, 'soldier, statesman, and an administrator of the first order', in the fourteenth century, heyday of collegiate foundations. 'At Oxford,' writes Armstrong, 'the foundation of Queen's precedes, that of New College shortly followed, the Spanish College. At Cambridge, Pembroke, Gonville, Trinity Hall, Corpus and Clare are all within twenty years of it.' From early days favours were showered upon the College by the Spanish monarchs, by the Popes and by the town of Bologna. Possessing its own lands like an Oxford college today, and similarly governed under statute by its Rector and Fellows, it enjoyed a privileged and independent position in relation to the university.

Throughout its history the chief danger to its existence has been the political connection entailed by its national character. Armstrong says that the Spanish domination of Italy, from the sixteenth century onwards, gave it a political complexion 'which was not favourable to its best interests'. It shared the the ups and downs of Spanish fortunes in Italy, and several times was near to foundering altogether. In the War of the Spanish Succession, the students were strong in support of Philip V, the choice of the Spanish people; the College was in consequence closed by the Austrians and only reopened after the conclusion of the War. Under Napoleon it was suppressed again, its properties confiscated, while paintings by Raphael disappeared from the walls and the fine fresco representing Charles V's coronation at Bologna was ruined. The establishment of the new Kingdom of Italy brought yet another danger and the College was temporarily sequestrated. An appeal to the Spanish government was, however, successful, and it survived.

It survived to undergo yet a new crisis with the Spanish Civil War; on its outbreak all the eighteen students departed. The College shut up, everything well kept, neat and in order, waiting for their return. (Who of them will return? I wondered.) There is always something rather moving about rooms through which so many tides of young life have flowed, particularly in the intervals of absence, when they are withdrawn and the old places wait. All was so familiar here: the little sets of sitting-room and bedroom, the small bookcase, the writing-table before the window. A fresh wind blew through the empty corridors like an Oxford college in vacation.

The friendly porter, so accustomed a figure, showed me round the loggia with its polished floor, its pictures and old chests, the little doors of Spanish chestnut inlaid with the Cardinal's hat that lead into the students' rooms. The common rooms were on a more comfortable scale, and more elegantly furnished than junior common rooms with us. There was the *sala da pranzo* with its bust of Cardinal Albornoz over the door, the *sala da te*, which appealed even more to an Englishman's taste, the *sala da conversazione*, a regular drawing-room such as we are not accustomed to in English colleges, with its fine Venetian mirrors and portraits of Spanish sovereigns, Queen Maria Christina and others. Then there was the *sala da giocco*, a long gallery with its billiard-table — 'a luxury', Armstrong wrote in the eighteen-eighties, 'to which even All Souls has not yet attained'. I must not forget the chapel with its fifteenth-century altar-piece, its fresco by Gian Bologna, a tablet commemorating Charles V's visit to the city. The excellent library, which escaped the French Revolution, I did not see; for the Spanish consul who occupies part of the College had taken the key with him.

I walked across the beautifully-kept garden, to the tomb of the founder with its painted recumbent effigy. The paths were bordered with blue irises, the south wall covered with climbing roses from which looked the windows of the upper rooms. There, at that passing moment of the Italian intervention in Spain — after the centuries of Spanish intervention in Italy — I paid my respects to the great ecclesiastic whose tomb had witnessed them all, founder, in just the generation before Chichele, of this Spanish All Souls in the Marches of the Romagna.

# XI

# THE OLD MUSIC SCHOOL AT OXFORD

FOR this early hour of the summer afternoon, a magic quiet has descended upon the stilled and sleepy room. Like Matthew Arnold, whom I think of, perambulating the classroom, reading poems out of a book while the scholars are bent over their examination task; or like Yeats, an old grey-haired senator walking up and down between the benches where the school-children are congregated watching; so I sit here at the long table in the music school, alone with all the desks and faces.

Outside, the enchantment of the bells of Oxford in summer has fallen upon the grey streets and green gardens of the city. We are borne down beneath the sounding waters. Time's tide sweeps by; no less inevitably, more felt, for the illusion given that this one moment is eternal. The noises of the city are caught up and cherished and given beauty, as if they too should not perish: the horn of a passing car, bringing back the snowy squares of Munich one February night; the quick ring of a bicycle; the rich 'gulge-gulge' of sparrows in the eaves, that I always associate with school on hot summer afternoons from childhood. But above all, the bells; fragile but immutable; eloquent of what victories, what past devotions; the nearest thing man had created to the flight of birds, until the coming of the aeroplane to ruin all.

Around the room there are the pale faces of the dead men who were here before us, looking out from their picture-frames; all of them looking down upon me with concentrated gaze, as if in accusation that there are others who have come and taken their familiar places.

There is Matthew Locke, a beautiful face, dark and oval, with high arched brows; the eyes have an awareness in their hazel lights, looking away from us as if greeting some friend whom we cannot see. In life he had plenty of friends, as we know from Pepys's Diary: 21 February 1659, 'After dinner I back to Westminster Hall, here I met with Mr. Locke and

Purcell, masters of musique, and with them to the coffee-house, into a room next the water by ourselves. Here we had variety of brave Italian and Spanish songs and a Canon of eight voices which Mr. Locke had lately made on these words, "Domine salvum fac Regem", an admirable thing.' There, in the Latin version of 'God Save the King', is a musical indication of the nearness of the Restoration. Locke is a West Country name, and as a boy Matthew was a chorister of Exeter cathedral, where on the old organ screen one may still see his name carved in full with the date 1638, and again 'M.L. 1641' — the year in which the hateful Civil War brought the cathedral services to an end.

However, in the long interval before they were resumed, Locke took to composing secular music to accompany masques and plays, when allowed to be played. He was no mean composer — one still hears his instrumental music, consorts for the viols, occasionally performed. But in the end he was surpassed by his pupil and protégé, 'the divine Purcell', with whose family the older man lived, and who composed a fine cantata on Locke's comparatively early death.

Two sombre faces of the seventeenth-century peer direct from their canvases: Christopher Simpson and Thomas Blagrave. Who were they, I wonder? The one a narrow wizened-looking man, appearing a Puritan sobersides rather like Governor Winthrop, with neat tassels at the throat, drawing together the pointed collar. The other jaundiced, puffy about the eyes— a pertinacious University politician?

Not at all: it only shows how appearances can belie, especially after the lapse of centuries. Christopher Simpson, so far from being a Puritan, was — like most musicians — a Cavalier. On the outbreak of the Civil War he at once joined the King's forces. After the defeat of the Royalist cause, 'the iniquity of the times reduced him with many others, in that common calamity, to a condition needing support'. He was taken into the household of a Lincolnshire Cavalier, Sir Robert Bolles, who was devoted to both Crown and music, who provided the musician with 'a cheerful maintenance'. It was this that gave Simpson the chance to write the works that brought him a competence. An accomplished performer on the viol, he wrote

K

mainly works of instruction on that instrument, such as *The Division Violist, or an Introduction to playing upon a Ground*, dedicated to his kind patron in 1659. Perhaps it was during this gloomy Commonwealth time that he was painted: hence the sombre impression he gives.

Nor was there anything more Puritan about decent Thomas Blagrave, made a member of Charles II's private band at the happy Restoration — in which he was 'a player for the most part on the cornet-flute, and a gentle and honest man'. Pepys knew him, and in his Diary records walking in the Abbey with him, 'he telling me the whole government and discipline of the Whitehall Chapel, and the caution now used against admitting any debauched person'. Very different from the Palace, we may say.

Here is William Gregory, iron-grey, with suspicious eyes and querulous eyebrows puckered. He had reason enough to be querulous. Of an older generation than those others, he was a musician in the household of Charles I and lost his job when the Civil War scattered them all. At the Restoration he was restored to his post, but he died not long after with arrears of wages still owing him from the impoverished Treasury.

There in the shadowy corner is a far more eminent musician, in flowered silk gown, Orlando Gibbons, who is now known to have been born at Oxford, though his youth was passed at Cambridge as a chorister of King's College chapel. A brilliantly-gifted executant, he was made organist of James I's Chapel Royal when only twenty-one. It was when the whole Chapel Royal was in attendance upon Charles I at Canterbury, to meet his new Queen Henrietta Maria, that Orlando Gibbons was suddenly struck down by a seizure, when still only forty-one — he had been baptised at St. Martin's, the city church up at Carfax, on Christmas Day 1583.

Not far away is the charming Henry Lawes, friend of the young Milton in the years before the cataclysm, for whom he wrote the music for *Comus*:

> Harry whose tuneful and well measur'd Song,
>   First taught our English Musick how to span
>   Words with just note and accent.

He looks jovial enough, though with upward questing turn of the eyebrow; in his hand, a scroll of music for a canon *a tre voci: Regi Regis, Regi Regis, Regum arcana cano.* How devoted they were to the Stuarts, these musicians; the Civil War was a tragedy for all of them. They lost their livelihood with the dispersal of the King's household, the closing down of the Chapel Royal, the cathedral services, the collegiate churches. As Lawes himself wrote, when he published his book of *Ayres* during the Interregnum, having 'lost his fortunes with his master, of ever blessed memory'.

Some lost their lives, like William Lawes, whose portrait too is here. We now know him to have been the younger of the two brothers — as indeed he looks in his portrait: 'Brothers in blood, in Science and Affection, beloved by those that envie their Renowne.' Where Henry, who wrote for voices, was the more popular, we learn that the younger, who wrote more for instruments, was the more original, writing in the more elaborate polyphonic style, a skilled contrapuntalist. Both brothers were favourites with the poets who also served that sophisticated and elegant Court, and whose poems and masques they set to music, before the condemned time closed in upon them. Of William's end we learn: 'in these distracted times his Loyalty engaged him in the War for his lord and master, and though he was made a Commissary on designe to secure him — such officers being shot-free by their place, as not exposed to danger — yet such was the activity of his spirit he disclaimed the covert of his office, and betrayed thereunto by his own adventurousness was casually shot at the Siege of Chester, the same time when the Lord Bernard Stuart lost his life. Nor was the King's soul so engrossed with grief for the death of so near a Kinsman and noble a lord but that, hearing of the death of his deare Servant William Lawes, he had a particular Mourning for him dead whom he loved when living and commonly called the Father of Musick.'

This phrase of the connoisseur king did not refer to William Lawes's age, for he was only forty-three when killed, but to his eminence as a musician. Here he lives for us again under the sweeping, rakish Stuart hat, the untidy hair brushed back on his shoulders, fringe coming down to his eyebrows. It is a clever,

humorous face, intelligent eyes and prominent nose giving a
hint of the adventurousness that was in his spirit, in his music
as in the determination that brought him to his early end.

In the centre, there is the best portrait of them all: a brilliant
Elizabethan picture of John Bull, the Court musician, as
bright now as the day it was painted. The portrait says, *anno
aetatis suae 27; in the year 1589.* There he is, stayed for good
and all at just that time of life: a youthful Elizabethan face,
long and ridged, auburn hair and candid narrow brow, neat
sparse beard and delicate lined lips. But the main feature of
the face, the cold grey eyes, are full of awareness of the sentence that time passes on all that is human, arrested only for a
moment while music is playing. The painter, painting him in
the year after the Armada, inscribed around the finished
picture:

> The Bull by force
> In field doth raigne
> But Bull by skill
> Good Will doth gaine.

Bull took his degree as Doctor of Music at Oxford in the summer
of 1592, in the month before Southampton was incorporated
as M.A. in time for the Queen's visit in September. Dr. Bull
seems to have had rather more of an erotic disposition than he
knew how to provide for; what with that and his Catholic
inclinations, he got into some trouble, and in James's not very
exacting reign he absconded abroad. He received a warm
welcome in the Netherlands, where his musical prowess — he
was a marvellous virtuoso on the organ — was respected.
He ended his days comfortably, with the consolations of the
Catholic faith, as organist of Antwerp cathedral.

Dr. Burney is here too, and Dr. Croft: good stout eighteenth-
century faces, more content, altogether more placid and solid;
certainly less pathetic, less remote, not ravaged in their time
by mischance or ill-fortune, but no less making their mute
protest against the ravages of time.

Last of all, among these musicians, one who was both
musician and painter, and prided himself upon his mastery
of the twin arts. For he has painted himself as an artist, holding
brush and palette; and on the table by him he has a roll of

music, inscribed in a clear Caroline hand, 'Canon a 3 in $y^e$ $5^{th}$ and $6^{th}$'. There are the notes, in an old notation, hard to follow; and the words — but the words express the universal theme: they say in the accent of their time what all these dead men if they had voices would say from the dark canvases:

> Thus, thus, at last wee must
> Reducèd be
> To naked boanes and dust.

# XII

# THE CAROLINE COUNTRY PARSON:
## GEORGE HERBERT

IT sometimes occurs to me, as I know it does to others, to see an historical period in an image, a pictured scene, a landscape of the mind, as if one looked into some old mirror and saw there the shapes, the figures it had beheld in that time past, the sunlight and clouds passing of three hundred years ago. When I think of the quiet, peaceful decade before the Civil War, when Charles was King and Laud building the garden-front of St. John's at Oxford, it is always early summer. I see the blue sky with white feathery clouds and those figures walking with grave seventeenth-century tread up and down the terraces of some great house, as it might be Wilton or Great Tew, where Falkland walked in the shades with Hobbes and Sidney Godolphin. It is Sunday; the church bells are stilled, yet there is music in the village away beyond the park-pale; and within, there is the drone of bees busy among the rosemary and musk and lavender: they have a nest in the church porch next the house. The figures upon the terrace group and regroup themselves while discoursing upon poetry and the times. I cannot hear what they are saying; now they pause — there is a rustle of satin upon stone — and look out over the parterres and English fields to where there is a cloud no bigger than a man's hand upon the horizon. A rain-storm threatens; the sky is lowering: the threat of the Civil War that came to break up that Caroline peace. The figures are driven in: the terraces deserted.

Such is the world that the thought of George Herbert conjures up in the mind. His poetry is the perfect, the ideal, expression of it, if not the most complete, because of its very unworldliness: it reflects the soul of that world.

Herbert is the best known of those religious poets of the seventeenth century who came from the Welsh Border. Herbert, Vaughan, Traherne: one wonders whether the Welsh admixture in their blood may not have given them their leaning to mysticism, their familiar vision of eternity in the transitory things of this world, their way of hearing

> Church-bells beyond the starres.

George Herbert was born at Montgomery, that steep Border town, where his family had been governors of the Castle for generations. One remembers the view out over the straggling town from the height where the Castle stood, the broad street at the foot, the cottage gardens bright with wallflowers, the fine church with the painted tomb of George Herbert's parents, Sir Richard and the Lady Magdalen. Their fifth son was one of those men of genius who owed everything to a remarkable mother, the friend of Donne, who wrote of her:

> No Spring, nor Summer Beauty hath such grace,
> As I have seen in one Autumnal face.

Left a widow, she brought up her family herself, the eldest of whom, Edward, was to become the soldier-philosopher, Lord Herbert of Cherbury, and early intended her clever youngest son for orders. But though, from the time he began to write, he dedicated himself to sacred poetry, he had other ideas about a career. With such a family background — and we learn that when young at Cambridge, as was perhaps only natural, he 'put too great a value on his parts and parentage' — he aspired to a career in the state. He became Public Orator at the university with that end in view. But ill-health dogged him all his life, and instead of becoming a self-important figure in affairs, conspicuous for a moment and then to disappear into oblivion, he became a priest and poet, a figure who has never been forgotten. It was long before he could bring himself to take the yoke. In 1625 his patrons, King James and the Dukes of Richmond and Hamilton, died, and Herbert took deacon's orders. Still he delayed, living in the country in various houses of friends, pursued by illness, consoling himself with music and books and, within, that struggle going on to subject himself to the will of God, from which sprang the poetry which moves us most in him.

Then, in 1630, he took the decision from which there was no

turning back. He married, took the living of Bemerton near Salisbury, outside the park gates of Wilton, and the next three years saw him set a standard in his calling which has ever since been remembered in the English Church as the ideal to which the country parson can look for inspiration. Canon Hutchinson, who understands all this with so sensitive a sympathy, sums up George Herbert's inner struggle:

The letters which Herbert wrote from Bemerton show how far he had travelled since his Cambridge days; they manifest an achieved character of humility, tenderness, moral sensitiveness and personal consecration, which he was very far from having attained or even envisaged when he was dazzled by the attractions of the great world. Above all, *The Temple*, in which he laid bare the long story of his inner life, with all its faults and its ardours, and *A Priest to the Temple*, which he wrote at Bemerton that he might have a 'Mark to aim at', reveal the man, both as he had been and as he had become. . . . The inward conflict which had lent such poignancy to the poems written in the period of indecision and inaction was quieted when Herbert went to Bemerton, and there are only occasional echoes of it. Many of the later poems breathe a spirit of content.[1]

Herbert's aim in his prose work, *A Priest to the Temple; or The Country Parson*, was to portray the character and rule of life of the ideal pastor: 'which also I will set as high as I can, since he shoots higher that threatens the moon, that he that aims at a tree'. His ideals, besides being the ripened fruit of his own spiritual struggle, were much influenced by his friend, Nicholas Ferrar, and the circle at Little Gidding. Herbert was minded to set such a standard for the country parson in his office as to lift him out of 'the general ignominy which is cast upon the profession'; the precepts which he enjoined were those that inspired his ministry during the three years when he was Rector of Bemerton. His own example, even more perhaps than his book, has been a lasting influence upon the gentle and faithful tradition of the country parson in England.

What is remarkable about Herbert is his combination of common sense, his feeling for the plain country folk (he, too, whose early ambitions were set upon Courts), with the rigorous

[1] *The Works of George Herbert*, ed. F. E. Hutchinson, pp. xxxvi–xxxvii.

standards of a dedicated man. He was an aristocrat not only in his spiritual and aesthetic sensibilities, but in the tone of authority with which he addressed his folk, whether labourers and ploughmen, or gentry, or noblemen. For example, he says:

If there be any of the gentry or nobility of the parish, who sometimes make it a piece of state not to come at the beginning of service with their poor neighbours, but at mid-prayers, both to their own loss, and of theirs also who gaze upon them when they come in . . . he [the parson] by no means suffers it, but after divers gentle admonitions, if they persevere, he causes them to be presented.

The Caroline parson would need to be a Herbert to take this high and mighty line with the gentry of his parish, let alone the nobility! One wonders if this was the course he took with his distinguished and haughty relations beyond the rectory gates and across the park-pale at Wilton?

With the simple country folk no wonder he was a success: his ideal rested upon such a strong foundation of sense and meticulous attention to duty. The country people live hard and by the sweat of their brow; therefore their parson must avoid all covetousness and give according to his means. He must be strict in keeping his word, plain in speech and apparel. He must know about tillage and pasturage, be well versed in cases of conscience; he must be moved himself to move others. The saint was a good psychologist.

When he preacheth, he procures attention by all possible art, both by earnestness of speech, it being natural to men to think that where is much earnestness, there is something worth hearing; and by a diligent and busy cast of his eye on his auditors, with letting them know who marks, and who not, and with particularising his speech now to the younger sort, then to the older, now to the poor and now to the rich.

Here speaks the practised speaker: the man who had been Public Orator at Cambridge. He knew his Caroline country folk well, 'which are thick and heavy, and hard to raise to a point of zeal and fervency, and need a mountain of fire to kindle them; but stories and sayings they well remember'. When he was at Cambridge he had compiled a collection of

'Outlandish Proverbs': the accumulated wisdom, the tradi-
tional wisecracks, of our country folk. No doubt he found them
useful in the pulpit at Bemerton.

The parson entertains his parish folk, his farmers, in turn,
and helps to order the poor, parting with some of his living to
them in hard times and helping them to find employment: one
sees something of the age-long work of the country clergy, along
with the J.P.s and parish wardens, in this. He does not disdain
to enter the poorest cottage, 'though it smell never so loath-
somely'. He sees that the church is swept, and 'at great festivals
strawed, and stuck with boughs'. He acts as a lawyer for his
flock, reading up the J.P.s' book and deciding issues between
them. No less he should know how to effect cures with simples
and herbs. One thinks of the old-fashioned plants, neglected
now, that are still to be found about old habitations in the
country, the simples our forefathers used. Herbert was much
in favour of old customs, 'if they be good and harmless; and
the rather because country people are much addicted to them,
so that to favour them therein is to win their hearts, and to
oppose them therein is to deject them'.

In the end we think of Herbert's last days as Izaak Walton
wrote of them in his Life, so well attuned to its subject: of
Herbert walking in to Salisbury twice a week to hear service
in the cathedral and afterwards play his part at a music-
meeting with friends (like many Englishmen of his class and
time, he played upon both lute and viol); of the simple folk in
the fields who 'did so love and reverence Mr. Herbert, that
they would let their plough rest when Mr. Herbert's saint's-
bell rung to prayers, that they might also offer their devotions
to God with him, and would then return back to their plough'.

Almost all of Herbert's poetry is concerned with this inner
world of experience, as against his contemporary Herrick's
frank acceptance of the good things of this world. A speaking
contrast those two Caroline parsons make, genial Herrick
with his quick eye for the flowers (and the maidens) of his
Devonshire lanes at Dean Prior, and the 'sainted Mr. Herbert'.
Yet they had much in common: their love of music, so true to
Caroline England, of flowers and birds and church bells, of
the ancient country customs and the country people; their

devotion to the English Church they served and by which they are remembered. And though Herbert was centred upon his inner spiritual life, in turning over his pages one comes upon the evidences, so many notes, of his love of the fragmentary beauty of this. Take one of his Easter poems:

> I got me flowers to straw thy way;
>   I got me boughs off many a tree:
> But thou wast up by break of day,
>   And brought'st thy sweets along with thee.

We see again the sweet-scented, rush-strewn churches of that age. Or when he writes:

> Sweet day, so cool, so calm, so bright,
>   The bridal of the earth and sky:
> The dew shall weep thy fall tonight;
>   For thou must die . . .

one can fancy that long-vanished summer day at Bemerton within view of the trees of the park, within sound of the Wiltshire Avon running softly down to Salisbury.

## XIII

## THREE CIVIL WAR FIGURES

### I. John Hampden

On 24 June 1643 there died a man who has left an undying name in the story of English liberty: John Hampden. Yet I doubt if he is much more than a name to us. We probably remember him as having something to do with Ship Money, though very vague as to what that was, from our school-days. Yet it so happens that Hampden's was one of the most appealing characters, one of the finest natures, that have ever come to the fore in English public life.

Hampden was by nature, like so many determined men, a moderate. He had no intention of overthrowing the monarchy, but wished to restrain it within the boundaries of the constitution, to see Charles I working *with* Parliament, not against it. And there is no doubt that Charles was proceeding along an unconstitutional course, raising forced loans, imposing taxes without authority, imprisoning people arbitrarily, governing without Parliament.

From his first entry into public life, Hampden joined the opposition to Charles. But it was not until the famous Ship Money Case that he became a national figure. In itself the extension of the charge for building ships from the coastal counties to those inland was not unreasonable. But the point was that it by-passed Parliament. If the King was to be allowed to go on extending the area of taxes in this way, there was no reason why he should not govern indefinitely without Parliament — and the people of England, not merely the gentry, had come already to regard Parliament as the defender of their rights and liberties against encroachments.

The Buckinghamshire squire, who came of a family that went back to the Norman Conquest and was very wealthy in land, rose to the occasion and challenged the King. The case was fought in the courts, and in the end a majority of only seven judges to five declared for the Crown.

It was a great defeat for the King. Hampden leaped at once into the front rank of men of the day. Clarendon says, in that wonderful style of his:

He grew the argument of all tongues, every man inquiring who and what he was that durst at his own charge support the liberty and property of the kingdom, and rescue his country from being made a prey to the Court.

And when the King was forced to call Parliament,

the eyes of all men were fixed on him as their *Patriae pater*, and the pilot that must steer their vessel through the tempests and rocks which threatened it. . . . His power and interest at that time was greater to do good or hurt than any man's in the kingdom, or than any man of his rank hath had in any time: for his reputation of honesty was universal, and his affections seemed so publicly guided that no corrupt or private ends could bias them.

Clarendon sketches his character vividly for us: as a young man his pleasure 'in all the sports and exercises and company which was used by men of the most jolly conversation'; then with marriage and increasing seriousness of mind, his retirement to 'a more reserved and melancholic society, yet preserving his own natural cheerfulness and vivacity, and above all, a flowing courtesy to all men'. There was his 'rare affability and temper in debate', his extraordinary persuasiveness, his tactical sense, his moderation and fairness. 'He was indeed a very wise man, and of great parts, and possessed with the most absolute spirit of popularity, that is, the most absolute faculties to govern the people, of any man I ever knew.'

Such was the character of John Hampden, as drawn by an opponent. If that was what opponents felt about him, we can imagine how he inspired his followers. The truth was that there was a bond of sympathy between constitutional Royalists and moderate Parliamentarians. If they had had their way there would have been no Civil War. But Charles could not be trusted; he let them both down — fatal, hopeless man that he was. He broke the law by attempting to arrest the five Parliamentary leaders, Hampden among them, and charging them with high treason. After that, Clarendon says of Hampden,

'He was much altered, his nature and carriage seeming much fiercer than it did before.' And then, in a famous phrase, 'Without question, when he first drew his sword he threw away the scabbard!'

When war broke out he became, though not a professional soldier, a most active commander in the field. He raised a regiment of his own 'green-coats', which soon became one of the best in the army. He was all in favour of forward aggressive action, as against the slow caution of Essex, the professional soldier whom Parliament made its general.

Next year, in June 1643, Essex moved forward as if to attack Oxford, the King's headquarters. The Parliamentarian troops were dispersed about Hampden's home country, with their centre at Thame, where Hampden had been a boy at the grammar school. Suddenly Prince Rupert shot out from Oxford in one of his swift cavalry raids. Hampden moved forward at once with his usual dash and intrepidity, and with what forces he could collect, to cut off Rupert's retreat. On Chalgrove Field, that long level stretch ten miles out along the road from Oxford to the south-east, Rupert turned upon his pursuers.

There, among the standing corn on a fair June day — one knows well the red poppies in that great field — the fight took place: Hampden's green-coats against Rupert's horse. Hampden put himself at the head of the attack; but in the very first charge he was shot, his shoulder broken. He was observed, Clarendon says, 'to ride off the field before the action was done, which he never used to do, with his head hanging down and resting his hands upon the neck of his horse'.

There is a touching tradition — and there is usually something in a local tradition — that as he left the field he looked up to the Buckinghamshire hills towards the house where in his youth he had married the first wife of his love, and whither he would have gone to die. But Rupert's cavalry covered the plain between. So he turned his horse and rode slowly back towards Thame. There he died several days later; local memory points out the Greyhound inn as the house. It is said that the King sent over Dr. Giles, the rector of Chinnor, to visit him in his last hours. Such were the courtesies that passed in the Civil War.

Hampden's death caused consternation in the Parliamentarian ranks. 'The loss of Colonel Hampden,' said one of their newspapers, 'goeth near the heart of every man that loves the good of his king and country, and makes some conceive little content to be at the army now he is gone.' Baxter, the distinguished Puritan divine, wrote in his *Saints' Everlasting Rest* that he thought of Heaven with the more pleasure because he should there meet among the apostles and divines of all ages, Pym and Hampden; and of the latter he said, 'One that friends and enemies acknowledged to be most eminent for prudence, piety and peacefulness, having the most universal praise of any gentleman that I remember of that age.'

The noblest tribute of all comes again from his opponent Clarendon:

He was a supreme governor over all his passions and affections, and had thereby a great power over other men's. He was of an industry and vigilance not to be tired out or wearied by the most laborious, and of parts not to be imposed upon by the most subtle or sharp; and of a personal courage equal to his best parts.

It is idle to speculate what would have happened if he had lived. Probably with his unique popularity and Pym's prestige — for they were the architects of Parliament's victory — they would have made a moderate, civilian settlement, more durable than the régime Cromwell imposed by force of arms. But that Hampden deserved the people's love in his own time, and to be something more than a name in the story of English liberty — with its reverberations overseas among our kinsfolk — there can be no manner of doubt.

## II. LORD FALKLAND

Of the three famous men, John Hampden, Falkland, Pym, who died in 1643 in the first year of the Civil War, Falkland was not the greatest — that title must belong to Pym — but he was perhaps the most sympathetic to us today. Something of his spell must be owing to the portrait Clarendon painted of him in his *History*: the most moving, as it is the most celebrated, of that gallery of masterpieces. Of their friendship the old Chancellor wrote years after in exile at Montpellier, 'From his age of twenty years he had lived in an entire friendship with the Chancellor, who was about six months older; and who never spoke of him afterwards, but with a love and a grief which still raised some commotion in him.' That commotion he still communicates to his readers.

The nineteenth-century historians were tougher — or more obtuse. Falkland, whose heart was not wholly with either side in the struggle, who was struck down in battle against Parliament for which he had more veneration than he had for the King, could not be expected to appeal to their obvious sympathies. Macaulay has a funny passage, full of high spirits and Philistinism, making a guy of Falkland's career: 'He was indeed a man of great talents and of great virtues,' it begins, 'but, we apprehend, infinitely too fastidious for public life'; and Carlyle dismisses him in a footnote about his clean shirt on the day of his death at the battle of Newbury, 20 September 1643. Falkland's position is to us understandable. To the Victorians, to whom everything was simpler, it was not. His tragedy was that of the moderate in time of revolution: he died in a cause with which he was not wholly in agreement, hating the struggle which rent the country and longing — as the great majority of people did — for a sensible course between the two extremes. But he was *caught* by his fate. A man of marked gifts and high promise, he was thirty-three when he died. True, we should not know much about him if it were not for Clarendon; but his career has a certain symbolic importance.

Lucius Cary, son of the first Viscount Falkland, was of West Country stock, like several of the poets who were the friends of his youth and whom he names in the couplet

> Digby, Carew, Killigrew and Maine,
> Godolphin, Waller, that inspirèd traine.

His mother was an Oxfordshire heiress, through whom he succeeded to the delectable houses and estates of Burford Priory and Great Tew. Upon the magnificent painted tomb of his grandparents in Burford Church one sees the little figure of the young Falkland kneeling, looking to the altar. In the

Bodleian there is his portrait: that affecting gesture of the hand laid upon his heart, the luminous, melancholy eyes, the look of refinement one notices in Caroline portraits against the hardness of Tudor, the brazenness of Restoration, types. Succeeding early to his estates, rich, youthful, with a passion for learning and a gift for friendship, Falkland made his house at Great Tew in the Cotswolds the resort of the best minds in the university, of the poets and wits from London. His first devotion was to poetry; and chief among the poets of his circle was Ben Jonson, who wrote a fine ode to celebrate the passionate friendship that subsisted between Falkland and Sir Henry Morison, whose sister he married when the brother died. Thither, too, came the cynical Suckling, who celebrated the gatherings in his *Session of the Poets*, Tom Carew, amorous but somewhat costive of verse, diminutive but gallant Sidney Godolphin, the much-travelled Sandys. As the years went on, Falkland ceased to write verse and turned his attention to divinity and philosophical questions. Suckling lamented:

> He was of late so gone with divinity,
> That he had almost forgotten his poetry,
> Though to say the truth, and Apollo did know it,
> He might have been both his priest and his poet.

The poets were succeeded more and more by the divines from the university. There was Gilbert Sheldon, Fellow, and soon to be Warden, of All Souls, born to be Archbishop of Canterbury. There were the amusing Dr. Earle, author of the delightful *Microcosmographie*; the witty Dr. Morley, whose promotion was held up for a time by a too happy reply to a grave, country gentleman who, puzzled by the new-fangled Arminian tenets, asked Morley what the Arminians held; and he replied, 'All the best bishoprics and deaneries in England.' Above all, there were John Hales, 'one of the least men in the Kingdom; and one of the greatest scholars in Europe'; and the subtle, questing intellect of Chillingworth, Falkland's mentor, who gave the philosophical tone to this circle.

It was that of a passionate belief in toleration. Chillingworth believed that the fundamental truths of religion were few and simple, and that they might be ascertained from the Bible;

L

he wrote an important book that was a plea for Christian unity on the basis of the widest possible toleration. Falkland followed his lead with a *Discourse on Infallibility*, and two tracts. He had determined to learn Greek; and, being fond of the society of London, he made a vow not to see it again until he had learned the language. He not only kept the vow, but ended by reading all the early Fathers. One sees the picture: the young patron whose poetry was without inspiration, his philosophy without originality, yet whose gifts of mind and sympathy kept the circle together.

Upon this charmed society there fell the thunderbolt of the Civil War. What added poignancy to their grief was that it was so unexpected. Clarendon describes the contentment and prosperity of those years before the storm; and to the trouble of mind they suffered they added the singular faculty of expressing it in poignant words. 'All things progresse toward the fatal declination of our time,' wrote an ordinary Kentish gentleman who watched Pym riding into London attended by hundreds of his supporters.

Falkland was elected to Parliament, and henceforth his life was a part of national history. He was thirty when he became at one step a leading figure in the Long Parliament, which contained a large number of names to become very famous. Falkland and Hyde were united with Pym and Hampden in the attack on the King's personal government and on Strafford, who was at once its instrument and victim. Falkland voted for his attainder, though he wished to spare his life; he led the attack on Ship Money; he went all the way with Pym in the onslaught upon the Prerogative Courts, the institutions of authoritarian government. He had no love for Laud and was willing to see a reform of the Church and the Bishops out of the House of Lords: he regarded that as a matter of expediency rather than of principle. He was a latitudinarian and a tolerationist.

But he stopped short when he saw that Pym was pressing forward to a constitutional revolution. The united House was divided in two by Pym's revolutionary manifesto, the Grand Remonstrance, which demanded that Ministers should be responsible to Parliament. Falkland opposed this invasion of the King's constitutional rights. After the decisive debate far into the night — Sir Philip Warwick describes the extraordinary scene — Falkland was left at the head of a large minority, the backbone of a party for the King, the origin of the Tory Party. It was to Falkland that the comparatively unknown Oliver Cromwell said that if the Grand Remonstrance had not passed he would have sold all he had and gone to America. 'So near was the poor kingdom at that time to its deliverance,' comments Clarendon.

Since he had broken with the Parliamentarian leaders and led the opposition to their course, the onus fell upon Falkland of advising the King. A man of honour, a man marked for responsibility from the moment of his entering into public life, he could not refuse the King his service, though he became Secretary of State with the greatest reluctance. Clarendon has a moving description of his dilemma, the call of duty against every inclination:

He had not the court in great reverence and had a presaging spirit that the King would fall into great misfortune: and often said to his friend that he chose to serve the King because honesty obliged him to it; but that he foresaw his own ruin by doing it.

The motive that weighed strongest with him was the hope of using his influence to bring about peace. 'When there was any overture or hope of peace,' Clarendon says, 'he would be more erect and vigorous, and exceedingly solicitous to press anything which he thought might promote it; and sitting amongst his friends, often, after a deep silence and frequent sighs, would, with a shrill and sad accent, ingeminate the word *Peace, Peace*, and would passionately profess that the very agony of the war, and the view of the calamities and desolation the Kingdom did and must endure, took his sleep from him, and would shortly break his heart.' All through the winter of 1642–3 he worked hard at negotiations with Parliament; if it had rested with him the Treaty of Oxford would have achieved peace. But there were intransigents on both sides, and in the end his efforts were wrecked by the influence of the Court camarilla and Charles's fatal devotion to Henrietta Maria, who had all the Frenchwoman's itch for meddling in politics.

Falkland was despairing and, when war was renewed, threw himself into the most dangerous and exposed positions: as he had done at Edgehill, so in the trenches before Gloucester, and at last at Newbury, where 'in this battle the Chancellor of the Exchequer lost the joy and comfort of his life'.

Historians have been very obtuse about Falkland's mind and motives, and how he came by his death. Clarendon is quite clear, and surely it is very simple. Falkland had courage and was 'naturally inquisitive after danger'; but it was precisely because he was known to long passionately for peace that he thrust himself in battle into the place of greatest danger.

In the end one thinks of him in those thyme-scented, walled gardens at Great Tew, walking with his friends among the violets and the limes before the War came upon them to scatter them for ever. Yet they will always have their place in our tradition, thanks to Clarendon's imperishable portrait of them.

## III. John Pym

John Pym was the architect of the English Revolution, which was, above all, a Parliamentary revolution. Though the name of John Hampden is better known to people today, Pym was a greater man: he was the real leader, the man who conceived the strategy. And very characteristic for an English revolutionary, he was essentially a moderate. He was no extremist, nor a mere talker, mouthing clichés which mean nothing, but a practical man of business who did not want a revolution but was impelled by circumstances and his own abilities to take the lead.

Pym was a West Countryman, of good Somerset stock, and owning estates in that county; one of the gentry whose rise to power was the dynamic force behind the whole struggle. But his father having died, he was brought up from his earliest years in Cornwall, where his mother married Sir Anthony Rouse, friend and executor of Sir Francis Drake. We are to think, then, of the young Pym growing up in that strong Protestant household at Halton among the cherry orchards of Tamar-side. Not many miles away, at St. Germans, there was growing up another young man, John Eliot, who became an earlier leader of Parliamentary opposition to the Stuarts.

Equally important for a youth whose whole boyhood was spent on the banks of the Tamar running down to Plymouth, in those years of the great voyages of Drake and his fellows, Pym was deeply interested in the colonisation of America. No nonsense about being ashamed of building an empire with these leading Puritans! The interesting thing is that the whole group of Puritan leaders who defeated the monarchy were imperialists. During the eleven years in which Charles I misgoverned the nation without a Parliament, Pym was the leading spirit, and the treasurer, of the Providence Company, formed to colonise one of the West Indian islands off the coast of Honduras.

With the summoning of Parliament in 1640, a larger scope opened out for Pym: he became the unacknowledged leader of the House of Commons. Charles I's inept policy had involved him in a war with Scotland and aroused the antagonism of the country. Clarendon himself tells us what magic the name of Parliament had at this time and how the whole country looked to Parliament for a remedy. Pym, by his experience, his judgment, his knowledge of business and procedure, his sense of tactics, became the leader of a united Parliament. It soon became evident that he was one of the two men in the country who understood all that was at stake, and had the strategic vision to guide events. The other was Strafford.

There is no doubt that Pym wanted to come to terms with the King and to avoid civil war. He was not an extreme Puritan; he was prepared to compromise over Church matters and retain the bishops (bishops have never been popular with Englishmen). But Pym saw, as Strafford did on the other side, that the real issue was whether government was to be responsible to Parliament or to the King.

Here was a new and revolutionary step to take. Many people wished to burke the issue or to patch up an accommodation. Pym had the statesman's faculty for grasping the essential issue. He saw further that with Strafford at his back the King would never come to terms. It was necessary to destroy Strafford: the destruction of that indomitable, tragic figure was the work of Pym. In all the manoeuvres necessary to bring him down, the impeachment, the bill of attainder, the intimidation of the King, the master hand was Pym's. He never made a mistake; his intelligence service was so efficient that he knew every move of the Court. 'Stone dead hath no fellow,' he said of Strafford.

Still the King could not be brought to terms. Pym brought forward that masterpiece of propaganda, the Grand Remonstrance, reciting all Charles's misdeeds and demanding that Ministers should be responsible to Parliament. Charles determined to arrest the five Parliamentary leaders in person: he made his descent on Parliament to find that they had taken refuge in the City. Pym realised that there could be no security with Charles, and that civil war was inevitable. He now came out openly as the leader of the war party, and undertook all preparations, diplomatic, financial, military.

The first year of the war, 1642–3, was full of reverses for Parliament, before its superior resources could be organised and brought into play. Pym suffered a grievous loss in the death of his friend, John Hampden. The reverses of 1643 forced Pym to play his trump card and bring Scotland in on the side of Parliament. Though stricken with cancer he carried through the negotiations to success: the alliance made the victory of Parliament as certain as it could be made, though Pym did not live to see its triumph. Within a month of his death he was made Master of the Ordnance — equivalent to being Minister of Munitions — on top of being his own Prime Minister and Foreign Secretary. No wonder that in these last years of his life he became known as 'King Pym'.

He died, worn out with the burden of his work, which he never relaxed in spite of mortal illness. If he had lived, no doubt there would have been a civilian settlement of the issues of the war instead of the military dictatorship of Cromwell. Pym would have had the immense prestige of having led Parliament through to success, and he would have seen to that. For all his ruthlessness as a leader in time of crisis, he was a civilian aiming at Parliamentary government. Responsible, representative government is the precious contribution the English-speaking peoples have to make to the world. It offers more hope of essential freedom of spirit than any other political form. In its evolution John Pym was a very powerful link in his day.

# XIV

# CLARENDON'S LIFE

How great, how varied and agreeable, are the riches of English historical literature. Perhaps not quite so copious as the French; but there is no modern literature other than French that compares in this respect. Yet there are classics of our literature of which few enough have heard, let alone read. How many have read Clarendon's *History of the Rebellion*, or his *Autobiography*, or Lord Herbert of Cherbury's, or Hervey's *Memoirs*, or the *Verney Letters*?

Horace Walpole knew a good thing when he saw one and pounced upon Clarendon's *Life* when it appeared. He wrote to Montagu, on 19 July 1759, 'Have you read my Lord Clarendon? I am enchanted with it; 'tis very incorrect, but I think more entertaining than his *History*. It makes me quite out of humour with other *mémoires*.' (He meant his own.) It is true that Clarendon's *Life* is in some ways a finer work even than the *History*, and at the same time it is far less well known. There are several reasons for this; the chief, perhaps, being that Clarendon did not intend the *Life* for publication, but for the private instruction of his children, and so he plundered the completed *Life* ruthlessly to enrich the *History*. The story of the composition of the *History*, of the reliability of different parts of it and of its relation to the *Life*, is a complex one, which has been worked out by Sir Charles Firth in the *English Historical Review* (1904). Most of the famous character sketches in the *History* really come out of the autobiography. What Clarendon did was to leave the latter a torso, by robbing it of much of what he had written about the Civil War and Commonwealth period; though the latter part, from the Restoration onwards, is very full. The result is that we are left with only half of what would have been perhaps the finest of English autobiographies, if we had it complete.

Then, too, it has never been properly edited. The only edition we have, published at Oxford in 1857, is an inadequate text, with no notes at all, no indication of the large passages which have been transferred to the *History* or of others that have not been printed in either. A new edition is what is wanted: a good job of work for some young scholar in this field to tackle.

All the same the *Life*, even as we have it, is a wonderful book. Clarendon wrote it when his powers were at their height, freed from the daily preoccupations of politics by his second and final exile from the country. The taste for character drawing, which people did so well in the seventeenth century, had grown upon him since his original composition of the *History* twenty years before; now he could let himself go, and the most fully-developed portraits all belong to this period. Since he was not writing for publication, he could afford to be far more frank than in the *History*, where one of his main objects was to defend Charles I. Clarendon's deep-seated loyalty prevented him from being too outspoken — besides he had the essential justice of mind and devotion to truth of the real historian; but the *Life* is more revealing of the hidden causes of events as he saw them. The sense of the play of personalities is absorbing; the somewhat ponderous politician turns out to be a subtler psychologist than the nimble wits that got him turned out of power. There is an exquisite feeling for the atmosphere of that chosen time before the Civil War when such personalities as Falkland, Sidney Godolphin, Selden, Chillingworth, George Herbert, Nicholas Ferrar had come to flower. Most of them had been friends of Clarendon's — close friends to whom his mind and heart were attuned. No wonder he was a *laudator temporis acti*, who spent much of his activity in politics on trying to make those good days come again, and when that failed him spent his last years in the dream of what that time had been — out of which he recalled the figures of the past with all their rich, warm colouring and made them live again for posterity. Above all, his *Life* is what an autobiography should be, a complete portrait of his own personality, with all his qualities and limitations, his fidelity, integrity, honesty, his ability and courage, his warmth of heart — and the truly monumental self-satisfaction which cannot but amuse the modern reader.

Sir Charles Firth says that Clarendon was 'one of the first examples in later English history of the man who begins in low estate and rises by his own abilities to the highest political office'. In fact he came from a good country family, well connected — his uncle and patron was Lord Chief Justice. The King himself wrote him a letter of recommendation as a youth to Magdalen College, of which the President, for some odd reason, took no notice; and so Magdalen lost the chance of having a second historian hardly inferior to Gibbon. (In spite of his great loyalty to the University, Clarendon, too, was distinctly critical of the studies and diversions pursued there.) He made a good match which brought him an estate, and as he says himself, lived as a barrister in good style, much above that of other lawyers. He kept the best company and enjoyed the patronage of the great. He 'well knew how to cultivate those advantages', beginning with the confidence Laud reposed in him. There is a vivid description of the Archbishop walking in his garden at Lambeth on the occasion when the young lawyer told him candidly how unpopular he was and how much it was due to the sharpness and inconsiderateness of his manner. Laud blushed for himself, and taking it like a man, had a particular regard for and trust in his young acquaintance ever after.

True, Clarendon was not an aristocrat, but a gentleman at a time when the gentry were extending their power and influence in the state beyond all expectation or precedent. It was that upward surge of power, a shift of social forces, that lay behind the Civil War — of which Clarendon had no notion, while Harrington had. Just like an actor in these events, he saw it all in personal terms, the mistakes of the King on one side, the aggressions of Parliament on the other. It makes him all the easier and more congenial reading.

In spite of his long years of exile, twenty-one altogether, Clarendon remained always the country-bred Englishman with his roots deep in the life of his country. From the beginning of the *Life* one notices this theme, as one does in the *History*: the different characters of English counties, their differences in custom, cultivation, even in weights and measures. It is so much taken for granted that it is not developed as a theme, but it is always there in the background. Clarendon's father, a Wiltshire country gentleman, served in the last Parliaments of Elizabeth, but after the Queen's death was never in London again, though he lived for thirty years after; his wife, to whom he was married above forty years, was never in London in her life:

the wisdom and frugality of that time being such that few gentlemen made journeys to London, or any other expensive journeys, but upon important business, and their wives never; by which providence they enjoyed and improved their estates in the country, and kept good hospitality in their houses, brought up their children well, and were beloved by their neighbours.

Clarendon was always an old-fashioned man in his prejudices, not the worse for being a bit out of date, a belated Elizabethan.

There is no more convincing country note than his story of how he was just reading to his father the passage in Camden's *Annals* about that John Felton who affixed the Papal Bull of Excommunication upon the Bishop of London's door 'when a person of the neighbourhood knocked at the door, and being called in, told his father that a post was then passed through the village to Charleton, the house of the Earl of Berkshire', with the news of the assassination of Buckingham by another John Felton. Clarendon deplored the influence of women in politics at Court, dating from Buckingham's removal and the emergence of Henrietta Maria; and no wonder when one considers her disastrous influence upon the country's affairs, or of Charles II's seraglio, which Clarendon had even more personal reason to resent. One appreciates as never before that the Elizabethan age, to which he looked back as an ideal, was a thoroughly masculine society; only one woman had her hand in politics then — and *what* a hand! There was no room for any others.

Clarendon's psychological insight is nowhere better displayed than in his account of the personal relations of Falkland and Culpepper with the King and Queen. Falkland was compliant enough with the weakness and humours of smaller men, where there was no question of flattery:

Yet towards the King, who many times obstinately adhered to many conclusions which did not naturally result from good premises, and did love to argue many things to which he would not so positively adhere, he did not practise that condescension, but contradicted him with more bluntness, and by sharp sentences; and in some particulars (as of the church) to which the King was in conscience most devoted: and of this his majesty often complained; and cared less to confer with him in private, and was less persuaded by him than his affairs, and the other's great parts and wisdom, would have required.

What a condemnation this is of Charles really; he preferred to listen to Culpepper, who told him what he liked to hear, and whose judgment was less good even than the King's.

Culpepper, on the other hand, had

with all this uncourtliness (for sure no man less appeared a courtier) and ungracefulness in his mien and motion, a wonderful insinuation and address into the acceptance and confidence of the king and queen, and flattery being a weed not so natural to the air and soil of the country where he had wholly lived, he was believed to speak with all plainness and sincerity; when no man more complied with those infirmities they both had, and by that compliance prevailed often over them. He had a very tragical way in expressing himself, to raise the fears and apprehensions of those who were naturally apprehensive of dangers; and by this means he prevailed marvellously with the queen in those matters to which she was most averse; by representing things as dismally to her as he could well do; and on the other hand to the king (who was naturally very sanguine) he was full of compliance; cherished all his hopes and imaginations, and raised and improved those hopes very frequently by expedients very unagreeable to the end proposed.

One sees the situation so well: the complex play of personalities holding up, and in the end frustrating, the ends they all wanted — as so often, and so intolerably, in human affairs.

And then a reflection occurs to one about Clarendon's rotund, elaborate style: those long involved sentences, with all the parentheses, are precisely fitted to express the complexity of the psychological situation. Better indeed than a modern style, which would split up the qualifications into separate sentences, where Clarendon is able to carry them along with the statements they qualify. Nor is his style for all its richness without edge; people can be ticked off very precisely in a subordinate clause. There is the Earl of St. Albans, who visits Clarendon in a crisis 'with all those compliments, professions and protestations, which were natural, and which he did really believe everybody else thought to be very sincere; for he had that kindness for himself, that he thought everybody did believe him'. Then when Clarendon had got through the crisis, Henrietta Maria was gracious enough to him, 'and from that time there did never appear any want of kindness in the queen towards him, whilst he stood in no need of it, nor until it might have done him good'. There was the treacherous Coventry, 'who had never paid a civility to any worthy man, but as it was a disobligation to another whom he cared less for'; or the slippery Shaftesbury, 'who was good at looking into other men's offices'.

One must not give the impression that Clarendon was peevish, though the *Life* was written as a defence of his career and actions; nothing is more remarkable than his magnanimity, in spite of being traduced and hounded out of public life. He does indeed betray a particular sensitiveness about the mimicry of him which brought him into ridicule at the easily amused, cynical, heartless Court of Charles II; one recalls the scene of that scapegrace Tom Killigrew, with the bellows for the great seal and the poker for the mace, strutting behind the pompous old Chancellor. What a target he must have presented to those wits and rakes, not to mention the royal mistresses, with his smugness and self-satisfaction, his honesty and integrity. And yet he was right: such qualities would never have been allowed to bring him down at the Court of Elizabeth, and after such services to the monarchy. It is not for nothing that the Stuarts became a byword for ingratitude.

Evelyn describes the portraits of his friends that the Chancellor had hung in the days of his glory upon the walls of Clarendon House. For consolation in exile, setting out upon his travels from the Scilly Islands where he had begun to write his great *History*, in Jersey walking upon the sands in the evening with the Governor, the day's work over, or in the hot streets of Madrid, at Montpellier in his last and final exile, Clarendon

loved to turn back in his mind to the garden at Great Tew —
and remember the friends of his youth, lingering over their
names and virtues. To his love for them we owe the unfading
freshness, the beauty of his two great books: into them both
there comes the scent of the musk, the roses and thyme of that
Cotswold garden in the high summer of the early seventeenth
century.

# XV

# PICTURES IN A DEANERY

WHAT could be a more delightful setting for an exhibition of old pictures than a house in a cathedral close — particularly when it is the close at Salisbury? The house was then the Deanery there, perhaps the finest of all the houses set down in that wide space, with views from its windows across green lawns and water-meadows, across rose-covered walls to the west front of the cathedral, the back with its cut hedges and grass walks leading down to the Wiltshire Avon? The idea of bringing together in one place a selection of pictures from surrounding country houses can never have been more justified. Nothing of the deadness, the intimidating professionalism of so many galleries: Dr. Tancred Borenius, in arranging these pictures, was able to imagine himself as an eighteenth-century dean with a taste for pictures and this fine house to put them in.

There are so many good things here that may not be brought together again for a long time; best of all in quality are the paintings of the late fifteenth and sixteenth centuries, mainly from Fonthill. They have, too, a common character, which makes them the more interesting: that of the Renaissance in Northern Europe, France, the Low Countries, England. In that order, for really the English contribution is very small: a miniature of Sir Philip Sidney, by Isaac Oliver, and a small painting of him in camp at Zutphen, which I do not remember ever to have seen reproduced. If a more English character were to be given to this room, it could easily have been done by bringing the Holbein portraits of Erasmus from Longford Castle, and of Sir John More from Wilton.

Practically every picture in this small room is of beauty and interest. There are two Clouets, both well known; one of Mary Queen of Scots, 'Le Deuil Blanc', in the white cap and high-necked veil prescribed as mourning for widows of the French royal house — a picture for which there is a study in the Bibliothèque Nationale; and a portrait of Charles IX, with that pale-olive Medici complexion and almond-coloured eyes, a small round hat with plume set on one side of the head, a pearl in his ear. There is a memorable portrait, by Corneille de Lyon, of Theodore de Beza, the Reformer, all in black against a green background, with full grey beard and fine blue eyes set wide apart. A less interesting portrait of the French school, one of Louise de Lorraine, has nevertheless an historical interest for us; for the daughter of the Duke of Lorraine was one of the ladies whose hand Henry VIII sought after the death of Jane Seymour, before he, so disagreeably for himself, became committed to Anne of Cleves. Surely this portrait must be one of those specially painted for the King — like the famous Holbein portrait of the Duchess of Milan — in the hectic rush round Europe for a wife in the years 1538–9, one that came to repose afterwards, the lady herself put aside or not being willing, in some private collection in the country?

The Sidney portrait — it is not certain whether it is an Oliver or no — is worth noting. It is a full-length portrait of him in armour chased in gold from head to toe — the effect is rather of a medieval picture with much use of gold leaf. Sidney is standing at a table covered with green velvet reaching to the ground, at the entrance to his tent; in the background a servant is holding his horse richly caparisoned. It is a curious picture; and though the face is a familiar Elizabethan face, with tall fine forehead, brown hair and moustache, is it certain that it is Philip Sidney? Might it not be his brother Robert, Governor of Flushing?

The masterpieces are those of the Flemish school. There is the Morrison Triptych — the centre panel a Madonna and Child with angels and saints adoring, the inside panels occupied by a St. John the Baptist and some saint holding a chalice, an exquisite figure with a lavender-coloured cloak over a grass-green vesture: the latter obviously painted under Italian influence. The backgrounds are filled with Low Country landscapes, a fifteenth-century brick house with truncated gable by a river with swans; the centre panel has a castle with river and wooden footbridge: all very well realised and naturalistic, the slow tide of that late fifteenth-century life now vanished for ever, yet leaving this image to us long afterwards of what once it was.

There are other expressions of that faith here: an *Adoration of the Shepherds* by Van der Goes, touching in its simplicity and very satisfying in its grouping of the figures. The hands are as distinctly characterised as are the faces, rustic, awkward, angular, and the little landscape in each corner, the angel appearing to the shepherds, the blue strange light upon the hillside: the essence of Christmas and all that has meant to generations of the faithful:

> Herdmen beheld thes angelles bright
> To them apperèd with gret light,
> And seid 'Goddes sone is born this night.'
> *In excelsis gloria.*

Perhaps this Van der Goes lacks the strange power, the absorbed ecstasy, of that fragment of a *Lamentation* in the library of Christ Church at Oxford. Nor are the two Mabuses, each of them a *Madonna with the Child*, more exciting; they are placidly, heavily Flemish. More appealing is the *Madonna and Child* of the Lower Rhenish school, lent by Mrs. Christie-Miller. This has more life and rhythm, the figures as round and substantial, but more lively and gay. The picture exfoliates children, cherubs after the German fashion, all too expressive of their cult of domesticity. The Virgin, a simple German girl, innocently proud, is seated on a low cushion, child on her knee, a crimson cloth of state held up behind her.

Going up the Dean's staircase (very measured and dignified), we pass some pleasant pictures of the English eighteenth century, a painting of old Lambeth from the river, and two of Samuel Scott, one of Covent Garden, the other of Lincoln's Inn Fields: both bringing home to us in the noble regularity of the architecture the disaster that has overcome London in this century.

And so into the Dean's gallery, a fine room on the first floor looking east and west, to the cathedral and the water-meadows. Here are gathered the bulk of the pictures, an eighteenth-century collection, in keeping with the character of that hypothetical collector, the Dean. There are two Canalettos, familiar scenes along the Grand Canal, one of Santa Maria della Salute, the other of the Dogana: with a little cleaning, they would show up, with the clear aqueous Venetian light upon them, bright and festive as the day they were painted.

The room is given up to English eighteenth century portraits mainly by Gainsborough, Reynolds, Hoppner and Lawrence, of members of the surrounding families, Herberts, Radnors, Burdetts, Methuens. Here they meet each other once more, or are at least on nodding acquaintance, after the long lapse of time. There is an attractive Reynolds portrait of Gibbon as a young man — and we remember that for a time, during the Seven Years War, he served as captain of militia in the neighbouring county. The embryo historian used his time to study military literature, and afterwards observed with some complacency that 'the captain of Hampshire grenadiers had not been useless to the historian of the Roman empire'. Here the young man is precisely painted — more so than most in the room — and it is a very precise young man that the artist has observed. He is depicted in pretty green coat with gold facings: priggish face, fair complexion, small mouth and pursed lips made for pomposity. One sees in and behind the young captain the great historian adumbrated, self-conscious, fat and pursy as he was to become.

Not far away is Rigaud's portrait of Nelson, also painted early in the famous subject's career, on his return from the West Indies station in 1780. It is a pleasant picture in which the most is made of the dominant blue of the naval coat and the rhythmical line it makes, cut in close to the slender figure. Here is a splendid example of Lawrence's art —very appropriately since the painter too was brought up in Wiltshire. (Son of the improvident host of the Bear Inn at Devizes, who liked to show off his boy's precocious talents to his guests: 'Gentlemen, here's my son. Will you have him recite from the poets or take your portraits?') Another portrait is the well-known one, subsequently engraved, of William Henry Miller, founder of the famous Britwell Court Library and of the no less famous — perhaps more so now — Christie-Miller family. Lawrence responded more to male beauty than to female: he was apt to make his young men glamorous — as in the case

M

of this sober Scottish bibliophile, who is presented in Byronic pose, hair romantically dishevelled, wearing a red velvet coat edged with fur, all the richer for the contrast with the green chair.

But the great surprise of the show to me, a stunning revelation, is a portrait by Tilly Kettle. Who was Tilly Kettle that he should be so good? This picture of an Indian nabob is as fine as the best of Reynolds and easily mistakable for one. Apparently Kettle had a very chancy career — is much known about him? But what a brilliantly gifted painter! It seems that his father was a London house-painter, who taught his son all he knew and then sent him on to the academy in St. Martin's Lane. He early achieved some success with his portraits, then in 1770 went to India, where he remained for seven years, painting native princes, dancing girls, grand viziers, Anglo-Indian nabobs, and made a fortune. He then came home to dissipate the lot, became a bankrupt, and took refuge in Dublin where I have come across him before. In 1786 he set out for India once more, to recoup himself, travelling by the overland route by Aleppo, where he died, still only in his forties.

What a loss to painting! What a story he would make! There must be work of his in India to this day, stowed away among the junk of extinguished rajahs' palaces, along with a good deal of treasure-trove — if only someone would make a systematic investigation among the ruins, the débris of empire. What a fascinating, if nostalgic, trail to follow! Here in Tilly Kettle is only one promising subject, among many: why has no-one given us a book about him?

The subject of this portrait is Alexander Davidson of Drumhall, Cromarty, who was Governor of Madras from 1785 to 1791. So it was before this period that Kettle painted him, when Davidson was a handsome youngish man, black hair and swarthy complexion, tanned by the Indian sun, the good healthy Scottish colour appearing through the tan. It is a fine head, shapely and poised, leaning slightly to one side, luminous dark eyes, a cupid's bow to the lips. He is wearing a sand-coloured coat with gold facings, grass-green waistcoat and lapels. A golden luminousness pervades the whole picture, such as Reynolds achieves at his best.

No less excellent are the two Zoffanys. One is of a family group with a boy flying a kite, very lively, full of movement and charm. In the other the interest is concentrated rather upon character. It is a conversation piece portraying the Hon. Charles Hope Vere with his sisters, Lady Christian Graham and Lady Charlotte Erskine: a satisfying composition, fresh yet sober in colour, the figures lively but staid, each distinctly visualised and characterised, yet well subordinated to the general scheme. One sister and her brother are seated on a blue-green sofa, each gold nail-head distinctly painted, the man in a brick-red coat, one hand in his waistcoat, the other holding a book dated 1782: he has an aristocratic horsey face, with large nose and coarse profile. The two ladies are in black satin, with white lace aprons and mob caps: the one on the left has a pert expression, looking direct at the painter, with a flowered work-bag on her wrist, spectacles and a book upon the round table by her chair. Lady Christian Graham in the middle looks older, more imperious, a less cheerful nature. There they are: two old tabbies and a tom: a charming scene, beautifully grouped, their expressions, their very selves naturally caught and precisely rendered.

In the parlour, the Dean's own taste as an eighteenth-century connoisseur has been allowed full play by Dr. Borenius. This is probably what he would have collected and brought home to the Deanery, if he had existed. The room is full of little Wouverman and Van der Neer landscapes, Pieter Neefs' and Saenredam's interiors of Dutch churches: very cool and evocative. But one goes down the Dean's stairs and out into the Close with an alluring vision of the use to which our deaneries may be put, when the day comes when deans can no longer occupy them.

# XVI

# SWIFT AS POET

## I

Of all the books that have come out in late years about Swift, there are few that are up to the subject. Middleton Murry's biography was, surprisingly, the best; but then Murry had a remarkable critical intelligence and even finer understanding, when away from his hobbies. Professor Louis Landa gave us an excellent specialist book on Swift and the Church. Professor Quintana limited himself to a study of Swift's mind and art as a writer.[1] This provides a careful survey of Swift's work, connects it up with the large body of research that has accumulated on the subject, and gives us enough of Swift's life to make it intelligible.

It is the background to Swift's thought, the various elements that entered into it from other thinkers, where they came from and how they affected him, that now need more study. There is this excuse, that there is no history of English thought in the seventeenth century, as there is of the eighteenth century, by Sir Leslie Stephen. One notices this lack most in regard to the problem of Swift's belief — or unbelief; for there was a strain of deism, or of definite unbelief, among English thinkers of that age, which must surely have left its mark on Swift's mind. Mr. Quintana notices the influence of Hobbes's materialism upon Swift's view of the imagination and his aesthetics generally; but it may be that that influence went further, to affect the whole of Swift's intellectual position, to instil scepticism into a mind not naturally sceptical, to denude him of any vestige of idealism in his view of the world and experience. There is a considerable body of deistic writing contemporaneous with Swift, which is part of his intellectual background: such writers as Shaftesbury, Toland, Mandeville. Mr. Quintana says that 'when the great Dean of St. Patrick's died in 1745, he had already ceased to be understood by the eighteenth

[1] Ricardo Quintana, *The Mind and Art of Jonathan Swift*.

century'. All the more reason to consider him historically in relation to his environment.

The question of Swift's religious convictions is central. On this point neither defence nor excuse is necessary; it is enough to understand him. 'It is not that Swift wavered in belief, nor that in conduct he failed to be guided by it,' says Mr. Quintana. 'In all these matters he was rigorously consistent, rigorously in accord with his theoretical premises.' But the point is whether these premises were in accordance with orthodox Christianity. I cannot but think that Archbishop Sharp, Queen Anne, the instinct of religious believers (typified by Dr. Johnson, who knew very well), were right about Swift. They scented that there was no religious belief in him. As for getting a bishopric, he was lucky to become a dean. Only an age when patronage was in the ascendant would have been so broad-minded; any other age would have expected a dean to believe.

Such conception of religion as he had was of an external and institutional character; there is no sign of personal belief. Even in the *Prayers for Stella*, the nearest in expression he achieved, there is more evidence of doubt than of faith or hope; whereas he frequently gives expression to the Manichee view that life is in itself an evil to be endured. Perhaps, however, one need not take him so seriously as he took himself on this point; he clearly enjoyed some parts of his own life — the years 1709–14, for example, the exercise of power, his many friendships, writing.

Mr. Quintana is at pains to rebut the charge that Swift was a misanthrope. Why shouldn't Swift be a misanthrope? Hatred of human beings is as legitimate a subject of art as love of them, and its possibilities more rarely explored. Nor need one be prudish about the scatological poems with their 'disgusting' imagery. They are often artistic successes, and are as much part of Swift's mind as the 'fine, satiric touch' — indeed more intimately part of his mind, all the more revealing of what kind of mind that was. The self-laceration of these poems may represent an excessive sensibility, turned back upon itself, turned inside out. 'I was to see Lady——,' he wrote to Stella, 'who is just up after lying-in; and the ugliest sight

I have seen, pale, dead, old and yellow, for want of her paint. *She has turned my stomach.* But she will soon be painted, and a beauty again.' In this one perceives the type of all those poems of physical disgust he wrote: they are due to a morbid degree of sensitiveness, acting upon a disillusioned temperament, to make him torture himself and others.

There was certainly an acute tension between defeatism in his view of human nature and an active temperament in himself, between reason and the emotions, in Swift's mind. He had no illusions about human nature, yet he did — perhaps unreasonably — expect men to be better than they are. He insisted always upon the moral responsibility of the person. In his outlook there was too great a dichotomy between Reason and the emotions; he thought of them as simply and necessarily in conflict and this increased the strain in his inner life. The tension bore fruit in his art, but it made for unhappiness in the man. Swift believed, in accordance with the materialism of Hobbes, that 'self-love, as it is the motive to all our actions, so it is the sole cause of our grief'. It is a forbidding view to hold, repressive of the emotional life, especially with a man so self-conscious as Swift: he at any rate was not under the illusions that most people are as to their motives. He girded at *la condition humaine*, but might he not have been a little happier if, realising how little disinterestedness there was in the world or in himself, he had made it more his aim?

As it was, his intellectual position was at every point that which his interests demanded and with which his person was identified. A churchman, he saw only the interests of his own sect; a Tory, of his own party; an Irish Protestant, he stood up for the Irish Church against both Catholics and Dissenters. If he had happened to be a Dissenter, or had remained a Whig, he would have been as vehement on the other side. Mr. Quintana comments, 'however ignoble his actuating impulses may have been, the ends which he achieved cannot be judged solely in terms of motive'. What is odd is Swift's consciousness of the situation and his acceptance of it. It is like his denial of any place to idealism in life, or to imagination in poetry: an abnegation springing from his fear of disillusionment. He realised all too clearly the discomfort of the latter, but did not allow for the necessity for a certain amount of illusion or even humbug to make life tolerable. As T. S. Eliot constantly enforced, human beings can bear very little reality. Swift stripped life to the bare bones.

Mr. Quintana insists upon the richness and fertility of Swift's later phase. 'Nothing is further from the truth than the idea commonly entertained regarding Swift's latter years of activity. He was still the great artist, producing verse and prose of undiminished brilliance and intensity, and he remained an imperious public figure.' So often this period is treated merely as an aftermath. Yet it is in this period that he produced *Gulliver's Travels* and much of the best of his poetry. All the more reason for not agreeing that *Gulliver* is inferior to *The Tale of a Tub*. There is a universality and a range in *Gulliver* which the earlier work does not compass; it has, too, a depth of experience and conviction, where *The Tale of a Tub* is more intellectual, cold and academic. *Gulliver* is the work that the world has chosen; that kind of universal consensus is not likely to be wrong.

## II

The poetry of Swift is an esoteric taste. There is hardly anyone in our literary history who has had a liking for it since his own time. Yeats is a notable exception, perhaps the only poet whose verse was directly influenced by Swift, and that is partly owing to their common Irish background, Swift's living tradition there and the cult of him Dublin. However, contemplating and brooding over Swift was an element in making the later verse of Yeats what it became, in content and temper. But apart from Yeats, nobody. This lack of appreciation springs from the dominance of the romantic tradition in our literature — the line that runs from Spenser, Shakespeare, the Caroline poets, to the great Romantics, Wordsworth, Coleridge, Shelley and the later. But for some time such poets as Skelton, Donne, Dryden, Byron have been coming back into their own. Perhaps this definitive edition may have the effect of enabling Swift to do so too.[1]

There is so much in his poetry that should appeal to this

[1] *The Poems of Jonathan Swift*, edited by Harold Williams.

age: its realism and ruthlessness, its exposure of the human condition, without pity or illusion, its stripping away of all pretences, its very nudity, its terse force, concentration and clarity.

Hitherto, Swift has been universally underestimated as a poet. To some extent he is himself to blame; for it has been partly due to that pride which made him careless, where Pope was so careful, about the publishing of his poems. It was Swift's foible to care more for the reputation of a gentleman than of a poet: 'I do not call him a poet that writes for his diversion,' he said, 'any more than that gentleman a fiddler, who amuses himself with a violin.' Swift left his verse publications in indescribable confusion until Mr. Williams came along to bring order out of chaos, as nobody had done previously. 'No part of his writing has been so neglected and mishandled by editors,' Mr. Williams says. Partly the neglect of Swift's poetry may be put down to the rapid change of fashion that came about after his death, in the latter half of the eighteenth century; and in part, too, to his consistent, half-humorous depreciation of his own verse:

> In Pope, I cannot read a line,
> But with a sigh I wish it mine.

But it does not say much for later generations of critics that they have been so ready to take a master of irony *au pied de la lettre*. Mr. Williams says that to the unhappiness of Swift's life there was added 'the misfortune of falling short of his friends, Pope, Prior and Gay, in the poetic content of his work. . . . In verse Pope was his superior. Gay and Prior had a more lyrical gift. Swift's genuis lay in the succession of Samuel Butler.' Swift was a less accomplished poet than Pope, and he had altogether less charm — though he was a more astonishing apparition, a stranger genius, and this appears in his verse no less than in his prose. But fall short of Prior? or Gay? Surely not.

In force, range, persistence, he is a remarkable poet. Swift expressed himself more fully and more continuously in his verse than in his prose. Mr. Williams allows that 'he was constantly turning verse as a common part of his everyday life, so much so that no part of his writing is as complete an autobiography'. He concludes, 'We are closer to Swift in his verse, and in his letters, than in his prose-writings'; and he quotes Dr. Elrington Ball's summing-up, 'Without knowledge of his verse a true picture of Swift cannot be drawn. In his verse he sets forth his life as in a panorama, he shows more clearly than in his prose his peculiar turn of thought, and he reveals his character in all its phases.' He took earlier to the writing of poetry, and in an early poem, the *Ode to Sir William Temple*, describes how everything that he writes turns to verse:

> In vain all wholesome herbs I sow,
>   Where nought but weeds will grow.
> Whate'er I plant (like corn on barren earth)
>   By an equivocal birth
> Seeds and runs up to poetry.

That in itself is evidence of his early bent; and though there comes a break after these poems, six years in which he is not known to have written any verse, the characteristic traits of Swift appear thus early. It is usual to mark a complete contrast between this first group of pindaric odes and the later poems. Yet in these first poems there is the declared intention of the satirist to lash mankind for its folly:

> My hate, whose lash just heaven has long decreed
> Shall on a day make sin and folly bleed.

There is 'that scorn of fools, by fools mistook for pride', the authentic note of contempt for mankind, the incapacity for contentment which such thoughts, in the human condition, must induce:

> Madness like this no fancy ever seized,
> Still to be cheated, never to be pleased.

There is the inhibiting doctrine that all knowledge comes only from memory, enshrined in a remarkable passage to which Yeats drew Mr. Williams's attention:

> But what does our proud ignorance learning call,
>   We oddly Plato's paradox make good,
> Our knowledge is but mere remembrance all,
>   Remembrance is our treasure and our food;

> Nature's fair table-book our tender souls
> We scrawl all o'er with odd and empty rules,
> Stale memorandums of the schools;
> For learning's mighty treasures look
> In that deep grave, a book.

All this in those first few poems, the neglected odes: the poems on which Dryden is said to have commented, 'Cousin Swift, you will never be a poet.' Evidently Dryden said something of the sort; for Swift underwent some kind of crisis, was silent for six years and then emerged with a totally different style, fully-formed, from which he never afterwards departed. But the themes were continuous and received their full development in the mature poetry.

There is a case for thinking that the more complete Swift is the Swift of the poems. There is nothing he said in prose that he did not say as well in verse; only the reputation of the author of *Gulliver* and of *The Tale of a Tub* has overshadowed the fact. There is all the savagery of the last book of *Gulliver* in *The Legion Club;* and there are a good many things among the poems that are hardly paralleled in the prose. The good-humoured, below-stairs fun of the remarkable early poem, *Mrs. Harris's Petition*, is paralleled in the late prose-work, the *Directions to Servants*, but with the added note of bitterness his experience of life had induced. It is revealing that it was in verse only that Swift expressed the precarious ambiguity of his relations with Vanessa; nothing like it in his prose. And how well that complex, poised state of mind, neither wholly one thing nor the other, is described:

> But what success Vanessa met,
> Is to the world a secret yet:
> Whether the nymph, to please her swain,
> Talks in a high romantic strain;
> Or whether he at last descends
> To like with less seraphic ends;
> Or, to compound the business, whether
> They temper love and books together;
> Must never to mankind be told,
> Nor shall the conscious muse unfold.

As to form, Swift's verse was a perfect instrument for the expression of what he intended; it, too, has greater variety than is usually realised. Even Dr. Johnson, whose criticism of Swift's poems was casual and unsympathetic, allowed this: 'They [the poetical works] are, for the most part, what their author intended. . . . All his verses exemplify his own definition of a good style, they consist of "proper words in proper places".'

The ends Swift set himself were too restricted or, at a deeper level, inhibited by his fear of giving himself away, of giving hostages to fortune in the realm of the emotions. One can appreciate the motives that made him repress his hopes and desires — his determination to have his life as far as possible under his own control, a rational control; the realisation of the insentience of the universe to the sufferings of men; his refusal to lay himself open to experience, especially in regard to sex. The paradox is that it is often those persons who go out of their way to reject experience for fear of the suffering it may entail, who suffer most. The searing irony of Swift's life is that the man who imposed so rational a control upon his emotions, should have ended by losing his reason. Mr. Williams concludes that if Swift had been prepared to let himself go, he would have been a greater poet, that 'he had something to give to English poetry that he never wholly gave'. On the other hand, it is that very sense of restraint that gives the impression of such power in reserve. And it is present, perfectly and precisely expressed, in all the metres and verse-forms he chose to write in.

The real criticism against Swift's poetry is not, then, on the score of lack of variety either of subject, or of metre, but rather a lack of variety in *tone*. But may not the same be said of many other poets whom the poetic tradition recognises without demur, Spenser, Shelley, Keats — though with them the tone is a different one? It may be agreed that Swift, for a poet, wrote too much from the head, and not enough from the heart; and it is not a good idea for a poet to write wholly from the head, never to allow himself freedom from the limits consciously imposed by the intellect. That is what Swift set himself to do, and the result we have to take for what it is. It is hardly just to demand that it should be something other than it is, as so many have done, and say, 'This is not poetry.' They start from a carefully selective view of what poetry should be — one moreover which is not sanctioned by the practice of the poets — and then impose that standard upon poetry like Swift's.

Naturally, with a dominantly intellectual approach and with his experience of the world what it was, Swift's creative impulse turned mainly to satire. He might have said with Juvenal, whom he modelled himself upon: 'Difficile est non satiram scribere.' And he was well aware of the criticism that might be pointed against him:

> Perhaps I may allow, the Dean
> Had too much satire in his vein;
> And seemed determined not to starve it,
> Because no age could more deserve it.

It is clear that this was the frame of mind that with him released the aesthetic impulse, that this was the psychological groove along which his inspiration and its expression ran most easily. There is a strong case for Swift's classicism, that controlled and deliberately directed emotion, as opposed to the romantic inspiration. For one thing his chief emotion was intellectual passion, a rare thing in an Englishman; which is perhaps why the English have never properly understood him or his poetry.

# XVII

# SARAH CHURCHILL IN OLD AGE

HERE is one of those books that give one all the more pleasure because they recall an earlier, more agreeable age, adding something fresh to our knowledge of it, bringing out new letters from houses that have meant much in the past. In this case Woburn, with its immense and varied inheritance, now in part dispersed — though nothing can or need disperse historic memories. The editor places these letters perfectly in their setting, tells us all that we want to know to make the story clear, works them skilfully into a characteristic conversation piece of the eighteenth century.

The letters are those of Sarah, Duchess of Marlborough,[1] written in her old age to her favourite granddaughter, Diana, Duchess of Bedford, whom she had brought up and loved with all the possessiveness of her nature. We all know what an astonishing personality Sarah's was: her beauty, her single-minded devotion to her famous husband, her forthrightness, candour and sincerity, her acquisitiveness and tenacity, the jealous spirit that went with it, her quarrelsomeness that made her so intolerable. She was a flame that scorched, rather than warmed, everything that came near her. Yet one would forgive her much for her magnificent answer to the Duke of Somerset: 'If I were young and handsome as I was, instead of old and faded as I am, and you could lay the empire of the world at my feet, you should never share the heart and hand that once belonged to John, Duke of Marlborough.'

Sarah, whatever her faults, had style: she was a woman made on the grand scale; and these letters reveal her at her most sympathetic. An old woman, crippled with gout so that she has to be carried about in a chair and often cannot wield the pen, she is as indomitable as ever and has such zest for life — and that is always irresistible. She is all for investigating new experiences, seeing new sights; those sharp eyes took in

[1] *Letters of a Grandmother*, 1732–1735, ed. G. Scott Thomson.

everything, her even sharper tongue commenting readily, and with a devastating candour, on everybody. The very intensity of her personality made her an admirable writer: she sees things with such a direct, clear vision; as she says about the finishing of her house at Wimbledon, 'My taste having always been to have things plain and clean from a piece of wainscott to a lady's face.' The indefatigable old lady in one day jolts along in her coach from Holywell, near St. Albans, to Woburn, sees all over the house, wearing out the invalid young Duke in the process — though here more considerately, 'I find he cannot endure to be thought ill, and therefore did not take any notice that I saw it, but contrived to sit down often as we talked over the pictures' — dines there, pushes on to Northampton, and the same night dictates a letter to her beloved Diana, describing it all.

So she marches along all the way to Scarborough — which was just coming into fashion as a spa — to drink the waters there for the benefit of her health. She does not seem to have noticed that she might have spared herself the pains, since she could have bought the waters bottled and drunk them at home. Of course the place did not meet with her approval when she got there:

My Lord Chesterfield is here and he told me my house was the envy of the place, but I think it a very bad one, very dirty and so noisy that I am going to lay straw in the street before my house to hinder the intolerable noise of the horses and coaches that go by my window. I have seen nobody yet that I know, but my Lady Gertrude Hotham and my Lord Chesterfield, who are both extremely well bred, and if anything could make this place tolerable, it would be their agreeable conversation.

She was pleasantly surprised by a visit from young Lord Cowper, who brought her a favour,

which is so extraordinary in this modern way of breeding that I was surprised at it, and asked one that is acquainted with him how he came to think of an old woman who was of no manner of use, to which I was answered that he loved me because I had been his father's friend. This is likewise a different way of thinking from the present age. He is an extremely honest young man and seems to have good sense. Those that know him say that he has a very good understanding and no vice. I think my Lord Grantham's daughter is a very lucky woman to be married to such a man, for it is certain she has no great title to sense from either side of her family, and had but £10,000.

Courtesy seems to have been hereditary in the Cowper family: for, years before, when Sarah had had to give up her apartments in St. James's Palace, on her quarrel with Queen Anne, the first Lord Cowper had been the only one of the Whig leaders, for whose sake she had sacrificed her favour with the Queen, to pay her a farewell visit. 'The only Whig that behaved himself like a gentleman to me,' she wrote.

However agreeable this interlude, it was the same old Sarah underneath, with her uncompromising comments on whoever or whatever earned her disapproval: 'There is no company here that one would not choose to be deaf and dumb than to be with them.' Her grandson, Lord Sunderland, comes in for a severe wigging:

if I were a young woman and was in circumstances to choose my lot, I had rather marry a man of sense with good morals than the Emperor of the world, that was a brute and a fool. My Lord Sunderland can't be called strictly the last, for as he speaks very little he imposes upon some. . . . Since he had money in his power, he has never disposed of any, that I have heard of, with any judgment; nor has he governed himself in any one action by the rules of reason. He seems to be very fond of his person, though not a very pleasing one, and to bestow a good deal of time upon dress, and which is not a great commendation, even in our weak sex.

In fine she winds up, 'By some of these accounts I send you, I think it is very plain that there is some tincture more or less of madness in almost everybody that one knows.'

Architects especially come in for her condemnation — she had had such an experience of them with the long warfare she had carried on with Vanbrugh over Blenheim Palace. Sarah, who had much common sense and hated pretentiousness, had never meant to have such an elephant of a building; and yet there she was, in spite of all her efforts, landed in the end with something like an English Escurial on her hands.

Architects? — 'I know of none that are not mad or ridiculous, and I really believe that anybody that has sense, with the best workmen of all sorts, could make a better house than any has been built these many years.' That was all very well in an aristocratic age, with standards formed by an *élite* which imposed its taste upon the whole society. But in an egalitarian society, where there is complete chaos in taste, it is of melancholy interest to watch in these letters how their taste was formed, how watchful it was of every detail of proportion, how sensitive to beauty.

Sarah greatly admired Southampton House, the town house of the Russells in Bloomsbury — alas, like so many of London's finest houses, completely vanished.

In this room at Southampton House, there is a set of blue and gold leather hangings which I bespoke and which is as fresh now as when it was put up. And I like it so extremely that I have bespoke the same to hang one of my rooms at Wimbledon. Southampton House is the handsomest, the most agreeable and the best turned that ever I saw either in town or country. There is everything in it that can be wished. He that built it (my Lord Southampton) has a great character, and I think that house represented one part of it very well.

It is a revealing comment and shows how conscious — and conscientious — people were about the houses they put up then; only in such circumstances and in such a society is a general standard of excellence possible. The letters are full of the detail which reveals the care they lavished upon every aspect of their houses: Sarah's enthusiasm for the rich effect of the combination of red damask hangings with white-painted panelling, the tall pier-glasses hung between windows to heighten the effect; her preference for simple mouldings as against the elaborate carvings of the previous century, her passion for light in a house.

Sarah prided herself on being a woman of sense. 'Sense' and 'reason', the 'rules of reason', were for ever on her lips or the tip of her pen: they were the tribute that the old Eve in her paid to the good form of the age. In fact she was the same impulsive, passionate woman she had always been; beneath the formidable exterior of the dowager Duchess there beat the same youthful heart that had exerted such a jealous hold upon John Churchill. It was power that was Sarah's foible; she exacted such submission that many of her family were forced to become enemies to keep any independence of soul.

In her last years Sarah met her match in her granddaughter, Lady Bateman, who took after her. We find the Duchess trying to force her favourite granddaughter to choose between her and Lady Bateman: 'But for Lady Bateman I must declare that I never can have any satisfaction in the conversation of anybody that has any commerce with her, I mean as to my own relations, for as to common acquaintances, I don't concern myself with what they do.' Diana must have been a clever, tactful girl to have slipped out of that dilemma. And then we find Sarah ending up, 'I think I am not in my nature at all partial, and I am the more persuaded my notions are right in this,' etc., etc. Of course, she was always right. Power was at the bottom of it all, it was her dynastic sense that was outraged. 'But this, with a great many other things I know, makes me see plainly, that she is a great favourite at Court, and that must be from the hopes the ministers have of dividing a family, who, if they were wise would be strong enough to make any ministry afraid of disobliging them.'

Sarah's trouble, as so often with persons of her temperament, was that she brought a good deal of ill-treatment down upon herself as the result of the intensity of her likes and dislikes. She was hardly treated by her daughters, the Duchesses of Marlborough and Montagu — disgracefully by the latter. For years relations had been broken off between them; and when the elder daughter, Henrietta, died, Sarah wrote:

You have judged very right in thinking that what has happened I should feel much more than I should have imagined formerly I could ever do. By which I am convinced that there is such a thing as natural affection, though I have heard many people laugh at that notion. . . . However it is a satisfaction to me that I did all that was in my power. But what do I dream of satisfaction when there are not two things upon earth at so impossible a distance as satisfaction and me?

She ends up with a picture of herself, as vivid as ever, reading Job for consolation: 'But I can say with Job that my eyes are

N

dim with sorrow, and my nerves are as shadows, and indeed
I think my circumstances is more like his, than anybody's
that I have heard of or read of.' This from the richest, and
the most celebrated, woman in Europe, widow of the great
Duke who had adored her all his life!

It is precisely that that makes her such a good letter-writer.
We — two hundred years away, and not among the exposed
circle of her relations — do not have to put up with the tan-
trums, the upbraidings; we have only to sit tight and be grateful for someone who is so unself-conscious, so natural and
immediate in her reactions, that she might even now be in the
room with us. Sarah was a born writer, though uneducated.
We see her as she saw herself, 'labouring like a pack-horse
every day' to save her grandson, the young Duke, from the
cheats; 'it is probable the Duke of Marlborough may think
£20 nothing; but it is a great deal in £46'. Now she is reading
Sir William Temple, having put by the Book of Job. Or she is
suggesting that Diana should get somebody 'to pick out what
is most ridiculous in the reign of King James the first, and read
to you. There is a great deal so tedious, that I pass it over,
but his love letters to the Duke of Buckingham are incomparable.' Sensible, unsqueamish age! She cannot abide powdered
hair in a picture, though Sir Godfrey Kneller painted her hair
like that:

I never knew anything of it till many years after his death
I saw it at his house in the country. . . . But it was a very odd
fancy in him to make my hair look like the Queen's [Caroline's]
when she came first into England, clotted all over with powder,
when I fancy the best thing I had was the colour of my hair.

Sometimes Sarah gives us a whole scene, in the manner of
the deliberate, considered artists among letter-writers. There
is a comic account of what happened to Queen Caroline in
Kensington Park:

Two or three days ago, Her sacred Majesty was in danger
of being ravished. She was walking from Kensington to London
early in the morning and having a vast desire to appear more
able in everything than other people, she walked so fast as to
get before my Lord Chamberlain and the two princesses upon
one of the causeways, quite out of sight. . . . My Lord

Grantham meeting a country clown asked him if he had met any person and how far they were off? To which he answered he had met a jolly crummy woman with whom he had been fighting some time to kiss her. I am surprised at the man's fancy. And my Lord Grantham was so frightened that he screamed out and said it was the Queen. Upon which the country fellow was out of his wits, fell upon his knees, cried and earnestly begged of my Lord Grantham to speak for him for he was sure he should be hanged for what he had done. But did not explain further what it was. And her Majesty does not own more than that he struggled with her, but that she got the better of him.

Caroline, who was a good sort, made no fuss about it, seems indeed to have been amused and taken it in good part. Sarah, for whom Caroline was much too able a woman for her to like, wished somebody would make a ballad of it; 'for when I was at Scarborough, I learned to sing and I fancy I could perform such a one very well without any graces'.

Or there is a conversation piece, like one of those characteristic pictures of the time — a Hogarth, for there is a spice of caricature about it — of Sarah, the Duchess of Manchester and Lady Bristol at play at Tunbridge Wells. Sarah did not approve of the last, 'for she is a mighty ridiculous woman, entirely wicked in all things. But though her actions are bad, I can't think her what one calls a fool. She is worthless, but there is a mixture of cunning and sometimes a good deal of wit and sharpness in her answers.' In spite of this unpromising beginning, a treaty of peace ensued and Lady Bristol persuaded Sarah to give a party at her house to play, and 'one of the chief preliminaries of this peace was that she should stake'. When Lady Bristol sat down to play she pretended to have lost her purse.

There was no remedy for that: so we played as well as we could. She sent several messages about for this purse and acted the part pretty well. And yet she said, there was eight or ten guineas in it and a double moidore. . . . When the play was over, I told her that I had often looked into my pockets for things and have not found them at first, having four little pockets in one great one. And I desired her to search again all her pockets, which are much the same as mine. She said she was sure, and had not it. Then I desired the Duchess of Manchester and I might search the pockets. And so we went to romps. But she struggled with us and got the better, for I would not carry the jest too far.

One sees in this glimpse, under the formality of the age, the horseplay. At the same time as they had greater elegance in life and taste, a fine creativeness in art, they were also coarser and more natural, both more formal and more spontaneous. Who would not prefer such a combination to the lowering of taste characteristic of a democratic age, standards geared to the lowest common measure of understanding and appreciation, a new social order intellectually and aesthetically confused?

The best side of Sarah comes out in her love for Diana. Early on in these letters she writes: 'Your desiring me to take care of myself for your sake is very kind, and I return it by assuring you that I desire to live only for you.' Her formal 'dear Lady Russell', or 'dear Duchess of Bedford', gives way to 'dear Di' and in the end 'dear Cordelia'. Sarah loved her for her sweet and considerate ways; she fancied that she took after her grandmother in this respect. 'Notwithstanding, I have had the same way of acting as yours has been to me, with all those that I ever loved; but you are charming in all your thoughts and actions.'

Over the later letters there is the shadow of a fear: Diana's health was not good. There was Sarah in these years engaged in building yet another house, her fifth, at Wimbledon, which was designed for Diana. Sarah was as insatiably interested as ever in pictures and furnishing, planning and projecting, what she was going to have at Wimbledon and what she was *not* going to have, her zest for life undiminished. But Diana's tenuous hold on life was failing; a grave fear gripped her grandmother's heart. At last the day came when Sarah had to get out the tent which the Duke had used on his campaigns — 'to think that it was your dear Grandfather's tent, when he did such wonderful things to secure the nation from being enslaved by the French King' — and have it set up on the lawns at Woburn so that her beloved girl might breathe.

In all the letters we never hear Diana's voice directly, but we can gather how kind and tactful she was with her tartar of a grandmother, how lovable she must have been. Alas, Diana never inherited the house upon which the old Duchess lavished such thought and care. By the time it was ready, the girl who held such a place in her heart was dead.

# XVIII

# HORACE WALPOLE AND
# GEORGE MONTAGU

VIRGINIA WOOLF made it difficult for anyone coming after her to review Horace Walpole's letters, with her essay on the impossibility of doing justice to the vast Yale edition of them, now marching improbably on towards its completion. So much work has gone into it, such mountainous collections, photostats of everything extant in Horace Walpole's hand — when there is not the original itself in the fortunate editor's possession — a great deal of the library at Strawberry Hill, now reposing at Farmington in parallel places according to their old shelf-marks, the books Horace printed at his press in the garden, the furniture, the portraits and pictures he had around him, the Gothick lantern that shed its dim unreligious light upon the staircase and watched the ageing Horace's gouty steps hobbling up and down.

What a wonderful work of re-creation Mr. Wilmarth S. Lewis has accomplished in his own life's work! — not only the devoted re-creation of a man, one of the most original figures in his time, and his collections, but his time, the age itself. If one wants to see the eighteenth century, the second half of it — Horace Walpole's *floruit* and apogee — one can study it, in scholarly authenticity and taste, in the perfect early eighteenth-century colonial house in that unspoiled Connecticut township Mr. Lewis has made famous. For, in addition to being scholar and connoisseur, he is himself an admirable writer. The collections he has brought there are not to be thought of as a museum; Farmington is a creative centre, whence this fabulous edition of the greatest of English letter-writers proceeds and further works of eighteenth-century scholarship may be expected in the future. For Farmington is closely *lié* with the neighbouring university of Yale — and no doubt will become more so — the repository of the Boswell Papers and so much other literary material of the English eighteenth and nineteenth centuries.

Fortunate Farmington, lucky Yale, to have thought of it in time!

The Yale edition of Walpole's correspondence with George Montagu, in two volumes, is not only the most manageable but the most intimate and sympathetic of all the sequences published.[1] It contains some of his finest letters, like those describing the executions of the Jacobite lords after the 1745 Rebellion, the funeral of George II and the coronation banquet of George III, the description of Walpole's visit after many years to his father's splendid Houghton with all its memories, the celebrated party at Vauxhall, that on the summer of 1759 with its victories and golden weather ('Our bells are worn threadbare with ringing for victories'). Apart even from these, which have become almost set-pieces with frequent quotation, Walpole is at his best, his gayest and most spontaneous, in writing to Montagu. They were friends from their school-days at Eton; they both belonged to the innermost circle of the grand Whig families; they knew everybody. While Walpole lived the busiest social life in London, or constantly entertained at Strawberry Hill, Montagu lazed his time away in the country and was content to hear what happened in the world from the most brilliant and vivacious letters anybody ever got. He was so indolent, and often unresponsive, that he did not deserve to have them. But the indolent and impassive frequently have an unaccountable attraction for the active-minded and sprightly; and so it was with Walpole and George Montagu.

To all the gaieties and charms of a Walpole correspondence there is added the psychological interest of the curious relation between these two. From the very beginning it is Walpole who makes the pace, the more interesting man making up to the less. 'Write soon,' he says, 'for I love your letters.' How often he had to repeat the request in the years that were to come, until even his vivacity flagged against such massive unresponsiveness and he was driven to complain. 'I hate you for being so indifferent about me,' Walpole writes; 'I live in the world, and yet love nothing, care a straw for nothing, but two or three old friends that I have loved these thirty years.' And again, just

---

[1] *Horace Walpole's Correspondence with George Montagu*, edited by W. S. Lewis and R. S. Brown, 2 vols.

before Montagu allowed their friendship to lapse into silence: 'But I grow old; and the less time we have to live together, the more I feel a separation from a person I love so well.'

Montagu was a lazy bachelor, a sort of Edward Fitzgerald, who dreamed his life away in the country, drinking his port, nursing the gout, dozing by the fire in his various country houses. Not that he had Fitzgerald's gifts; but all the same he was not without talent. He was a very good letter-writer, when he chose to exert himself — as we can now see from this first publication of his letters in full; he was well read, interested like Walpole in antiquarian things, humorous, amusing. The real passion of his life, as with a good many bachelors who do nothing about it, was for his family, the Montagu clan, the Cues as they are called all through their correspondence; anything about the doings of any of them was grateful news to him sunk in rustic contentment at Greatworth or Adderbury; any family portrait he could pick up, or Walpole for him, was grist to his mill and went into his collection. He, too, was something of a collector, in this a follower of Walpole's; and they both shared a romantic sensibility to nature. He was as proud in his quieter way, of his own Greatworth as Horace was of Strawberry Hill. 'My Greatworth begins to put on its pretty looks,' he writes in April 1763, 'and I amuse myself with washing its face and powdering its hair, and I hope for a country lass you will not find her quite inelegant.' One misses the lyrical note of Walpole's love for Strawberry, 'where [May 1761] my two passions, lilacs and nightingales, are in full bloom. I spent Sunday as if it was Apollo's birthday, Gray and Mason were with me, and we listened to the nightingales till one o'clock in the morning.' Or the sharpness of a poet in his observation: 'observing [May 1763] all the way I came the proof of the duration of this east wind, for on the west side the blossoms were so covered with dust one could not distinguish them; on the eastern hand the hedges were white in all the pride of May'.

With such a friend, the nervous, highly-strung Walpole could be perfectly at ease. He wrote Montagu all the gossip of the town, all the events and happenings, the grand occasions of public life as well as the tittle-tattle of private life. But the small-talk, the amusements, amenities, extravagance were those of a society that was intensely political at heart, of an aristocracy that ruled England and made an Empire. It is that that gives a solid foundation to all the bubble and effervescence on the surface, that makes the difference between Horace Walpole's 'town' and Proust's Faubourg. Walpole himself was an active politician who worked and intrigued hard for his side — Macaulay forgot this, among other things, when he treated him as a mere light-weight, and the Victorians followed suit. Almost the deepest thing in Horace was his pride in his father, the great man who ruled England as Prime Minister longer than anyone else and who ended his career under a cloud. His son never forgave anyone who had contributed, however many years ago, to his father's fall. (It is all the more piquant because of the doubt as to Horace's paternity — many thought that he was the son of Carr, Lord Hervey, whom he much more resembled.) And so we have the unforgettable portraits of Newcastle for ever behaving absurdly on the public stage, making a fool of himself at George II's funeral:

He fell into a fit of crying the moment he came into the chapel and flung himself back in a stall, the Archbishop hovering over him with a smelling bottle — but in two minutes his curiosity got the better of his hypocrisy and he ran about the chapel with his glass to spy who was or was not there, spying with one hand and mopping his eyes with t'other. Then returned the fear of catching cold, and the Duke of Cumberland, who was sinking with heat, felt himself weighed down, and turning round, found it was the Duke of Newcastle standing upon his train to avoid the chill of the marble.

The Duke was an Aunt Sally for everybody, but even his Duchess comes in for a comic insinuation from Walpole: 'On Tuesday the operation of shaving was happily performed on the upper lip of her Grace the Duchess of Newcastle by a celebrated artist from Paris sent over on purpose by the Earl of Albemarle.'

The two old bachelors talked antiquities, books, projects for planting, building, printing, improving; and, for want of better, they talked bawdy. 'Dick Edgcumbe is shut up with the itch; the ungenerous would ascribe it to Mrs. Day, but he denies it, owning, however, that he is very well contented to have it, as nobody will venture on her.' Lord Calthorpe has gone mad and walks down Whitehall with red ribbons in his hair to insist on seeing the King. Lady Townshend falls madly in love with the Jacobite Lord Kilmarnock at his trial. We are kept well posted in news of the health of Mr. Chute of the Vine: he is always in or out of bed with the gout, and nothing else happens to him at all, except an occasional chaste visit to Strawberry Hill. 'Here I am with the poor Chutehed, who has put on a shoe but today for the first time.' 'The poor Chute rose from the gout, and Lady Carberry who can raise nothing' are not at Frogmore.

How much we have to be grateful for to this friendship which has left us such a portrait, with all its colours, its lights and shades, of that age and world! One still derives some sense of it from the gaping windows and broken fanlights of those streets in and around Arlington Street. 'From my earliest memory, Arlington Street has been a ministerial street.' But how much more one gets from these letters! Two days before her death Lady Hervey wrote to her son: 'I feel my dissolution coming on — but I have no pain — what can an old woman desire more?' The brave, stoical, *sensible* eighteenth century, besides its elegance, its colour and gallantry!

As one reads these letters, something happens to one. The eyes wander away from the printed page; one loses oneself in a dream, as in listening to music; one sees the world through the eyes of Horace Walpole; it is his world that one sees. It is the summer of 1753 once more; George II is king, and the garden at Strawberry Hill is at the height of its beauty; it is the hottest day of the summer and in the evening the Duc de Mirepoix, the French ambassador at the Court of St. James's, walks slowly in the *beau milieu* of Brentford Town, without any company but a brown lapdog with long ears, two pointers, two pages, three footmen and a *vis-à-vis* following him. Or it is May in 1763, and Miss Pelham is entertaining a party *al fresco* at Esher: a magnificent dinner, cloaked in the modesty of earthenware; French horns and hautboys on the lawn. They walk to the belvedere on the summit of the hill, where a threatened storm only serves to heighten the beauty of the landscape, a rainbow on a dark cloud falling precisely behind the tower of a neighbouring church, between another tower and the building of Claremont. Or it is March 1766, and it is snowing in Paris where Horace is on a visit to Madame du Deffand, and clouds of dust are whisking about the streets and quays, edged with an east wind that gets under one's shirt: 'I should not be quite sorry if a little of it tapped my lilacs on their green noses, and bade them wait for their master.' A few weeks later and he is at Livry in the *forêt de Bondi*, at the little pavilion where Madame de Sévigné used to write to her daughter: 'on one side of the garden leading to the great road is a little bridge of wood on which the dear woman used to wait for the carrier that brought her daughter's letters'.

What is it that makes the snow, or the maytime, of two hundred years ago so affecting? If we could say, we should lay our finger on the nature of poetry or music. We feel about Horace Walpole as he felt about Madame de Sévigné: it is this sense of the past, apprehended through that prism which reflects its beauty, that gives his letters, like hers, their poetry. For Horace Walpole, like Proust, was a poet: a poet who found the perfect form for his vision and experience of life.

# XIX

# THE LETTERS OF JUNIUS

THE *Letters of Junius* are like the *Sonnets* of Shakespeare in one respect, that they have provided material to create a major mystery in our literature and an immense amount of argumentation, largely superfluous. There was indeed far more reason for it in the case of the *Letters of Junius*, for their authorship was an extraordinarily well-kept secret. There has never been any doubt as to the authorship of the *Sonnets*, and the bulk of informed opinion has always held that they were written to and for the obvious person, Shakespeare's patron, Southampton, and that the only possible rival poet was Marlowe. Nonsensical conjectures all over the place, with no sense of time, dating or character, hallooing after a supposititious inspirer, Mr. W. H. — when they are the obvious initials of the person who had got the manuscript — are entirely modern and fabricate a needless mystery.

There *is* a mystery about the *Letters of Junius*, namely, how their author, who was well enough suspected to be their author at the time, managed to escape having them pinned down to him. The answer is that, for one thing, he was a backroom-boy in a government department, very shy and secretive — and, we now know, an intelligence-man; and, for another, he was not only fairly well covered, but was probably well protected.

All the suspicious circumstances have always pointed to Philip Francis as their author, and to no other. It is only fair to say that most informed opinion has always thought this, as Sir Leslie Stephen summed it up conclusively in his article in the *Dictionary of National Biography*. But that has not prevented fifty fools from putting forward fifty different people at various times as candidates for Junius, and a small library has been written to settle or, rather, to confuse, his identity.

As with Shakespeare and the *Sonnets*, these people have a vested interest in mystification, in keeping up a needless mystery.

It so happens that a recent investigation has put the computer on the tracks of Junius and Philip Francis and found, what is not surprising — when all the circumstances, historical, political, personal, literary, cohere — that their verbal usages are one and the same. But what is new, offers a new track to explore, is that when Philip Francis was in France in 1772, offering his services as an intelligence-man, and actually achieved an interview with the Foreign Secretary, the reference appears in the latter's papers as *un nommé Junius*.[1]

What were the *Letters of Junius*? Why did they make such a sensation in their time and retain their interest long after the original circumstances which brought them forth had vanished? Who was Philip Francis?

The *Letters* were a series of contributions to a London newspaper at a critical and embittered period — the end of the first decade of George III's reign. The first appeared in the *Public Advertiser* on 21 January 1769, the last on 21 January 1772, so that this unknown author held the attention of the public, stirring up feeling against the government, lashing Ministers with all the resources of a brilliant invective, agitating, arousing opinion, exciting the most intense personal animosities, during a period of three years.

The period was in many ways like the disgraceful Baldwin–Chamberlain epoch which reduced British policy to incoherence, allowed Germany to make a second bid for world-power so that the war had to be fought all over again. — Very much as happened with France in the two decades after Pitt's victorious war, the fruits of which were thrown away, and the country let in for a second struggle all over again with the American Revolutionary war. It was a period of incoherence, confusion, party-scuffling without real leadership, after the Seven Years War, under the genius of Pitt, had elevated Britain to the highest summit of power it has ever known.

After the war was over the governing circle turned away from the great man under whose star it had been won and gave itself up to the delights of faction fights, which were exploited by George III, whose political intervention only increased the confusion. The pity of it was that the one man of genius, William

---

[1] I am indebted for this information to Mr. Rohan Butler.

Pitt, played into the hands of those smaller men by the mistakes he made and at times was incapacitated by illness, so that he was effectively kept out of power. Meanwhile, the American Colonies were provoked and teased into rebellion; our enemies on the Continent, France and Spain, were enabled to recover the initiative; the Navy, which Pitt had left stronger than the combined fleets of France and Spain, was out-numbered at sea; the Army got demoralised, and Pitt's able generals displaced to make way for yes-men.

Above all there was a fatuous spirit of self-complacency, exuded by the government (so like the 'National Government' of 1931–9), a spirit of levity which led them to appoint inferior men to crucial posts and to keep out men of energy and ability. The Prime Minister, Lord North, who was a sort of Baldwin of the time, popular with both King and people, himself said on one occasion of the army officers he had appointed: 'I do not know what effect they will have upon the enemy; I only know that they make me tremble.' The upshot of that unfortunate decade in our history was the loss of the American Colonies, and the ascendancy won by seven years of struggle, 1758–63.

Junius was a devoted follower of the great Lord Chatham, who at the end of 1768 had recovered from his two years of illness and reappeared like an avenging spirit upon the scene of his former triumphs to find all in confusion. George III's Government — like the so-called National Government — spent all its energy in clinging to office at all costs and had none left over to look after the long-term interests and safety of the country. They had alienated the people and divided the country by their determined exclusion of the Radical Wilkes from Parliament, who, three times elected by the voters of Middlesex, was as many times excluded from the House and in the end somebody else declared elected in his stead. Meanwhile the really important issues, vital to the future, went by default and the Government fumbled and stumbled into alienating America.

Chatham emerged from retirement determined to reverse all this. He formed a united front with the Whigs to drive this effete Government out, hoping to return to power himself while there was yet time. In the campaign which he launched, his most effective weapon in the Press was the unknown, mysterious

'Junius'. The freedom of the Press was all the more important since Parliament was partly bought, and most of its members anyway incapable of appreciating what the long-term interests of the country demanded, the crisis with the American colonies approaching. Junius made it his business to fight each of these campaigns, since it was the Government's aim to muffle up Press criticism as well as to lull the country into a sense of false security.

Junius was in the possession of weapons which made him a formidable adversary. In the first place he *knew* everything: he had the inestimable advantage over so many political writers on the fringe of politics that he was inside and knew what was going on — often things of so private and personal a nature that his letters threatened political blackmail. That, added to his anonymity, redoubled his power: nobody knew where these blows came from or where or on whom they might fall next. Then, in an age which appreciated such things, he had an effective style, polished and classical, excoriating, like Tacitus. Only one political writer of the time came up to him, and that was Burke, which made some people suppose that Burke was Junius. In fact their two styles were very different; where Burke's periods are rich and variegated, coloured with romantic imagination, Junius's sentences are swift, incisive, and envenomed.

When somebody pleaded that the Prime Minister — as it might be Baldwin — was a virtuous man and had done some good, Junius replied in a flash: 'You do good, my Lord, by stealth — and the rest is upon record.' Here is his description of the ministry, fiddling while the Empire was foundering:

While the fate of Great Britain is at stake, these worthy Councillors dispute without decency, advise without sincerity, resolve without decision, and leave the measure to be executed by the man who voted against it. This, I conceive, is the last disorder of the State.

Anybody who came to the defence of the Ministry received more than he bargained for. Sir William Draper, a retired and well-sinecured officer, took up his pen on their behalf. Junius asked:

After selling the companions of your victory in one instance, and after selling your profession in the other, by what authority do you presume to call yourself a soldier? . . . Are your flatteries of the commander-in-chief directed to another regiment, which you may again dispose of on the same honourable terms? We know your prudence, Sir William, and I should be sorry to stop your preferment.

He attacked Ministers and their appointees mercilessly, and in nearly every case he proved to be right. Here was his comment on General Burgoyne, the dilettante dandy who owed his promotion to favouritism:

Let me ask your Grace for what military merits you have been pleased to reward him? He had a regiment of dragoons, which one would imagine was at least an equivalent for any services *he* ever performed.

This was the popular figure who achieved the surrender at Saratoga: the Government had withdrawn Carleton, the ablest British general in America. The country had to pay a terrible price for the years of incompetence and smug self-complacency — 'the years that the locusts have eaten', as Sir Winston Churchill described the 1930s.

Junius did not fear to indict George III, who was ultimately behind it all. He did not hesitate to imply that if they persisted in their course, a revolution would be the only remedy:

The prince who imitates their conduct [the Stuarts'] should be warned by their example; and while he plumes himself upon the security of his title to the crown, should remember that, as it was acquired by one revolution, it may be lost by another.

But Junius and his great leader, Chatham, were kept out by the mediocrities the country preferred, who clung obstinately to power — until the country went down to defeat and the loss of America.

Philip Francis was a young civil servant who had been in the Secretary of State's office, was for a short time secretary to Chatham, and at the time of the Junius Letters was in the War Office. He had a great deal of inside information about what was going on, and it seems that he got more information

from sources higher up in politics — from Lord Temple,
Chatham's brother-in-law, and Calcraft, who was a go-between
Chatham and Francis. There was much in common between
Chatham's tone and temper, his unbridled language and unrestrained passion, and Junius' envenomed invective; Junius
sometimes sent him advice and Chatham adopted the very
phraseology he suggested. As a civil servant Francis was de-
barred from saying in public all that he felt and wanted to say
— though there was no such stringent rule in those days as in
ours. He was one of the circle of young men who believed that
Chatham 'could save the country and that nobody else could'.
In that he was right enough; and since he held it with intense
conviction, who can blame him for doing whatever he could to
warn the country of its danger?

As a man, Philip Francis was not at all a nice one — which
was what we should expect from a master of political invective.
He was extremely clever, with a gift for languages and writing,
immensely industrious and methodical, restless and ambitious,
with the furious energy of a man bent on power and perpetually thwarted of it. The circumstances of his birth were against
him in that aristocratic age; it must have maddened him to
see power always going to the mediocrities whom he despised.
Even the good-tempered Burke felt it hard to put up with;
Francis, who did not put up with such treatment with impunity
— for he was as vain and arrogant as he was able and ambitious
— turned venomous.

What could he expect? He was the son of an impoverished
clergyman, with an Irish background. The analogy to Swift
does not seem to have been observed, yet he was growing up in
Dublin only a decade or so after Swift's famous, no less scathing
*Draper's Letters*. Here is the literary background to the *Letters of
Junius*: this is the tradition they came out of.

Disappointed of his hopes of power in England — like Swift
— or indeed of ever being effectively on the winning side,
Francis went into exile. For Philip Francis it was gilt-edged
exile to India. He had been thinking of retreating from his
disappointments, like Oliver Cromwell, to America, where
Francis purchased himself a nice estate of a thousand acres in
Pennsylvania. But in 1774 this retired War Office clerk got the

o

job of member of the Legislative Council of Bengal, under Warren Hastings, at £10,000 a year. Think of it! — £10,000 a year, with the pound at the value it commanded then, and no taxes to pay whatever. He proceeded to devote himself to making the life of the great pro-consul miserable — when Warren Hastings saved British rule in India at the crisis of the American war, practically single-handed. For, of course, Philip Francis thought he ought to be Governor-General. Nobody else thought so, not even his own extreme Whig friends when they got their chance.

All that is another, and a fascinating story, highly dramatic in its turns and chances — told by Macaulay, with extreme partisanship, from Philip Francis' point of view.

For, of course, Philip Francis was a Whig doctrinaire, wedded to Whig principles — though these offered no impediment to the unscrupulous pursuit of his own interests. Inspired by the courage of contempt, he had no fear of attacking the great, however powerful; contempt was the nerve of his style, in writing as in life, allied to a reckless daring. What he really hated was mediocrity; he also detested any authority over and above himself; he made a great show of moral disapproval of the corruption in politics in his time — though this did not prevent him from making a fortune. Though he missed power, he made money.

In the end, he was a snake. The Tories made a great mistake to tread on him.

# XX

# CARLYLE'S PAST AND PRESENT

It is difficult for us of our time and generation to appreciate Carlyle. So many things come between us and him. In the first place that appalling style, with its repetitiveness, its over-emphasis, its perpetual note of adjuration, its shrillness and exaggeration, with no soft tones at all, the trumpets always braying and rather discordantly: it makes him almost impossible to read. Then there is the insensitiveness, the dislike of art for itself, of music and painting, the philistinism of the Scotch peasant. No less serious, there is his German monomania, the confusion about what he thought of the relation between Might and Right, his intellectual muddle. There is no doubt that the Victorians overrated him; and that the older textbooks on the literature of the age were wrong in placing him at the head of it. Newman, for whose intellect Carlyle expressed great contempt, should have had a larger place; in some ways his mind foreshadowed the more subtle and critical intellectual issues of our time.

Yet for all his defects Carlyle was unmistakably a man of genius. He was that unattractive kind of genius, a prophet. All prophets are misfits; and that throws a flood of light on the source and conditioning of their 'message'. Perhaps one should not complain of their repetitiveness, or what would become of the books of Jeremiah, Isaiah, Amos — or for that matter, of of Marx and Lenin? Or of D. H. Lawrence? Repetitiveness is one of their strongest weapons, the way they get their message across. But the very fact of their being misfits means that they see more vividly certain shortcomings and defects in society and people around them. It also means that they often miss the unobtrusive good which is being done quietly by ordinary folk to whom they give no credit. What the understanding of their prophetic character in terms of modern psychology does is to make us chary of accepting their *judgment* about the things they so vividly, so vehemently, and often usefully, condemn.

Judgment is precisely what they have not got; what much-despised statesmen like Peel and Gladstone and regular thinkers like Mill had, Carlyle not. On the whole, considering his vehemence, and how much he lived by his intuitions, it is remarkable how much he was in the right.

Anyone who wishes to tackle Carlyle at his best might take *Past and Present* as an introduction. It is a book very symptomatic of its time and still has something to say to us today. It is the best and the most balanced of the books Carlyle devoted to the Condition-of-England question, which so exercised men's minds in the 1840s and left such a mark upon contemporary literature.

And well it might! For the hungry forties were the turning-point in the development of the Industrial Revolution, a dark and dangerous tunnel which the country had to traverse before it emerged into the daylight and prosperity of the Victorian era proper. There was mass unemployment on an unprecedented scale, fruit of the maladjustment of the new powers of production to the mechanism of distribution; the price of corn soared while men went hungry in the country districts no less than in the towns; the discontent of the working class expressed itself in the agitation of the Chartist Movement, that of the new middle class in the campaigns of the Anti-Corn Law League. It was a very disturbed decade, which culminated, on the Continent, in the revolutions of 1848. All these forces the writers of the time were conscious of in their different ways, Dickens, Disraeli, Tennyson, Arnold, Clough. In his *Life of Carlyle* Froude has a most interesting passage on the intellectual ferment of those years, and what it was that made younger men like himself turn to Carlyle.

Carlyle focused these discontents and gave them expression in a way that arrested attention. It is not that the thoughts which he had were very original; the actual thought is not subtle, or remote, but simple and even platitudinous. It was his way of putting it that was striking, his vehemence and sincerity. And he had a peasant's horse-sense about ideas: his intuitions were often more right than the intellectual views of the academic thinkers — for example, about *laissez-faire*, the Poor Law, and factory legislation. The sublime certainty and self-righteousness of the Victorian economists has a modern parallel in the equally doctrinaire fixation of the economists in the 1920s on free trade, the gold standard and no controlled economy. Carlyle, for all that he was no economist, was often quite right as against these *a priori* second-raters.

He begins his book with the contrast of an England wealthier than it ever had been before and yet with two million people out of work, in workhouses 'pleasantly so-named because work cannot be done in them . . . they sit there, pent up, as in a kind of horrid enchantment', or in receipt of out-door relief. He had been shocked by the scenes of want he had witnessed in East Anglia the autumn before on his ride through it in pursuit of material for his Cromwell; he was still more shocked by the condition of things in Glasgow, Manchester, Stockport and elsewhere revealed by the papers and blue-books, the reports which Edwin Chadwick was beginning to compile and of which Marx was to make such use later. He went on to point to the dilemma of over-production and under-employment which was a recurrent trouble of *laissez-faire* capitalism. He put it very effectively: so many shirts that 'hang there by the million unsaleable; and here, by the million, are diligent bare backs that can get no hold of them'. The operatives who made them are in want, without bread; and yet 'there is not a horse in England, able and willing to work, but *has* due food and lodging; and goes about sleek-coated, satisfied in heart. And you say, It is impossible.' Carlyle replies: 'It is impossible for us to believe it to be impossible,' and to those who are responsible, he says: 'Do you depart quickly; clear the ways soon, lest worse befall.'

He addressed himself to the aristocracy, the ruling class, for they had all the power and only they could amend it. It is interesting that the mission of this son of the people should have been directed to the upper and middle class; and that Marx and Engels, those scions of the middle class, should have turned to the people. Both had their influence in different ways; it would be a pity to exclude the effect of either upon the social ameliora-tion which was a grand feature of the nineteenth century. Carlyle appealed to the conscience and political interest of the rulers; Marx and Engels did their best to organise the workers to push for themselves. (They must have been wonderfully disillusioned after a lifetime of entertaining such hopes of them.) Carlyle, with more immediate point, tells the ruling class that since they are in possession of the land, they owe it good governance; and if they did not do their duty, worse consequences would follow. He always had the vision of the French Revolution at the back of his mind. So had they, and in fact, in the confusion of the forties, led by Peel, the 'pilot who weathered the storm', they did not do so badly. The English governing class gave this country far better leadership in the nineteenth century than the governing classes on the Continent gave their countries.

There were, of course, spells of faltering leadership, as at the end of Whig rule in the late thirties, or the way in which England muddled into and through the Crimean War. Carlyle hated the popular humbug of the age and the politicians whose ideas of leadership were publicity and playing down to the mob. He has an excellent portrait of Sir Jabesh Windbag, type of all these. 'Windbag, weak in the faith of a God, which he believes only at Church on Sundays, if even then; strong only in the faith that Paragraphs and Plausibilities bring votes; that Force of Public Opinion, as he calls it, is the primal Necessity of Things.' The regular type of the politician who tells the people what the people like to hear, until they wake up and find themselves where they did in 1939–40. Have we never come across a Sir Jabesh Windbag in our time?

Carlyle's anti-democratic bias is constant. But in this book it is held in restraint; he does not lose his sense of balance as in his later political writings, *Latter Day Pamphlets* and *Shooting Niagara*. In *Past and Present* he was content to insist upon the need for sincere, candid, able leadership.

In these years, while he was writing *Cromwell*, he had the heroic days of the Commonwealth all the time before his mind. Since he knew that in fact only a few rule, he was above all anxious that the right ones should be chosen. Liberty he attached less importance to than economic security: in that a true man of the people. 'Liberty, I am told, is a divine thing. Liberty, when it becomes the "Liberty to die by starvation" is not so divine.' It is here that Carlyle links up with the socialist trend of thought in his age. He goes further:

Liberty? The true liberty of a man, you would say, consisted in his finding out, or being forced to find out the right path, and to walk therein. To learn, or to be taught, what work he actually was able for; and then by permission, persuasion, and even compulsion, to set about doing of the same.

This leads on to his gospel of work:

Consider how, even in the meanest sorts of labour, the whole soul of a man is composed into a kind of real harmony, the instant he sets himself to work! . . . Blessed is he who has found his work; let him ask no other blessedness. He has a work; a life-purpose; he has found it, and will follow it.

Carlyle had been struck by the medieval Chronicle of Bury St. Edmunds and its portrait of Abbot Samson, who bore rule there nobly and restored the fortunes of the house: an effective ruler after Carlyle's own heart. This middle section of the book, the historical, which most people will find the most readable, sets off the rest of the book very well. Carlyle, who had such difficulties with his writing and filled the house at Cheyne Row and his correspondence with his groans, had no difficulty with *Past and Present:* he wrote it straight off at white heat in the first seven weeks of 1843.

And the reason why so many people regarded him with such respect, with something like veneration, in his time?

Of course, the Victorians liked preachers, and responded to preaching. Here was a preacher of genius. But he came from the people — there was his difference in that upper and middle-class society. Yet he was an educated man, with six or seven languages at command — better educated than they were, with a richer literary culture. Nevertheless, it was not this that gave him his originality and force, the conviction he communicated. That came from the freshness of his vision, the angle from which he saw the problems of society, the raw experience of his own impoverished, peasant youth. Thus he saw things so much more intensely, in flesh and blood, than the cool, middle-class calculators of the Utilitarians, of the Philosophical Radicals, of the *Edinburgh Review* — with all of whom he had some association, yet broke with them all. He just could not fit in; yet he knew, from experience, where the shoe pinched, what the facts about human nature were, where the doctrinaires and the intellectuals were wrong.

Nevertheless, he was an intellectual too — only with far greater imagination, a more original humour, a penetrating perception of character and singular gifts for expressing it all. (He was the foremost exponent of the German influence in his time: it did him nothing but harm.) The combination of his gifts, his intense moral sincerity, his earnestness and his energy, with his class-origins, made him something of a portent: his view opened up vistas unglimpsed by the conventional *bourgeois* intellectuals of his time. They, though not all convinced, had the sense to appreciate this and learn from him.

Then, too, as G. M. Trevelyan — an aristocrat who was a great admirer of Carlyle — used to insist, there was a marked contrast between the early Carlyle, full of compassion and sympathy, and the later, when the fires had burned down, weary with the long contemplation of the record of human folly in history and politics, with no faith or hope or compassion left — for folly exhausts compassion — with only the husks to feed on, the cult of power in itself, and for the rest a smouldering contempt.

# XXI

## MACAULAY'S ESSAYS

AMONG the number of remarkable books whose publication distinguished the year 1843 was Macaulay's *Essays*. We owe their appearance at that time to the Americans. Macaulay had previously considered publishing his reviews in book form and turned the idea down. For all his cocksure certainty he was a modest man. He did not think so highly of his essays as the public did. 'The public judges, and ought to judge, indulgently of periodical works,' he wrote to the editor of the *Edinburgh Review*. 'They are not expected to be highly finished. Their natural life is only six weeks.' But his hand was forced in the matter. When, not content with collecting and publishing his reviews (without permission or remuneration) in the United States, American publishers sent over copies in their hundreds to this country, Macaulay was forced to act. We have reason to be grateful. So far from being confined to a natural life of only six weeks, the *Essays* have survived a hundred years. Few works have been so severely criticised, or shown to have more serious errors; and yet there is no doubt that they will go gaily on to their second century. To what do they owe their survival?

First and last, they owe it to their immense readability. The inscription upon Macaulay's statue in the ante-chapel of Trinity at Cambridge, which says that he was the first to write annals in such a way that the truth was more readable than fiction, has an element of exaggeration in it, when you think of Gibbon and Hume before him, not to mention Tacitus. But all the same it lays hold of the essential fact about Macaulay: he is the most readable of historians. The difficulty with him is not, as with some others (the uncongenial Freeman, for example), to take him up but to put him down: the eye races through those exciting, easy pages, fearful lest the chapter or the essay come to an end too soon. And the *Essays*, though not up to the standard Macaulay reached in the *History*, reveal this particular quality at its highest.

Whatever we may think of his point of view, and however much we must take exception to what he says, there is no doubt about the pleasure he has given now to generations and will continue to give. Sir George Otto Trevelyan tells us that the demand for Macaulay went up and down, in the nineteenth century, with the demand for coal. Did that reflect Victorian reading habits? Anyhow I can imagine no more cheerful and stimulating companion for winter evenings by the fireside — if there are coal-fires nowadays. As Macaulay himself says of the pleasures of reading: 'Plato is never sullen. Dante does not stay too long.'

And the *Essays* are incomparable for young people who are just beginning to take an interest in things of the mind. How many people owe their first intellectual stimulus to the *Essays*! (The appreciation of the *History*, a maturer work, comes later.) Arthur Balfour, in his *Autobiography*, has expressed the obligation of those hundreds of people, with minds worth speaking of, for whom the *Essays* opened a door to higher things. One can see why this should be: for all that Macaulay was a man of affairs, and even a man of the world, there was something curiously unadult, ungrown-up about him. After Dickens the most famous writer of his day, he remained something of a boy to the end of his life.

What, then, are the qualities which give the *Essays* their appeal?

They have a power of holding the attention to an exceptional degree. And this arises from the fact that their style is essentially conversational — but the conversation is dramatic, declamatory, exciting. In fact the *Essays* are debates. Macaulay in his generous way gave Southey the credit for first hitting upon this form of historical essay; he said that he had merely improved upon it. But what life and vivacity Macaulay gave to it! You can hear the voice, the torrent of that astonishing conversation, which made some people protest (cf. Greville's *Memoirs*), though, like Greville, they usually ended by submitting, fascinated, conquered by him. Again and again one has the sensation of listening to a vivacious discussion among that brilliant circle of young men at Cambridge, or to the famous talk at Holland House. There is all the dramatic excitement of opposing ideas being argued out. There are the intellectual high spirits on every page — always an irresistible quality. There is plenty of good knockabout fun. One cannot but enjoy his attack on Montgomery's *Poems* — would there were someone with a pen like his to deal with the Montgomerys of our day — or his onslaught upon the intolerable prolixity of Professor Nares:

> The work of Dr. Nares has filled us with astonishment similar to that which Captain Lemuel Gulliver felt when first he landed in Brobdingnag, and saw corn as high as the oaks in the New Forest, thimbles as large as buckets, and wrens of the bulk of turkeys. The whole book, and every component part of it, is on a gigantic scale. The title is as long as an ordinary preface: the prefatory matter would furnish out an ordinary book; and the book contains as much reading as an ordinary library. We cannot sum up the merits of the stupendous mass of paper which lies before us better than by saying it consists of about two thousand closely printed quarto pages, that it occupies fifteen hundred inches cubic measure, and that it weighs sixty pounds avoirdupois. Such a book might, before the Deluge, have been considered as light reading by Hilpa and Shallum. But unhappily the life of man is now three-score years and ten; and we cannot but think it somewhat unfair of Dr. Nares to demand from us so large a portion of so short an existence.

And so on.

I used to think that this might be somewhat unfair on poor Dr. Nares; but having tried to read his book, I now sympathise with Macaulay.

Besides high spirits, ceaseless vivacity, firm sense of phrase, a vivid historical imagination, clear-cut and accurate, something more is needed to explain his success as a writer. On the technical side the clue is to be found in his admirable, his infallible power of construction. Macaulay had, what few writers have, an unfailing sense of the paragraph; he took trouble to shape paragraph on to paragraph, like a builder shaping stone to stone, so that the structure rises clear and takes one with it. Whatever it may be, whether argument, or scene, or narrative, he carries the reader along with him. Other factors help to explain his unexampled success, in his field, with the public in his own time. He was a deeply conventional man, a

Philistine of genius; his work appealed to, was the very expression of, the conventionalism, the Philistinism of the Victorian age. He was a moralist of a rather crude kind; he spoke straight to the heart of a society which, almost inexplicably to us, saw everything in moral terms. To him, as to them, everything was either black or it was white. And so we get the fatiguing antitheses in which he saw, altogether too simply, the characters of Warren Hastings, Clive, Marlborough, Bacon, Dr. Johnson, Horace Walpole. Whatever we may think of it as history, there is no doubt that it makes for good reading.

Macaulay's defects were the defects of his qualities. He was very square-cut, definite, downright. He had much of the positiveness of the eighteenth century about him. His taste was formed on Addison, that proto-Victorian, and the writers of the age of Queen Anne. This meant a notable limitation of sympathies — though, even then, those were broader than many of his latter-day critics realise. It was Macaulay, somewhat surprisingly, who said: 'We know no spectacle so ridiculous as the British public in one of its periodical fits of morality.' (If it had not been for that magisterial 'we', it might have been Matthew Arnold speaking.) His essay on the Restoration dramatists shows him a good deal less sympathetic to Puritanism than might have been feared from the son of Zachary Macaulay, brought up in the strictest circle of the Clapham sect.

The pity is that Macaulay had such power, such unique vividness, that when he was wrong, as he often was, he has impressed his own version upon the English mind more firmly than the truth. His treatment of Warren Hastings and Marlborough are outstanding cases in point. One might almost say that his misrepresentation of Hastings was responsible for the Indian attitude towards the history of British rule in India. What people other than the English would have been so careless of their own case, so unjust to themselves, as to prescribe the reading of Macaulay's essay on Warren Hastings in their schools and universities? The English have a weakness for depreciating their great men. Most people must still be under the impression that Marlborough, though a splendid soldier, was a bad man. That is the view that Macaulay has fixed upon us.

It is untrue that Marlborough was a bad man: he was a cold, contriving, controlled man; but in addition to his genius as a soldier, he was a humane man, not without a heart. Sir Winston Churchill's Life of his ancestor has disproved Macaulay once and for all.

Nevertheless, the exaggeratedly high standards which Macaulay stood for were an important element in forming the Victorian outlook. Though the Victorians kidded themselves a lot, they were genuinely high-minded.

It is interesting to note Macaulay's own modest estimate of his *Essays*:

In spite of the applause and the profit, neither of which I despise, I am sorry that it had become necessary to republish these papers. There are few of them which I read with satisfaction. Those few, however, are generally the latest, and this is a consolatory circumstance. The most hostile critic must admit, I think, that I have improved greatly as a writer. The third volume seems to me worth two of the second, and the second worth ten of the first.

That gives one a useful clue to the correct estimation of the *Essays*; what is needed is a dependable guide to them for the use of the unwary.

# XXII

# THE NEGLECTED FROUDE

## I

COMING up through Devon the other day, the slopes of Dartmoor in view from the train, succeeded by the spacious green landscape from Ivybridge to Brent, then the reddened waves curling in to the foot of the red cliffs by Teignmouth, I derived a pointed pleasure from reading that book of a Devonshireman, Froude's *The Nemesis of Faith*.

Of all the great Victorians Froude is the writer now most neglected and most worth while reviving. There is so much in him that should appeal to our age; in some ways he had more affinities with the twentieth century than with the nineteenth: the strain of scepticism in him for one thing, the historian's relativism that made him see religions more as myths and men's philosophies as rationalisations of their interests and desires; his independence of mind, detached from either party in politics, which saw the cardinal importance of good leadership to a people rather than the empty *clichés* of demagogic appeal.

And what an excellent writer, what a good natural style! So infinitely preferable to Carlyle, to whom he deferred, like the rest of the Victorians, as a major prophet. I am not sure whether, in addition to writing better, he had not more to offer in what he said, certainly more balance, than Carlyle had. Froude was the better historian, a better, if less original writer, a more sceptical, a more subtle, intelligence.

Perhaps one should not be surprised that such a man was so controversial a figure to the Victorians. They liked their categories to be distinct and clear:

> Every boy and every gal,
> That's born into the world alive,
> Is either a little Liberal,
> Or else a little Conservative.

One was either a Protestant or else a Roman Catholic, either a High Churchman or a Low Churchman, a little Englander or an Imperialist. James Anthony Froude fell not between two stools, but among them all. The younger brother of Hurrell Froude, Newman's early colleague in the leadership of the Oxford Movement, and as such a protégé of Newman, the young Anthony found that he could not believe his nonsense, lost his faith and became an agnostic. So to all the Tractarians he was an apostate, and Oxford rejected him as an unbeliever. When he found faith, of a kind, through Carlyle it was an unsectarian sort of Protestantism that made him glorify the Reformation in his *History of England*. This redoubled his offence in Oxford eyes. In his early years a liberal modernist, his love of the sea and his devotion to the Elizabethan seamen made him an Imperialist. This got him detested by Gladstonian Liberals and Little Englanders like Professor Freeman. At the same time, though an Empire man, neither he nor Carlyle could stand the cynic and *poseur* in Disraeli; over his pro-Turkish, anti-Russian policy they were in agreement with Gladstone. Where were they to go?

All this is only to say that Froude was himself, a highly individual and original man of genius. Though he fitted into none of the categories, he was read by more people than any other historian, except Macaulay. He had a regular public of scores of thousands. This did not endear him to the academics, whom for the rest he consistently out-wrote; nor did the fact that he did not seek their society: he enjoyed that of cultivated public men, Lord Lansdowne and Lord Caernarvon. A handsome, out-of-doors man, a keen yachtsman and angler, he was also a favourite with clever women, like Lady Derby and Mrs. Carlyle. Perhaps it was too unfair — but in return he was treated with great unfairness. In the end, the best academic of them all, Bishop Stubbs, admitted: 'Froude is a man of genius, and he has been treated abominably.'

All the same, it is a little difficult to understand quite why Froude was so much harassed and attacked. Every book of his provoked an outburst of criticism and controversy from the first to the last. His personality itself was regarded, I think very unjustly, as in some curious way questionable. It was a strange,

and characteristic, fate that shrouded his greatest friendship
and the chief intellectual influence in his later life, that of
Carlyle, in a more resounding storm of controversy than any
other.

Yet he was read. He held people's attention. He had admirers, if few defenders and no followers. He was a lonely
figure, at the same time as he was much sought after and a
distinguished person in society. But the incessant criticism had
an effect upon him, though he kept himself in restraint and
hardly referred in his writings to the detraction which followed
him all his days. Lytton Strachey has tried to put the vendetta
with which Freeman pursued Froude in a comic light; in reality
it was anything but comic, and shows up Strachey as always
ready to sacrifice truth to a joke. On Froude the ceaseless
attacks had the effect of driving him in upon himself, making
him aloof and reserved, and giving him a rather cynical air in
public contacts — though with his intimates he was an open
and brilliant talker on a wide range of subjects. In his last illness
he insisted that his letters and private papers be destroyed.

The result is that he is much less well known than many
lesser men among the Victorians. If we had only had something
comparable to Sir George Otto Trevelyan's classic *Life and
Letters of Macaulay* . . . The materials for it were there all right:
the background of that brilliant family of brothers, the master-
ful figure of Archdeacon Froude, the enchanting countryside
of the Dart where they were all brought up, the Oxford of the
Oxford Movement with Froude's close contact with its leaders,
the friendships with Matthew Arnold, Clough, Carlyle, the
life in Wales and on the Devon coast with its open-air interests,
angling, sea-fishing, sailing, the voyages he made all over the
world, like his West Country forebears, the Forgotten Worthies
whom he recalled in a famous essay. I cannot help thinking
that he was unlucky to have had quite so much trouble. *The
Nemesis of Faith* is chiefly known for having been publicly burnt
by the Sub-Rector of his college at Oxford when Froude was a
young Fellow. It is deserving of attention on more serious
grounds and for its own sake. Its subject is the ferment of thought
about the foundations of faith stirred up by the Oxford Movement, the dilemma of belief which was such a critical issue

to sensitive minds in the mid-nineteenth century, especially to those brought up in a clerical environment like Froude, whose livelihood and career were involved in it.

We need not pay much attention to the story: it is the autobiography in it that counts. And though Froude was forced to disclaim that it was autobiographical, in a preface to the second edition (1849), in fact there was no mistaking the parallel between his hero's case and his own. Markham Sutherland has the same struggle with his father, the same difficulties about the clerical career — which, like Froude, who stopped at deacon's orders, he drops — the same intellectual doubts about the inspiration of the Bible, the divinity of Christ, the historic and exclusive claims of Christianity, the same horror of the doctrine of eternal punishment. Religions were mainly myths; truth was not to be found in either of the rival armies that claimed so loudly to be her champions. At the same time as he dis-believed in any of the particular revelations which made such exclusive — and mutually conflicting — claims to allegiance, 'a profound belief in God and in God's providence lay at the very core of his soul'. The stage is set for the historian of the Reformation in England, when God had shown himself to be distinctly on the Protestant side.

Incredible as it may seem, Froude was sometimes charged, on the basis of what he wrote about himself under the guise of Edward Fowler in his first story, 'The Spirit's Trials', with moral cowardice. One would have thought it an act of great courage on Froude's part to have published the book at all. It lost him his Fellowship; it lost him (fortunately for him) a job in Tasmania; for a time he had to depend upon the generous-hearted hospitality of Kingsley. The old archdeacon, who had bought up and destroyed as many copies as he could of his son's previous book, *The Shadows of the Clouds*, cut off supplies at this second offence.

Both books are chiefly interesting from the autobiographical point of view. The story 'The Spirit's Trials' in the first book contains a shocking indictment of the bullying at Westminster when Froude was a boy there. It is said that he suffered from hernia as the result of his physical maltreatment. He certainly had to be taken away, and he fancied that it made him a moral

P

coward. Later, he tells us, he had to face the weaknesses that such treatment engendered in him, and he was able to conquer them — but not till years after. These two books of the 1840s tell us, under a thin disguise, the story of his intellectual and moral struggle. Those years in which he wrote them were the formative years, when he worked out, after the disturbance that Newman made in his mental life and the agitation had subsided, the position from which he confronted and carried out his own life's work.

There is much more to interest the reader in both books, especially in *The Nemesis of Faith*. I doubt if anywhere one gets a more intimate sense of the source of Newman's hold over the young men of his generation at Oxford. Froude could never forget his fascination, and, far as he moved away from him in intellectual position, he always thought of him as one of the two men of indubitable genius of the age: Newman and Carlyle. Forty years later he wrote a study, 'The Oxford Counter-Reformation', in which he speaks of Newman, now a Cardinal, immensely old and celebrated, with the same inner feeling for him as when an undergraduate he heard that voice from the pulpit at St. Mary's. He had brought Newman in as the *deus ex machina* at the end of the *Nemesis* — an extraordinary instance of the fascination, almost a kind of wish-fulfilment, for the man from whom he had departed:

How often in old college years he had hung upon those lips; that voice so keen, so preternaturally sweet, whose very whisper used to thrill through crowded churches, when every breath was held to hear; that calm, grey eye; those features, so stern, and yet so gentle.

He finds exactly the right phrase to describe the personality that flowered from such sensitiveness under such self-discipline; he speaks of the 'silvery loveliness of character' that resulted from it.

Then, too, we can trace in the moving descriptive passages of these little volumes the evocative cadences, the foreshadowings of famous pages he was to write at the height of his powers:

The old black wood lies round the house as it lay then, but I have no fear now of its dark hollows, of the black glades under its trees. There are no fairies and no ghosts there any more; only the church bells and the church music have anything of the old tones, and they are silent, too, except at rare, mournful, gusty intervals.

Where did he get the secret of such silvery cadences? Where, indeed, but from Newman himself? The apologist of the Protestant Reformation was the Cardinal's greatest pupil.

## II

Froude was the only historian of the nineteenth century whom we can place beside Macaulay and Carlyle, or not far short of them, for his gifts as a writer and his appeal to the reading public. Like them he was no constipated academic historian; though, just as Macaulay was an authority on seventeenth-century England, so Froude was a master in the field of six-teenth-century history, his masterpiece a great book in several volumes, *A History of England from the Accession of Henry VIII to the Defeat of the Armada*. More delightful, and more easily appreciated, are Froude's four volumes of historical essays, *Short Studies on Great Subjects*.

Froude, like Macaulay, had a marked gift for narration; he was a wonderful story-teller, with a vivid, coloured, flexible style, charged with emotion, capable of rendering everything he felt. He had an acute sense of drama in history; his description of such a scene as the execution of Mary Queen of Scots is justly famous, and appears in the *Oxford Book of English Prose*. He had a subtler sense of character than Macaulay, if not so sharp a perception of human shortcomings as Carlyle.

This being so, it is not surprising that Froude should have tried his hand at a novel. As a young man, his first books were two slight autobiographical novels, *The Shadows of the Clouds* and *The Nemesis of Faith*, which earned him some notoriety. In his maturity, a famous historian, he turned aside to write a novel which I think a fine one, yet which won no success at all. I prefer *The Two Chiefs of Dunboy* to many Victorian novels, to those of Froude's brother-in-law, Charles Kingsley, for example. How to account for not the writer's but the public's failure to appreciate it?

I think it is entirely due to the absence of a 'love-interest', or indeed of any women at all, in the book. But it is an absurd limitation, to expect every novel to deal with the theme of love as if that were the only subject in all human experience for the widest and most diverse of literary forms. It is a man's world that is depicted — which adds to its interest and freshness, as with *Moby Dick* or *Kim* or *Treasure Island*. How bored one is apt to feel the moment one finds one's feet set upon the trampled and soggy paths of ordinary sexual emotions, at finding oneself let in once more for the weary developments of this particular aspect of human relations, under a cloud of feminine sensibility — to which the modern novel seems to have succumbed!

Nothing of this in Froude — with the result that his novel is forgotten, though it has memorable qualities. A warm but not uncritical admirer of Froude, I had always thought that the *Two Chiefs of Dunboy* must deal with that last episode in the Irish war at the end of Elizabeth's reign: the desperate defence against Carew, the threat to blow the castle up, the surrender, the razing of it to the ground, so that when one visits that remote spot there is nothing left but a hump under the grass. Later, a house was built higher up the slope looking down on the creek.

Froude's story deals not with the vanished castle but with the later house; it is placed not in Elizabeth's reign but in the eighteenth century, not long after the 1745 Rebellion. The essential situation is unchanged — so like Irish history: still the possession is contested between the old Irish owner, Morty O'Sullivan, a rebel and exile who has fought for the Pretender and now lives the life of a soldier of fortune, privateer and pirate, and a new English 'undertaker', Colonel Goring, who had done execution on the Jacobites at Culloden, a belated Calvinist of a seventeenth-century type, such as fascinated Froude and his master Carlyle.

The conflict between these two gives us the story, and at every point it holds the attention — the attention of an adult mind interested in the historic issue of Irish policy, indeed of all government, the problems of authority and liberty. The story is a symbolic one: it clinches and concentrates the whole issue of the relation between England and Ireland in these last centuries. But the characters are not mere symbols: they are fully conceived and finely drawn, especially those of the two protagonists, Morty and the Colonel. The other men are no less convincing, the sinister Sylvester — all that is most odious in an informer, treacherous and revengeful; the leading men in Dublin, the magnificent and cynical Primate Stone, Speaker Shannon and others. These are described rather from the outside. But there is one character in the book, who plays no part in the action, yet fairly clearly speaks for Froude himself: the other Froude, the sceptic, never wholly submerged by the Calvinist lava of Carlyle.

Fitzherbert — an academic, a Fellow of Trinity — 'distrusted enthusiasm, and his temperament inclined him to the sceptical tendencies of the age. . . . When men talked of duty and disinterested motives. Fitzherbert generally believed them to be either fools or rogues. He used to say that on the rare occasions when he had gone against his own interest to do something which he thought right, he had found invariably that he had better have left it alone. Once or twice he had gone out of his way to be kind to people at his own cost. He had always had his face scratched for it. They would take what he gave, but they never forgave him for laying them under an obligation.' One recognises the overtone when a writer is writing of himself. It is a recognisable expression of the resentment he felt at the treatment he received from Carlyle's niece over the great biography — one of the three finest in our literature.

The scenes are as exciting as the changes of atmosphere — the way a disaffected countryside moves sensibly from sullen acquiescence to overt intimidation with a subtle transition in the balance of power. Colonel Goring gets an early intimation of what is in store for him when he comes upon the skull of a tithe-proctor who had been buried alive in the wastes high about Dunboy. The duel with Morty at the gathering of the O'Sullivan clan, where the Colonel carries off the honours, is exciting and admirably done. So is the chase of Morty's ship by a government frigate and his breath-taking escape through an unmarked, impracticable passage from Bantry bay into the Kenmare river. Froude had sailed all these waters and knew them well: no-one ever wrote better than he about sailing. For the scenes in the extravagant, patrician society of Georgian Dublin, Froude drew upon the historical memoirs of the time: they make a striking contrast. The ambush at the forge to which Colonel Goring is enticed to be murdered and Morty's own end, the burning of the house over his head, are equally exciting. I wonder no English film-company has thought of filming the book. They would have the advantage of the scenes being laid in what Froude himself thought the most beautiful country in the world.

Froude wrote of it with the pellucid clarity of the sea itself:

Bally Quoilach Bay is an estuary of the Kenmare River, lying between Ardgroom and Dursey Island, and immediately opposite to Derrynane. The entrance is covered by a long, flat-topped rocky Island, ground smooth by glaciers, which forms a natural breakwater, while inside there are hidden shoals and reefs, through which there is but one passage, that twists and winds like a snake . . . Inside, however, when these perils are all passed, there is in one corner of the bay a quiet basin into which even the swell of the open ocean fails to penetrate, with a bottom of sand which slopes up gradually to a beach of powdered sea-shell. At a little distance is the mouth of a small river, like that where Ulysses landed in Phoeacia, and here too Kings' daughters and their maidens may have washed their house-linen and spread it to dry on the shingle, for the spot was the favourite haunt of sea-rovers.

There are many such descriptive passages throughout the book. Froude's biographer, Herbert Paul, held that 'for distinction of style and beauty of thought it may be compared with the greatest of historical romances'. In situation and subject it reminds one most of *Redgauntlet*. Froude has been usually regarded as hostile to the Irish; but this book bears witness not only to his perceptive understanding of them, but to a wide range of sympathy with them. As Herbert Paul says, 'he would have done anything for the Irish, except allow them to govern themselves'. It is pleasant to think that one of the warmest admirers of the book was the magnanimous Gladstone, who was very much on the other side politically, particularly over Ireland.

As for Froude's prescience — he owed it to his freedom from party-ties, to his independence, his honesty and candour of spirit that he saw much farther than conventional people without his originality — there are evidences throughout the book. It is an historian's novel and so gets all the points right as few historical novels do — even if, at the same time, it suffers from a little too much comment and explanation. Here is Froude's real belief: 'Any country may have its liberty, when there is manhood there that will live free or die . . . A brave people always wins in the end, for it costs more to hold them than to let them go.' To which someone replies: 'A dale of blood would be running before we could drive the redcoats out, and a dale more would run among ourselves when we had seen the last of them and the land was our own.'

That, too, proved to be true. Anyone visiting Dunboy today will find the ruined and blackened shell of a Victorian country-house, cows and sheep walking in and out of doors and windows, the pleasure-grounds waste and overgrown, the trees forlorn and torn, the whole scene one of eloquent desolation.

# XXIII

## KILVERT'S DIARY

### I

KILVERT is a real literary discovery.[1] Just before the war there came to light some twenty-two notebooks containing the diary of this young Victorian clergyman. It makes fascinating reading; for, even apart from a liking for diaries in general, this one had exceptional qualities. It gives a sensitive and observant picture of country life in the 1870s, mostly of Radnorshire and central Wales, where Kilvert was a curate, but also of the West Country, for his home was in Wiltshire, and during this year, 1870-1, he visited a good deal in Cornwall, Devon and Somerset. Above all, he wrote like an angel; his gift was for prose rather than verse — though his verses are charming enough. The result is an addition to literature. In an odd way, the discovery of this unknown curate reminds one of the resurrection of Gerard Hopkins, though Kilvert was a gentler, less original genius than that.

Kilvert came from a good West Country family; and, though he spent most of the years covered by his diary as a curate in a remote part of Wales, he did not think of it as exile, but lived a full and enjoyable social life. He was a welcome guest at all the country houses round, especially at Clyro Court, in his own parish, with the family at which he was on affectionate terms. He was evidently sociable and likeable, though he had a gift for solitude too, and can say: 'I have a peculiar dislike to meeting people, and a peculiar liking for a deserted road.' He was an out-of-doors man who liked riding, fishing and, above all, walking — that old-fashioned pursuit of the intellectually-minded. Not that he was an intellectual; he does not appear to have been much of a reader; his reactions to public events — the Franco-German War, the Mordaunt case — were conventional enough. He was something more and better than that; he was an artist, with a passionate love of life.

[1] *Kilvert's Diary*, ed. by William Plomer, 1938.

He noticed everything; and his position as parson opened all doors to him. Very few people could have kept such a diary. It was not only the life of the country gentry that he knew but also of all the country people — farmers and labourers, the villagers, the poor. He notes their superstitions and beliefs, their good looks — he was extraordinarily sensitive to physical beauty whether in women or men, though particularly in girls. He was no less attracted by natural beauty, by mountains and hills, birds and flowers. And he was an artist in expressing his passion. The Diary is full of such passages as this:

The peewits were sweeping, rolling and tumbling in the hot blue air about the tall trees with a strange deep mysterious hustling and quavering sound from their great wings.

Or this, which reminds one of Hopkins by its phrasing:

Last night there was a sharp frost, the crescent moon hung cold and keen, and the stars glittered and flashed gloriously. Orion all in a move of brilliance.

There is a beautiful passage describing what he calls the Easter Eve Idyll — the custom of dressing the graves in the churchyard with flowers on Easter Eve — and concluding with an imaginative phrase:

As I walked down the Churchyard alone the decked graves had a strange effect in the moonlight and looked as if the people had laid down to sleep for the night out of doors, ready dressed to rise early on Easter morning.

It was a very varied, pulsating, natural life in that Welsh countryside that he observed so lovingly. There was always something interesting happening in Clyro; there are stories enough in the Diary to stock a short-story writer. Kilvert's account of the funeral of his great-aunt, Miss Maria Kilvert, the house in the College Green at Worcester, the haughty, un-friendly servants who knew that the wilful old lady was leaving her money away from the family, the service, the Canons, the reading of the will, show that the diarist had the makings of a novelist in him — it reads like Trollope.

What would he have become had he lived? With his social

gifts, perhaps a canon, or an archdeacon? He died when he was still under forty, leaving behind him this exquisite Diary and a few poems. But we are grateful for what we have, for he is a distinguished addition to the Victorian age. What a pleasure it is to immerse oneself in that secure Victorian life — archery and croquet on the lawn, tea under the trees, picnics on the un-spoiled Cornish coast, grapes and claret on a grassy bank, pleasant dinner-parties at Clyro Court, the busy kindly life centring upon the Church. The characters of the Diary have as full and rounded a reality as in the best novels; they have the substance of life, and live in the imagination.

## II

The second volume of *Kilvert's Diary* strengthens the impression that here we have an original work of beauty and charm, a book that is an addition to literature. The work to which it most closely approximates in character is Dorothy Words-worth's *Journals*. *Kilvert's Diary* does not come behind hers in its quality of observing physical beauty of every kind, whether of landscape, sky, flowers, men or women, or in the power of rendering it directly, sometimes with an acute nostalgic effect. He surpasses Dorothy Wordsworth in the humanity of his diary: he had an extraordinary degree of sympathy for people, as marked as that for flowers and animals. It is clear that they responded to him, and the result is in the breathing lifelikeness of his book, the stories of their lives simple people tell him, the intimate apprehension of character, the convincing portraits of the people of his Welsh and Wiltshire countrysides, his sus-ceptibility to the charm of young women and girls, which, held in as it had to be in his position as a Victorian clergyman, went near at times to oversetting him. He sometimes trembled on the brink, like the occasion when he nearly got out of the railway compartment to pursue the country girl he fell for, a couple of stations before his own. Poor Kilvert! It is clear that he was spoiling for marriage. That he was not already married was not his fault: it was due to the difficulty of his social position; after seven and a half years of his curacy at Clyro, to the lovely Brecon and Radnorshire background of which the Diary owes so much, he was still without a living. He does not seem to have had any push; he was a man of extreme sensibility and charm, an artist, a man with a touch of genius.

The one advantage which Dorothy Wordsworth has over him is that she lived among men of genius. Kilvert, though he was of good family and passed his life with the best of country society, knew nobody in the literary world. This volume of his Diary ends with a visit to William Barnes, the Dorsetshire poet, also a clergyman — and that was his highest flight in this sphere. In a sense he lived to himself, and wrote for himself; hence the integrity, the transparent sincerity, of his Diary. Is there not a romance in the discovery of this unknown figure, a young Victorian clergyman whom nobody knew, yet who wrote as well as Dorothy Wordsworth?

I place his Diary among the best half-dozen or dozen ever written in England. It is the quintessence of the countryside and country life, in that last age when it was still complete and entire, unravaged, and people thought it would go on for ever, as it had always been, essentially unchanged. No need to emphasise how well he wrote of it:

The oatladen waggon came creaking and swaying and sweeping the hedge along the edge of a brow high above the house and then down a steep rough path into the rickyard.

Or again:

A group of people were sitting in the churchyard among the graves, and one woman was dressing a green grave with scarlet and white flowers near one of the vast black yews.

Or:

The western sky was in a splendour and every branch and twig stood out clear against the glow and the two twin sister silver birches leaned towards each other and kissed each other in the dusk.

### III

What is the secret of Kilvert? He has this mark of genius, among others, that he has the faculty of making us insatiably curious about him. We want to know *all* about him, as we long to know what sort of man Tennyson was, or the mystery of Newman, or what it was that happened to Gerard Manley Hopkins. We should like to know so much more about what went on in him, what happened to the girls he fell in love with and what to him in the end. He has the appeal of holding a secret for us; there is something elusive about him. At the same time as we are in close touch with him, share his tremulous sensibility, there remains something withdrawn. He was that rare creature, a diarist who was not in the least egoistic, nor even introspective. What he shares with us is his own apprehension of life, completely and without reserve; but life viewed always in its aesthetic aspect, *qua* beauty, as one who was essentially an artist saw it.

Kilvert's is not the usual clergyman's diary at all; nor even like Parson Woodforde, who was so much concerned about eating. Very little in Kilvert's Diary about eating: only the dinner he gave to his farmers his first year at Bredwardine. But that sounds a good one: 'white soup, roast beef, boiled chickens and ham, curried rabbit, stewed wood-pigeons, beef-steak pie, potatoes and stewed celery, plum pudding, custard, plum tart, mince pies, apricot jam tart'. No, the point about Kilvert is that he was really a poet in prose. When the Diary first appeared I described it as the nearest thing to Dorothy Wordsworth's *Journals*. It is pleasing now to find Kilvert's mother presenting him with Dorothy Wordsworth on his birthday, and her name invoked on his last page. He pays a visit to Brinsop Court and the sitting-room where 'dear Dorothy Wordsworth spent much of her time'.

When the last volume opens, he is still acting as curate to his father at Langley Burrell in Wiltshire, having returned from Clyro in Wales, where so much of the story in the first two volumes passes. At once, from the first page his spell is upon us. Here is Seagry Mill in May, Kilvert lying back on the river bank while his father fishes:

It was a glorious afternoon, unclouded, and the meadows shone dazzling like a golden sea in the glory of the sheets of buttercups. The deep, dark river, still and glassy, seemed to be asleep and motionless except when a leaf or blossom floated slowly by. The cattle by the mill plashed and trampled among the rushes and river flags and water lilies in the shallow places, and the miller Godwin came down with a bucket to draw water from the pool.

It is a perfect landscape, like a small Constable; and that is the kind of thing that Kilvert can do on every page. More often, he is rendering life, from close-up observation and with the tenderest sympathy for every kind of human being. Every door was open to him, not only the squire's, the surrounding gentry and clergy but also the farmers and the poor. Still, the world they all inhabited was a secure and quiet one: their greatest disasters an occasional railway accident, or a shipwreck. What occupied much more of the foreground were such matters as the Squire's dismissal of old George Jefferies from leading the singing in church, the installation of a harmonium which almost led to a breach between manor-house and rectory. 'How strange it is that the Squire is such a distant man about music,' says Alice Matthews. It is a world of rural deans, and tea on rectory lawns under the trees and, after tea, archery or croquet, or picking flowers in the meads of Wiltshire for decorating the church, of pretty Victorian girls looking over the parapet of the bridge while the river flows by. And all the while there is one, a little apart, watching life itself flowing by, trying to catch it on the wing, to ensnare a momentary aspect of its beauty, with what quivering sensibility, with what nostalgia for what is passing, even as it passes. Here is Christmas Day, 1874:

This morning we plainly heard the six beautiful fatal bells of Bremhill ringing a Christmas peal through the frosty air.

Next day, St. Stephen's Day, he goes to visit a sick child who is in pain, hoping to read her to sleep:

The light shone through the night from the sick girl's chamber window, the night was still, an owl hooted out of the South and the mighty hunter Orion with his glittering sword silently overstrode the earth.

On Christmas Day:

As I came home the sky was black and thick with snow, but through the gloom one great lone star was burning in the East. We have seen His star in the East.

There is, however, more to Kilvert than this lonely recording of natural beauty. When he gets back to Wales his Diary quickens with an intenser life; he loved the Welsh, their warm, more percipient, more emotional life — so much so that he fancied he had Welsh blood. The characters become more vivid, more strange; there is Priscilla Price, who lived with her idiot step-daughter, could remember the coronation of George IV and tell him all sorts of human oddities such as he loved. He once asked James Meredith:

'James, tell me the truth, did you ever see the oxen kneel on old Christmas Eve at the Weston?' And he said, 'No, I never saw them kneel at the Weston, but when I was at Hinton at Staunton-on-Wye I saw them. I was watching them on old Christmas Eve and at 12 o'clock the oxen that were standing knelt down upon their knees and those that were lying down rose up on their knees and there they stayed kneeling and moaning, the tears running down their faces.'

It is like Thomas Hardy: curious to think that these two who were so near each other in spirit, and writing at the same time, should have known nothing of each other. But then, it is part of the romance of Kilvert that nobody should have known of him as a writer, and then within a few years a new figure should have been suddenly added to English letters from that vanished Victorian world.

# XXIV

# RUDYARD KIPLING

KIPLING offers the most notorious case of the depreciation, indeed the consistent denigration, of a man of genius after his death. Not even Tennyson had to endure such wilful mis-understanding, such perversion of critical justice. It must be admitted that both of them offered sufficiently obvious targets to the mean-spirited, incapable of understanding the positive content of their work or accounting for the extraordinary extent of their appeal, *on several levels* — to use a cliché of the Leavis School. This depreciation of a man of genius by the men of taste is a phenomenon of some significance, not without its distasteful elements. There is, for one thing, that of sheer envy — as one of these critics was recently candid enough to admit: the envy of the mere critic for the indefeasibly creative writer.

There is, first of all, the question of political bias. All his life Kipling naturally attracted the opposition of anti-Imperial-ists, liberals of the Left. He was taken too simply as the laureate of the British Empire, as in effect he was, at its Victorian apogee, at its brassiest period just before and during the Boer War.

There are two observations to make on this. Kipling's attitude was very different from what it is commonly misrepresented as being. It was not that of a vulgar boastfulness, but of a constant emphasis on moral responsibility, on duty and service, on the obligations of Empire, the trust confided, the true worth demanded of such a position in the world, the need to justify it by works — as it certainly was justified in India. The very moralism may not be to our liking, but that was its nature.

And there is something more curious — Kipling's extra-ordinary intuitive sense told him how tenuous it all was, that the whole fabric hung by the thread of service and could so easily vanish. The famous hymn, *Recessional*, written at the time of the Diamond Jubilee of 1897, which expresses the essence of Kipling's gospel of Empire as a trust under God, has the lines —

> Lo, all our pomp of yesterday
> Is one with Nineveh and Tyre.

How prophetically he spoke!

There is, further, the elementary mistake in criticism of judging a man's work by whether one agrees with his opinions. Kipling has been the foremost victim of this crudity: the attitude towards him depends very much on whether the viewer is a man of the Right or of the Left, and, since intellectuals incline mostly to the Left, it is in that quarter that least justice is done him and his reputation is most maligned. A critic of better judgment and sense of justice, who happened also to be more genuinely liberal, Quiller-Couch, once said to me: 'I detest his opinions, but I adore his genius.'

This leaves over the question whether Kipling's opinions were so detestable, or so wrong. For myself, I think not.

There is the further question whether the manner in which he expressed them was not more uncongenial than what he said. We must take into account some historical circumstances here — the time in which he was writing, the late Victorian inheritance, Edwardian oracularity and opulence. There was Kipling's own personal inheritance, the earlier brassiness, the youthful knowingness that always remained with him, the iteration, the preaching. There, in a word, is the most distasteful of his characteristics of style, and, as with D. H. Lawrence, it comes from the Nonconformist background.

And what of the vulgarity? The men of taste make such heavy weather of this, as with Elgar, and are equally impercipient. Taste has nothing whatever to do with creativeness — is often a hinderance to it, discourages it, may even destroy it, if the creative impulse is not robust and strong. If it is, it often goes along with vulgarity. What about Dickens, or Balzac, or, for that matter, Shakespeare?

I am not arguing that it is a good thing in itself, but it springs out of something more important to creation than mere good taste — contact with the common facts of life, common people, their emotions and affections, their weaknesses and strengths, the broad range of men's experience, rootedness in the human condition. What is important is to transcend this, express it in works of art; and that Kipling certainly did.

For he was at the same time a most conscious artist, with unexpected affinities: the pre-Raphaelite particularity of detail, the hard gem-like surface, the taste for the exotic, the strange, the highly-coloured. He was affected, too, by both the realism and Parnassianism of contemporary French literature. He was a connoisseur of words, of technical phrases, full of stylistic tricks — some of which one may not like — as clever as one of his own monkeys (of whom he always gives such an unfavourable portrait).

This makes a very strange apparition — as Henry James and Stevenson, themselves men of genius, saw upon the young Kipling's appearance over the horizon: the combination of the common with the esoteric, the vulgar with the sublime, the journalistic with the prophetic, the knowing and the technical with the intuitional and inspired.

Really, what unfair advantages Kipling had! The simple truth is that he was a wonderful writer, and it all came to him as easy as ABC, for he *was* inspired. (See his autobiography, *Something of Myself* — one of the most revealing of books, in spite of its marked reticence, about the ways of a writer.)

Lionel Curtis, who knew Kipling well, used to tell me that he was really two men: there was the *Morning Post* reactionary, who hated everything about the modern world and thought it was going to the dogs (isn't it?); and, on the other side, there was the visionary, with his extreme intuitive senses, the gift of second sight, the prophetic, the truly inspired. No one bore more obviously the stigmata of genius.

Kipling certainly had his reward. He was in touch with, and always capable of expressing, the life of common people, particularly of men in their work, at their most characteristic and revealing. The poets of the 1930s merely talked of going to the people; Kipling went. It is doubtful if any writer of such voltage and power has made so effective an impact on them since Dickens. For at the same time as Kipling gave us his pictures of army life — and not so much of the officers (as with

Q

Tolstoy) as of the men themselves — they rewarded him by singing his songs, as they marched to the Boer War, '*Boots*', and '*Stellenbosch*' and '*Pay-pay-pay*'. No great writer was ever a more effective one with the people; perhaps that is what the men of taste find it so hard to forgive.

But what of the issue of cruelty, so often preferred against him by the elect, by the so sensitive, those people who make their sensibility their chief claim upon our attention? Kipling does not flinch at portraying cruelty, and there is cruelty in his stories as there is in life — as there is in Shakespeare, and in other great writers giving a full portrayal of life on all its sides. Would Kipling be such a great writer, so comprehensive and so true to life, had he omitted it?

The men of taste write as if Kipling *liked* cruelty; I read it quite differently. A deeply sensitive man, as we know he was, he is tortured by it in a story like 'The Record of Badalia Herodsfoot'. But he is not sparing us any more than he spares himself — that is how I read it; and the mode in which it is told, the slightly offhand manner, the public school stoicism, do not take me in. It is the story of a man who had known suffering himself, had in fact an intense capacity for suffering, underneath the stoicism, and was to know much more. The sense of suffering suffuses his later work.

What about 'Mary Postgate', so often attacked, made a shibboleth of? It is a different case. It has hatred in it — hatred of the Germans. Any why should it not? — when one considers that the Germans destroyed Kipling's world, our world. Even if there are people so exquisitely moral as to condemn this — leaving aside the fact that that attitude among us had the practical effect of encouraging the Germans to do what they have done in the past century (I agree with Kipling) — even if I were to concede the point in ethics, I certainly do not in aesthetics. Why should hatred and indignation be denied expression in art? That would be to limit it, to exclude from literature some of the greatest works of Swift and Voltaire, Tacitus and Juvenal. The fact that you may not like the situation or the point or the mood is no reason for not seeing that 'Mary Postgate' is a brilliant and terrible story, though I do not myself rate it so highly as 'Badalia Herodsfoot', a masterpiece.

Altogether, Kipling was a far more complex, more strange and tortured spirit than either his detractors or admirers realise — certainly than those simple souls, the captains, colonels and knights-at-arms. For one thing he was not so much an Englishman as a Celt. He was in the marrow of his mind and being — that part from which he created his work — a Celt, one of those small, dark, swarthy men whom the English drove into the recesses of the Highland zone, in the rugged north and west of the island, and who have emerged very notably in our time to add to the variety of the nation.

This is the simple explanation of a good deal that was thought mysterious about Kipling, and of something that was even ambivalent in his attitude. Kipling himself, though he did not say much about it, was more conscious of the fact than, say, Matthew Arnold, of whom the same clue holds.

The Celt in all his variants from Builth to Bally-hoo,
His mental processes are plain — one knows what he will do,
And can logically predicate his finish by his start;
But the English — ah, the English — they are quite a race
  apart.

In telegraphic sentences, half nodded to their friends,
They hint a matter's inwardness — and there the matter ends.
And while the Celt is talking from Valentia to Kirkwall,
The English — ah, the English — don't say anything at all.

It is already a Celtic trait to be so much in love with the English. Lord Baldwin, Kipling's cousin — like him descended from Highland Macdonalds and Welsh Joneses — had it: he conducted a long love-affair with England. 'Understand Baldwin?' Lloyd George once said. 'Of course you can't: he's one of us.'

And Kipling had all the stigmata of the Celtic temperament: an extraordinary gift of intuition, the quick inner sympathy that enabled him to enter into the lives of all sorts and conditions of men — he had even the Highland gift of second sight. It was all this that enabled him to penetrate the *inner* experience of India and give it classic expression in *Kim*, as no other Westerner has done. It is amusing that it should not be the professional political sympathiser but the imperialist of whom this is true. Similarly during the Boer War, it was this laureate of empire with his instinctive sympathy for the fighting soldier who had most understanding of the other side. Take, among others, that fine ballad 'Piet' on the theme of 'respect for the man I fight':

Ah there, Piet! — 'is trousies to 'is knees,
'Is coat-tails lyin' level in the bullet-sprinkled breeze;
'E does not lose 'is rifle an' 'e does not lose 'is seat.
I've known a lot o' people ride a dam' sight worse than Piet.

Then, too, there is the prophetic, the *bardic* note. Kipling was a true prophet; he senses very well the way things were going in the modern world, the weaknesses of democracy, in our own society, in the Empire, in the affairs of the world. Do you know that passage at the end of his *History of the Irish Guards in the Great War,* i.e., the first German war? ' "The prisoner at the Bar", as men then styled Germany, being entirely at home [i.e. after the Armistice and during the occupation] was saving himself to continue the War underground when time, occasion, and dissension among his conquerors should show him his chance. But of this there was no fore-knowledge.' That was written as early as 1922. It was not the intellectuals like Keynes who were right, but men of profound intuition instructed by the historical sense, like Kipling and Churchill. We should have done better to listen to them.

But, of course, it is not popular to be a prophet, especially with the English. And at the end of his life, with genius un-dimmed — indeed, his last stories are the finest he ever wrote, sombre, rich, symbolic, with a deep reading of life — Kipling was a disheartened man: he knew he was not listened to. Now is the moment — the time has come round for him — for us to make reparation.

Among other qualities I like to think of as peculiarly strong among Celts is an intense feeling for place — and here Kipling had a power of evocation equal to, though tenderer than, the fierce intuitive genius of Carlyle. One observes it all through his work, in poems and stories, not least in the *Letters,* written wherever he was, though never more exquisitely than in such magical stories as 'They', or the poems that light *Puck of Pook's Hill.*

Of course, a great deal of Kipling is rhetorical in expression — not all the English like that. But rhetoric is as valid a mode of expression in literature as any other; otherwise how are we to appreciate French literature, in which rhetoric is so very strong an element? All Kipling's sympathies — not only the more superficial sympathies of politics, but also the more profound—were French. And that is revealing: not Teutonic, particularly not in their German manifestation; and with the show the Germans have put on for the twentieth century, who can wonder at that?

I note, too, his particular brand of humour, which is naturally that of exaggeration, like the Irish — observe his instinctive sympathy with them all through his history of the Irish Guards — rather than the modern (entirely modern) English humour of under-emphasis. Why should the under-emphatic, the comedy of understatement, the straight face, the poker face, the elimination — even the punishment — of the pun, be thought the only tolerable sort of humour? It is only a temporary fashion. Why should we Celts be expected to conform? We have our own idiosyncrasies, qualities and quirks of personality to offer. The English world would be much duller and less coloured without us. Do not overlook in Kipling this last characteristic I shall mention: the combination of an extreme sensitiveness with an acutely personal pride.

Nevertheless, it was England that conquered and annexed this Celt, as is the way — to become one of its brightest and proudest luminaries.

> I followed my Duke ere I was a lover,
>   To take from England fief and fee;
> But now this game is the other way over —
>   But now England hath taken me! . . .
>
> As for my comrades in camp and highway,
>   That lift their eyebrows scornfully,
> Tell them their way is not my way —
>   Tell them England hath taken me!

His imaginative discovery of England may be dated to the year 1902 when he came to settle in Sussex, after not only travelling all round the world but also living in three continents,

India, South Africa, America. Few writers have *seen* as much of the world as Kipling. Very rarely has the simple act of settling in the English countryside reaped such a harvest in the imagination. Kipling was at once inspired by it. He wrote to an American friend, 'then we discovered England which we had never done before . . . and went to live in it. England is a wonderful land. It is the most marvellous of all foreign countries that I have ever been in!' Years afterwards he wrote in his autobiography: 'Just beyond the west fringe of our land, in a little valley running from Nowhere to Nothing-at all, stood the long, overgrown slag-heap of a most ancient forge, supposed to have been worked by the Phoenicians and Romans, and since then uninterruptedly till the middle of the eighteenth century. The bracken and rush-patches still hid stray pigs of iron, and if one scratched a few inches through the rabbit-shaven turf, one came on the narrow mule-tracks of peacock-hued furnace-slag laid down in Elizabeth's day. The ghost of a road climbed up out of the dead arena, and crossed our fields, where it was known as "The Gunway", and popularly connected with Armada times. Every foot of that little corner was alive with ghosts and shadows.'

These were the ghosts and shadows that were given shape and substance in the marvellous series of stories that followed in the next decade and that fill especially the two volumes, *Puck of Pook's Hill* and *Rewards and Fairies*. *There* is the inspiration:

> See you the ferny ride that steals
> Into the oak-woods far?
> O that was whence they hewed the keels
> That rolled to Trafalgar . . .
>
> See you the dimpled track that runs
> All hollow through the wheat?
> O that was where they hauled the guns
> That smote King Philip's fleet . . .
>
> See you our little mill that clacks,
> So busy by the brook?
> She has ground her corn and paid her tax
> Ever since Domesday Book.

These stories and poems illuminate every page in the history of Britain, indeed they tell its whole story: from the Romans (remember 'A Centurion of the Thirtieth' and 'On the Great Wall'?), through Viking invasions and Norman Conquest to Gloriana and Armada days; from Edgehill to the Fleet guarding the North Sea that guaranteed our security and freedom, saved our lives, in 1914–18. Though no-one ever felt with more intense grief at what a cost:

> 'Have you news of my boy Jack?'
> *Not this tide.*
> 'When d'you think that he'll come back?'
> *Not with this wind blowing, and this tide.*

And one cannot read his *History of the Irish Guards* without feeling the undercurrent of anguish that runs through it all.

Before the war of 1914 brought to an end that happy world, and the long good fortune of our insular history, he had paralleled those stories with a series of poems, out of the same inspiration, that grew ever finer. The journalist-poet, who had started with *Barrack-Room Ballads* and *Departmental Ditties*, writing in soldiers' vernacular, became the pure poet of 'Merrow Down', 'The Way through the Woods' and many later poems.

Perhaps I may be allowed to turn didactic, as he was, and lay down two propositions. The historian is in some difficulty when confronted with works of historical fiction: they so rarely ring true, in the historian's ear, to the age they profess to evoke. Even *Westward Ho*, which I so much enjoyed as a boy, I cannot away with now. But I never feel that with Kipling's historical tales; it may be partly that they are so charged with poetry, the magic so potent, but it is also that the intuition is faultless and true.

Secondly, Kipling's last stories, far less well known and appreciated, are his finest — such extraordinary stories as 'Uncovenanted Mercies', 'The Wish House', the deeply-moving 'The Gardener', springing from the loss of his only son in the war. The writer of fairy-tales had moved into the zone of tragedy; some of these stories plumb the depths of experience, solitary and alone.

Lastly, no writer was more intimately part of the history of his time: the laureate of the last phase of British rule in India, that unique episode in world-history, the noblest bearer of the imperial idea. 'I hope you don't mind my using the word British Empire' — I quote Sir Winston Churchill. 'It is quite a good word in its proper place.' Remember — as his detractors do not — that Kipling's attitude was never that of a jingo chauvinism: he always underlined the moral responsibilities of government, obligations, duty, true worthiness. His Methodist forbears spoke out in him. So with the Boer War — the soldiers, the fighting-men spoke, never more directly, through him. So with the Navy in the penultimate phase of its long history, the naval struggle with Germany — Kipling spoke for the seamen, for engineer and rating as for captains courageous.

Of all English poets no-one has more widely expressed the life of the whole nation, or been more authentically the voice of its people. We heard a lot from the poets of the 1930s about poetry making a real contact with the life of the people; but it was Kipling who wrote it, not they. The men rewarded him by singing the songs he wrote for them — such songs as 'Boots' or 'The Absent-Minded Beggar' — on their way into battle.

When Disraeli died Lord Salisbury said, 'Zeal for England was the consuming passion of his life.' It is no unworthy passion for an outsider to cherish.

> Take of English earth as much
> As either hand may rightly clutch.
> In the taking of it breathe
> Prayer for all who lie beneath.
> Not the great nor well-bespoke,
> But the mere uncounted folk
> Of whose life and death is none
> Report or lamentation.
> Lay that earth upon thy heart,
> And thy sickness shall depart!

Kipling's spirit comes through his writing as clearly and movingly as ever, for it is a quality of genius to transcend history, not to be subject to time.

The Anglo-Indian in his background and make-up is

obvious; stranger is his intuitive penetration of Indian life, so esoteric to the Westerner, no secret to the author of 'The Miracle of Purun Bhagat' or *Kim*.

In these as in so many of his works, as in Kipling himself, there is the eternal Boy. Genius seems often allied with an arrested emotional development; the emotional life remains at that level — hence the power and reality of the evocation. (Witness, perhaps, one third of his work, not only the *Jungle Books, Just So Stories, Puck of Pook's Hill, Rewards and Fairies*, but many of the other stories and poems.)

The shy, unsatisfactory way of treating sexual love has often been noted — an inability to grapple with it directly, embarrassing in a story like 'The Brushwood Boy'. Nor has the unconscious emotional element escaped attention. Nothing would have more shocked Kipling or perhaps the Anglo-Indians, the officers who adored him, than to have had this made explicit. But the fact is that this was a large, if unrecognised, element in their nature, and one of the psychological forces — the comradeship, mutual loyalty, self-sacrifice, service — that bound the Empire together.

Nevertheless, though Kipling's emotional life remained on that level — with him parenthood seems to have meant essentially sharing in the fantasy-life of his children — his art never ceased to develop and grow.

It is a further irony, with this so famous, so little-known, man that his greatest works are much the least popular and appreciated. These are the stories of his last period, occupying his last three volumes. They are the finest work of all, philosophical and tragic, haunted by pain and grief, sometimes difficult because of symbolism and overtones that one cannot always catch. When one does, as when in 'The Gardener' one recognises the most touching of themes — that of the Magdalen in the garden of the Agony — it is a moment of illumination that one never forgets.

They are written with all the old mastery, but sometimes in an elliptical manner, with such conciseness, everything extraneous cut out, that they are rendered difficult. Even late Henry James is nothing compared with it. In his last phase Kipling added a dimension to his work: those late stories have a sombre poetry; they light up dark places of the soul, the fears and anxieties of men approaching their end, the consolations of the spirit, of having run a good race. They have something of Greek tragedy, something Miltonic, about them.

In the end Kipling had the greatest good fortune that can befall a writer: he completely fulfilled himself in his work, and in his own lifetime was already recognised as a classic.

## An Introduction to *Kim*

The present President of India, the philosopher Radhakrishnan, once said to me that of all Western books about India *Kim* was the best: its author, Rudyard Kipling, really understood India. The reasons for this judgment are quite simple: Kipling knew and loved India deeply; he was a great writer with astonishing gifts of intuition; *Kim* was written at the summit of his powers, carefully and slowly, after long meditation and maturing; among the many works of genius that he executed, *Kim* occupies a central place.

What luck he had with it, what providential, inspired luck! For it is an inspired work, as Kipling was an inspired writer — as he has told us in *Something of Myself*, if the imp of inspiration were not sitting on the end of his pen then nothing would go well. But, we may properly comment, if it were, the result was often a masterpiece. However, with this masterpiece he was taking no chances: there is both inspiration and careful preparation in it, the magic of genius and perfect craftsmanship.

But think of the advantage of the material he had to go into it, fertilised by his own experience: there was the whole life of India to draw upon; at any rate, of Northern India from the hot valley of the Ganges and the plains of Central India to the cool mountain air of the North West Frontier, the eternal snows of the Himalayas. I often think what an advantage Tolstoy had as a writer: he had to go only to the road at the bounds of his estate at Yasnaya Polyana, and there was all the life of Russia flowing by — primitive, medieval, modern; soldiers, traders, country people, monks, mendicants, pilgrims.

Kipling had even richer fortune with the idea of the Grand Trunk Road, from the Ganges up to Peshawur, along which the crowded, jostling, fantastic life of an even more exotic world,

Oriental and timeless, endlessly flowed: a river of human life in all its coloured variety. To take the life of the Road for his theme was an inspiration: it enabled him to string all the disparate episodes and experiences loosely together without imposing a unity that might have detracted from the authentic truth. At the same time that it presents a world of acute, poetic observation, it is also a world of inner imagination and fantasy. On the third level, it is almost a work of allegory: the old Tibetan lama whom Kim serves and reveres is engaged in a Search, a search for a river that will yield him some ultimate wisdom about the meaning of life.

Though a highly original work, *Kim* belongs to a well-recognised *genre* of literature, the picaresque: not so much a novel as a romance, consisting of loosely connected adventures strung out along the road. The most famous of all works of this kind is *Don Quixote*, and Kipling's *Kim* is not unworthy of that masterpiece of the world's literature.

It is a book that grows with one, like all truly great books. I read it for the story when I was young, though never have I forgotten the atmosphere, exotic and poetical, the feel and smell of India and the East. I read it with excitement and pleasure, and am glad to say that the book has lost nothing of all that for me; but to it there is now so much else added: knowledge of life, philosophical reflection, appreciation of character. Above all, it is a splendid and rich work of art.

Kipling had an immeasurable advantage over visiting observers of the scene — over E. M. Forster, for example, with his *A Passage to India* — for in his case India had entered into his heart and veins, into the unconscious experience out of which lasting works of art are born, with his earliest memories. Kipling was born in India — in Bombay in 1865 — now a century ago, and spoke the vernacular with his nurse and Hindu bearer as early as he spoke English. From their lips he learned the tales, the proverbs, the folk-wisdom of India; coming into the drawing-room as a child, he had to be reminded to speak English with his parents. His feeling for India, its people and their ways and traditions, was thus instinctual, going back to the beginnings. It is out of the instinctual, the unconscious and subconscious life that art is formed, not so much out of the cerebral, the intellectual, the merely clever — though Kipling was as clever as a monkey, too.

At the age of six he was brought back to England for his schooling, which lasted some ten or eleven years. At seventeen, in 1882, he went back to India for another seven years, the impressionable years of early manhood that formed him as a writer and confirmed his experience of India. All his early writings, his poems and short stories, his articles and reporting as a journalist, were about India: the poems and stories about army life, the sharp and disillusioned observation of British life in India that made him world-famous, when still quite young, with *Plain Tales from the Hills*.

During these years of intense hard work on newspapers, along with his early creative writing, of sweltering in the printing office down in the plains in the hot weather or up in the cool air of Simla, he was writing at a romance about the life of Lahore, *Mother Maturin*, which was never published. This was the germ of *Kim*. Ten years after he had left India for good, in the fall of 1899, he took up the idea of an Indian romance again. This time all went well. '*Kim* took care of himself,' Kipling tells us. 'The only trouble was to keep him within bounds. Between us we knew every step, sight and smell on his casual road, as well as all the persons he met. . . . At last I reported *Kim* finished. "Did *it* stop, or you?" the Father asked. And when I told him that it was *It*, he said: "Then it oughtn't to be too bad."'

It is in fact a work of love, arising out of Kipling's love for India, fulfilling it in that mood of nostalgia, of dream and regret and farewell that so often is at the root of the making of a work of revealed art.

Kipling had great luck again with his parents, on both sides. His father was an artist in his own right, some of whose work we see in the decorations and illustrated editions of his son's works. More important was the rôle he played as mentor and adviser to his famous son. The son tells us how often he took the manuscript of *Kim* to his father to be talked over and smoked over, and how much the book owed to his father.

There is a portrait of the Lahore Museum, of which his father was for a time curator, in the first chapter: the Wonder House. The old lama, who dominates *Kim*, talks with him: 'the curator smiled at the mixture of old-word piety and modern progress that is the note of India today'.

Through his mother, a Macdonald, Kipling had Celtic blood, Scots, Irish and Welsh, and through this came his strange, psychic gifts, his interest in the occult, his extrasensory perceptions, of which there is evidence in *Kim* as in all his work. The truth is that, in addition to being a very original writer he was no less a strange one, a very odd apparition on the horizon of English letters — as Henry James and Robert Louis Stevenson perceived at the time.

Kipling's mother, the daughter of a Methodist minister, was one of four sisters. Two of the sisters married Pre-Raphaelite artists, Burne-Jones and Sir Edward Poynter, while a third became the mother of Lord Baldwin, the Prime Minister. The Pre-Raphaelite influence is very marked in *Kim* with its intense visual realisation of the landscapes — never have the landscapes of India been so painterly described — in the sharp, precise colours, in the interest in antiquities, the rich effects of jewels. Compare the wonderful evocation, from real life, of the jeweller's shop at Simla.

The book speaks for itself, leaps up at one from every page, brilliant and loving. But notice the characters: in the lama Kipling's *daimon* ran away with him to create an immortal, wise, old holy man. He is really the decisive creation in *Kim*, even more important than Kim himself. And that is revealing: it means that Kipling's creative genius was more powerful and compelling than his cerebral intentions. For the character of the lama flowered into a creation of unforgettable moral beauty: the holy man incarnates the patience, the wisdom of the East, the subjugation of self, the fully achieved human spirit. Though the lama is an old Tibetan monk, he is really India, he speaks for the East.

Notice the rhythms of speech in which the Indian characters speak: Kipling has found an equivalent, convincing and poetic, for all of them: the Tibetan and the Pathan, the Mussulman Mahbub Ali and the Babu, Huree Mookerjee, who begins as a caricature with his mish-mash of English clichés and ends as a man, courageous and resourceful. And there is a speaking portrait of the old lady, widow of a hill-Rajah, autocratic and warm-hearted, a grand specimen of the tartar species.

The English characters are lay-figures, indeed caricatures: the Church of England Army-chaplain, who is portrayed without sympathy, the Catholic priest, portrayed with rather more, because he is closer to understanding the Indians. For Kipling is looking at the British in India through the eyes of the Indians, without illusions. The Sahibs are stupid and have 'dull fat eyes'; their conversation, to the lama, is 'without dignity', and 'they dance and they play like children when they are grandfathers'. To the uncouth and uneducated drummer-boy all natives were 'niggers . . . yet servants and sweepers called him abominable names to his face, and, misled by their deferential attitude, he never understood'. Kipling evidently found this unforgivable, and thought him a fool for not knowing the native language. On the other hand, to be fair, Mahbub Ali pays the English a compliment: 'the English do eternally tell the truth, therefore we of this country are eternally made foolish'.

Kipling was something much deeper than the old-fashioned Imperialist he was on the conscious and declamatory level of his brain: he was a visionary and a prophet.

What are we to think of Kim himself?

The story in a picaresque romance is not important, and it is merely suggested, the more excitingly, in *Kim*. The boy is an orphan-child of Irish parents out of Indian Army life; he has gone native and lives by his wits. His sharp wits, when he is discovered and identified, fit him for training for the British intelligence service, necessary in the days of the Raj. In those days the Russian menace across the North-West Frontier was a perpetual bugbear to the Government: its place has been taken today by the more actual menace of the Chinese.

All this is only incidental to the real subject of the book — Kim's wonderful apprehension of India, which was Kipling's, his loyalty to the lama from whom he learns wisdom and love. How well one recognises his characteristics: his sharp eye and resourcefulness, the schoolboy knowingness, the sheer cleverness, the intuition, those night-walks into the small hours, like those Kipling had a habit of taking, by which he apprehended the mystery, the sights and smells, the dangers, the inexhaustible variety of India. For Kim *is* Kipling.

The book then is a kind of allegory of Kipling's relation to India, nursing mother of his genius, to whom he owed inspiration: a poetic vision of an India that has undergone a transformation and yet remains immutable.

# XXV

# THREE AMERICANS ON ENGLAND

## I. NATHANIEL HAWTHORNE

NATHANIEL HAWTHORNE was in England as Consul at Liverpool for four years, from 1853 to 1857, the time of the Crimean War. It stands to reason that his *English Notebooks*, kept with conscientious care and a trained eye for detail in observation, hold a great deal of interest as a faithful portrait of the Victorian age in its heyday by a very critical and curious observer. Yet it was only in the year of Pearl Harbor that a full and reliable text, edited from the manuscripts in the Pierpont Morgan Library, was published in America.[1] After Hawthorne's death Mrs. Hawthorne published a bowdlerised version of her own, dominated by her standards of Victorian decorum. The later editor claims that 'out of the restored journals . . . a new Hawthorne will emerge: a more virile and a more human Hawthorne; a more alert and (in a worldly sense) a more intelligent Hawthorne, a Hawthorne less dreamy and less aloof than his biographers have represented him as being.'

Perhaps Mrs. Hawthorne was to blame for the unfavourable judgment on the Journals which Henry James expressed in his book on Hawthorne. He could not see what Hawthorne's motive was in keeping them. In fact, Hawthorne's creative faculty, though it ran clear and true, was not a strong one. He had just finished his three chief novels, the American romances. This was his first journey abroad. He was by instinct and long years of solitariness a careful observer. What more natural than that he should record the Victorian scene — and from a very advantageous look-out post, the Consul's office at Liverpool? There, there were the extraordinary stories he came in contact with every day, of American sailors maltreated to death on their ships, of the odd flotsam and jetsam of American life upon the European tide-line floating through his office, the drunken and

---

[1] Nathaniel Hawthorne, *The English Notebooks*, edited by Randall Stewart, 1941.

disreputable Doctor of Divinity to whom the innocent novelist, greatly to his surprise, had to read a lecture in morals. What more natural than that he should write down their stories? The pity of it is that he had not more years of life in which to write them up when he got back to America. (He was only sixty when he died.)

For an English reader the *Notebooks* provide a fascinating pictorial record of that vanished world. It is like turning over a book of Victorian plates, an early volume of the *Illustrated London News* (the editor of which, Dr. Mackay, father of Marie Corelli, was an acquaintance of Hawthorne's). But what comes as a surprise is how sensitively patriotic Hawthorne was. Himself the most English of American writers, he was acutely touchy and on the *qui vive* about America; and there was much in the robust and insensitive Victorian attitude that made him wince. He was torn between two feelings: the resentment which made him cry out at the beginning of his stay, 'I shall never love England till she sues to us for help', and the underlying emotion which made him speak, when his stay was over, of 'the deep yearning which a sensitive American — his mind full of English thoughts, his imagination of English poetry, his heart of English character and sentiment — cannot fail to be influenced by, the yearning of the blood within his veins for that from which it has been estranged'. In the *Notebooks* one can watch Hawthorne passing in the course of his stay from the one point of view to the other.

Then there is the interest of Hawthorne's everyday life in England: his fascination for the street life of Liverpool and London: the civic banquets ('turtle-soup, salmon, woodcock, oyster-patties, and I know not what else'); Ambassador Buchanan dropping a hint about the Presidency (he became President) and calling Queen Victoria 'a fiery little devil'; literary breakfasts with Monckton Milnes, the Brownings, Miss Martineau and her trumpet; the extraordinary appearance and eccentric ways of Tennyson; stories about Dickens; Herman Melville dropping into the Consulate for a chat; Sebastopol night at Liverpool; the bells of Westminster ringing for the opening of Parliament. 'Really, London seemed to cry out through them, and bid welcome to the Queen.'

R

There is then a double, perhaps a triple, interest in the *English Notebooks*: as a portrait of early Victorian England; as a revealing record of the American ambivalence towards the old country, particularly acute in a New Englander; as a self-revelation, if still reserved and withdrawn, of the most eminent of American novelists, excepting always Henry James.

We must keep in mind the period at which the *Notebooks* were written, now more than a century ago, the circumstances in which Hawthorne grew up and that formed his mind. So far as England was concerned — and in their isolation, three thousand miles away from the wicked Old World, it was England that the Americans were chiefly conscious of, and that constituted their chief point of contact with it — Hawthorne's background was that of the two wars with the mother-country out of which the United States was forged. Hawthorne was born in 1804, only twenty years after the Revolutionary war had come to an end; he was ten when the War of 1812 ended with Andrew Jackson's victory over the British at New Orleans. In our longer perspective we can now see that these two wars were the most unfortunate in modern history: they were so superfluous, and they left such a difficult legacy between the old country and the new, such a complex for the Americans, for more than a century.

These wars should never have taken place. If we must hold Britain as more responsible for the Revolutionary war, on the ground that — even if too much to expect of any eighteenth-century power — she should never have attempted to coerce the colonies, on the other hand, we can now see (as Hawthorne could not) how his own state of Massachusetts forced the pace and made the Revolution. If it hadn't been for Massachusetts there would have been no American Revolution. In any case, the Colonies would have had to work out their own form of self-government in the next two decades when Britain was fighting for her life against the French Revolution and Napoleon. The tragedy of it was that the new country should have come into existence the way it did, in strife and war with the old. It is the way things happen in history, but it is not necessarily inevitable, and it is all the more regrettable.

If Britain is to bear the larger share of the responsibility for the Revolutionary war — though both sides were in part to blame — she certainly did not want or expect the War of 1812. She was strained to the uttermost in her long struggle with Napoleon and conceived that she was fighting for the liberties of Europe against a militarist tyranny — as she was — and needed every ounce of naval strength to hold out. After the revolt of the Colonies her ships were seriously undermanned: Trafalgar was won with the aid, reluctant or otherwise, of a good many pressed American seamen, even Nelson's *Victory* could not do without them. In fighting a life-and-death struggle with Napoleon Britain might reasonably have expected aid, not to have to take on the new United States too. However, in this instance New England did not want the war either: it was forced on partly by the expansionist aims of the South, hoping to get Canada this time.

One cannot expect Hawthorne to have appreciated this: he was no politician and no historian. He would have been brought up in the romantic legend of the Revolution, the historical myth in which nations are apt to view their origins. The mother-country was a bully, the Colonies her innocent victims: no conception that there was much to be said on both sides, even if more to be said for the American. On the other side, we may fairly say that then as now, and all the way along, there has been a far greater degree of ignorance among the British about America, than among Americans about Britain. It is understandable enough, but all the same such a degree of inspissated ignorance is galling. And the English — rather than Scots, Welsh, Irish or Cornish — in their self-contentment are apt to be condescending. It is perhaps the fundamental reason — along with a natural envy — why Scots, Welsh and Irish have such a complex about the English. Perhaps the American may be consoled retrospectively by reflecting that, if they were three thousand miles away, think what we others have had to put up with on the spot!

Considering all this, considering the nature of these inextricable complexes, it is remarkable how generous Hawthorne is — in that very American, for the Americans are the most generous of all peoples in the world. Still, there remains the complex, the ambivalence, and that is what is interesting to trace.

He begins, 'an American is not very apt to love the English people, as a whole, on whatever length of acquaintance'. As to that, we shall see as the acquaintance lengthens. Then there is the intolerable English condescension, so wounding to a young people uncertain of itself — or perhaps most of all to New Englanders who were so certain of their own superiority. 'Not an Englishman of them all ever spared America for courtesy's sake or kindness . . . There is an account to settle between us and them for the contemptuous jealousy with which (since it has ceased to be unmitigated contempt) they regard us.' This seems a bit strong: perhaps here wounded feelings went rather beyond what was quite justified. And then: 'I shall never love England till she sues to us for help.' That day has certainly come: twice over in this century the very existence of Britain has been saved by the Americans.

But it is not long in the *Notebooks* before a feeling of love for England comes breaking in. At the beginning, naturally enough — for Hawthorne had not been abroad before — everything is compared, rather to its disadvantage, with American standards. The cathedral services at Chester and at York were disapproved of for not coming up to the standards of William Ellery Channing. 'In America, the sermon is the principal thing; but, here, all this magnificent ceremonial of prayers and chanted responses and psalms and anthems, was the setting to a little meagre discourse, which would not at all have passed muster among the elaborate intellectual efforts of New England ministers.' Simple as this comment is, it is fascinating to the historian, for it sums up just the difference between Old England and New England. The ceremonial, the ritual, the liturgy were just what the Puritans left Old England to escape. But who today would opt for a sermon by William Ellery Channing as against Byrd's five-part Mass or his Great Service, or Tallis or Orlando Gibbons or Purcell, Elgar or Vaughan Williams? The survival value of the liturgy, as of art, is far greater than that of all the 'elaborate intellectual efforts of New England ministers'; all over the English-speaking world the liturgy of the English Church survives, but where are the New England Puritans?

Coming from such a background Hawthorne's comments on

painting, on architecture, on the arts in general, are unbeliev-
ably naïve. At the National Gallery he glimpses a small picture
of Venus, 'naked and asleep, in a most lascivious posture, with
a Satyr peeping at her with an expression of gross animal
delight and merriment'. On Etty: 'the most disagreeable of
English painters is Etty, who had a diseased appetite for
woman's flesh, and spent his whole life apparently in painting
them with enormously-developed bosoms and buttocks. I do
not mind nudity, in a modest and natural way; but Etty's
women really thrust their nakedness upon you so with malice
aforethought, and especially so enhance their posteriors that
one feels inclined to kick them.' There's Puritan Philistinism
for you! Upon all the accumulated treasures of the British
Museum: 'we do not recognise for rubbish what is really
rubbish, and under this head might be reckoned almost everything one sees in the British Museum; and as each generation
leaves its fragments and potsherds behind it, such will finally be
the desperate conclusion of the learned'. In our time the Americans have compensated, perhaps over-compensated, for that
— nowhere are there finer museums or grander collections now.
We see that Hawthorne's comments on art are worthless, while
he recognised his utter ignorance of architecture. One thing
that is boring among even educated inhabitants of a new country, to cultivated denizens of an old, is the absence of visual
responsiveness to the architecture of the past, the inability to
tell between one thing and another.

However, it was not Hawthorne's business to write about art,
but to be a novelist, it is his observation of the human scene
that counts. Here is the squalor of Victorian Liverpool:

Almost every day I take walks about Liverpool, preferring
the darker and dingier streets, inhabited by the poorer classes.
The scenes there are very picturesque in their way: at every
two or three steps a gin-shop; also filthy in clothes and person,
ragged, pale, often afflicted with humours, women nursing their
babies at dirty bosoms; men haggard, drunken, care-worn,
hopeless, but with a kind of patience, as if all this were the rule
of their life; groups stand or sit talking together around the
doorsteps or in the descent of a cellar; often a quarrel is going
on in one group, for which the next group cares little or nothing.

Sometimes a decent woman may be seen sewing or knitting at the entrance of her poor dwelling, a glance into which shows dismal poverty.

Hawthorne had no high opinion of the appearance of middle-class women. 'An English lady of forty or fifty is apt to become the most hideous animal that ever pretended to human shape. No caricature could do justice to some of their figures and features: so puffed-out, so huge, so without limit, with such hanging dew-drops and all manner of fleshly abomination — dressed too in a way to show all these points to the worst advantage and walking about with entire self-satisfaction, unconscious of the wrong they are doing to one's idea of womanhood. They are gross, gross, gross.' If that seems a bit prim, it is counterpoised by a tribute to the 'women of the lower classes', who 'have a grace of their own which is not to be found in American women of the corresponding class'. He was much impressed by a servant-girl out of a place: 'her charm lay on all her manifestations, her tones, her gestures, her look, her way of speaking, and what she said, being so appropriate and natural in a girl of that class. Nothing affected, no proper grace thrown away by attempting to appear lady-like — which an American girl *would* have attempted, and succeeded in, to a certain degree.'

Americans who do not know England still have an absurd idea of the oppressiveness of class there. Hawthorne saw for himself that 'somehow or other different classes seem to encounter one another in an easier manner than with us . . . I suppose the reason is that the distinctions are real, and therefore need not be continually asserted.' Hawthorne has a point there, and he observed at that time a greater naturalness and ease in consequence. 'Here, a man does not seem to consider what other people will think of his conduct, but whether it suits his convenience to do so and so. It may be the better way.' Certainly life in England is easier on the spirit and incurs less psychological strain — Americans appear to have a much higher rate of neurosis. (Some would say that the English today are altogether too easy-going and display far too little of the effort and initiative that made Victorian England the first power in the world.)

We watch Hawthorne in process of becoming converted or, perhaps rather, acclimatised.

It is always a wonder to me how comfortable Englishmen know how to make themselves — locating their dwellings far within private grounds, with secure gateways and porters' lodges, and the smoothest roads and trimmest paths, and shaven lawns and clumps of trees and every bit of the ground, every hill and dell, made the most of for convenience and beauty, and so well kept that even winter cannot disarray it. And all this appropriated to the same family for generation after generation, so that I suppose they come to think it created exclusively and on purpose for them. And really the result seems to be good and beautiful — it is a home: an institution which we Americans have not. But then I doubt whether anybody is entitled to a home, in so full a sense, in this world.

What a curious and revealing qualification to impose — so Puritan and so desolating!

One notices this twitch on the rein, this tendency to qualify, in the midst of his growing enthusiasm for English ways of life, the countryside and even the climate.

I question whether any part of the world looks so beautiful as England — this part of England, at least [the Lake District] — on a fine summer morning. It makes one think the more cheerfully of human life to see such a bright, universal verdure; such sweet, rural, peaceful, flower-bordered cottages: not cottages of gentility but real dwellings of the labouring poor . . . And the climate helps them out and makes everything so moist and green and full of tender life, instead of being dry and arid, as human life and vegetable life is apt to be with us. Certainly England can present a more attractive face than we can, even in its humbler modes of life. To say nothing of the beautiful lives that might, one would think, be led by the higher classes, whose gateways with broad, smooth, gravelled tracks leading through them (but where none but the owner's carriage, or those of his friends, have a right to enter) you see every mile or two along the road winding into some proud seclusion. All this is passing away, and society must assume new relations; but *there is no harm in believing*[1] that there has been something very good in English life — good for all classes — while the world was in a state out of which these forms naturally grew.

[1] My italics.

No harm, indeed! — it was but the truth. The way of life of the English country gentry was the best balanced, offered the best model in its relationship to nature, its sense of obligation to landscape and the society around it and even to culture in its widest, most catholic sense, of any social class recorded in history. Hawthorne was quite right about this, and with the intuitive foresight of a poet he saw, at the moment of its apogee, that its day would pass. '*Society must assume new relations.*' Something very precious has been hit and damaged wherever possible in our time, well-nigh overwhelmed by the urban and suburban spread of the twentieth century. England is now a suburban country, with a suburban culture. Does it show any advance on the achievements of eighteenth- and nineteenth-century society that created and ruled a world-empire, made the Industrial Revolution (which underlies modern civilisation), and in the realm of culture nourished the greatest of modern literatures (along with the French)? There was indeed 'something very good in English life — good for all classes' — it was not only perceptive of Hawthorne to see it, but generous of him to express it. It is passing away, but what is taking its place is so inferior that it hasn't even any idea that what it is replacing was good.

Hawthorne was more generous; he was a superior spirit. 'I shall always wonder the more at England, which comprehends so much, such a rich variety, within its little bounds. If England were all the world, it still would have been worth while for the Creator to have made it, and mankind would have had no cause to find fault with their abode — except that there is not room enough for so many as might be happy here.' When Hawthorne was here there would have been a population of under twenty million in the little island. We are now getting on for sixty million, and the little island has grown no bigger. There will shortly be hardly standing room — while everything is done to encourage people to proliferate and stay there.

Hawthorne noticed, as something exceptional yet characteristic of the English, in his time, that 'in England all people, of whatever party, are anxious for the credit of their rulers'. It is doubtful whether this could be said today — as we have 'progressed' into the welfare-state the spirit has become in-

creasingly one of envy and the disclaiming of responsibility:
nobody is 'anxious for the credit' of anybody else. Certainly
no-one could say, as Hawthorne did in 1854, 'these English are
strangely proud of having a class above them'. Was there anything wrong in that attitude — it certainly showed a more
generous spirit? The answer depends on one's view of the
capabilities of average humanity.

At the beginning of his stay Hawthorne was already prepared to credit the English with kindness of heart. On saying
goodbye to a family acquaintance who was returning to America
he found the lady sad at leaving England, 'where she has met
with great kindness, and the manners and institutions of which
she likes rather better, I suspect, than an American ought. She
speaks rapturously of the English hospitality and warmth of
heart. I likewise have already experienced something of this,
and apparently have a good deal more of it at my option. I
wonder how far it is genuine, and in what degree it is better
than the superficial good-feeling with which Yankees [i.e.
New Englanders] receive foreigners — a feeling not calculated
for endurance, but a good deal like a brushwood fire. We shall
see.' Later on in his four years' stay he saw, and was able to
say, 'how thoroughly kind these English people can be when
they like, and how often they like to be so!' It is good that he
should have felt that, even in those early days of queasy Anglo-
American relations, of American inferiority complex and
English condescension. The situation has greatly changed since
then — Hawthorne himself threw out that 'by 1900, probably,
England will be a minor republic, under the protection of the
United States'. But the instinctive kindness of these peoples —
the kindest-hearted in the world — has not changed, for at
bottom they *are* one.

Underneath all the prickliness Hawthorne had that feeling.
Though this was his first visit to England he constantly had the
sense that he had been there before; as he went about the
English villages, he found them 'unlike anything in America,
and yet possessing a kind of familiar look, as if it were something
I had dreamed about'. Unconscious affinities are so much more
revealing than conscious ones: it was the feeling of inheritance.
Somewhere in Warwickshire, he did not know the name of the

place, 'I had a feeling as if I had seen this old church before and dimly remembered — so well did it correspond with my idea, from much reading about them, of what English rural churches are. Or perhaps the image of them, impressed into the minds of my long-ago forefathers, was so deep that I have inherited it; and it answers to the reality.'

It was like T.S. Eliot's idea of East Coker, where his ancestors came from, and in the church of which his ashes now rest. Hawthorne's ancestors came from Wilton. 'My ancestor left England in 1635. I return in 1853. I sometimes feel as if I myself had been absent these two hundred and eighteen years — leaving England just emerging from the feudal system, and finding it on the verge of Republicanism. It brings the two far separated points of time very closely together, to view the matter thus.'

And, in Westminster Abbey in 1855: 'an American has a right to be proud of Westminster Abbey, for most of the men who sleep in it are our great men as well as theirs'.

Yes, indeed: all that we have is part of their inheritance.

## II. WALLACE NOTESTEIN

The particular quality of Wallace Notestein's *English Folk*, and its value, are due to its author being an American. Only an American could have written it, observing us and our ways through the ages so closely and yet from the outside, with affection yet with a spice of irony, noting the things we take for granted, the unconscious assumptions, the codes of conduct in our past. In this book a number of English men and women out of the last four centuries are studied almost as museum pieces: the types which are so continuous against the background of their countryside, yeoman and labourer, tailor and shopkeeper, country gentleman and his lady, the old county families.

Yet they are not merely curiosities out of the past; they are studied and re-created with too much inner sympathy and understanding for that. Professor Notestein is an authority on the seventeenth century, to whom we owe the fine edition of the Commons' Journals coming out under his guidance. Not content with devoting years to research among documents and archives, routing out old diaries and letters, he knows our countryside as few of us do; has walked over it, meeting country people, staying with them, talking with labourers in the pubs, learning by heart the village lore.

Now he has written a book about England, drawing not only upon his store of information about the past, but revealing his care for what has lived on into the present, a knowledge of places and persons altogether exceptional in one living outside the country. It must have given him pleasure to be able to say with a little flourish, when writing of Nicholas Ashton, a hunting squire of the seventeenth century, who knew Ribblesdale and his Lancashire well: 'Two points that he spoke of, Scout Stones and Brennan Stones, are not set down in the ordnance maps today, but the latter is still known to keepers and shepherds.' And there are similar touches everywhere to remind us that here is someone who knows his England well.

His appreciation of the country is wide and varied, and he paints his characters firmly in the setting of their respective landscapes: Parson Woodforde in his Norfolk, Lucy Lyttelton riding about Worcestershire as a child — and very well she described it in her diary — the Berkeleys in the lower Severn valley, so much of which belonged to them. All the same, one suspects that Professor Notestein has a particular liking for the North Country and its people: he has drawn so many of his figures from there: Thomas Tyldesley, the Jacobite squire, a Catholic, and a good hunting man, whose estates lay in the Lancashire lowlands, between Myerscough and the sea; Thomas Bewick, the engraver, who was born and bred in the upper valley of the Tyne; Adam Eyre, whose farm looked down upon the little River Don. Of this last, he says:

> Yorkshire yeomen were possibly of a tougher fibre than those of the Southern Shires. They lived in a country from which it was hard to extract a living; they were used to long, dark winters and raw, searching winds. . . . Even the epitaphs in the churches of the moorlands are those of a stern people, who knew their rights and remembered their wrongs.'

He loves best the England of the seventeenth century; and who can blame him? For it was then that the language was at its freshest and most poetic, and people often showed a quaint courtesy and mutual respect. A tailor writes in his diary of his wedding night, 'the music hearing that we were awake came and saluted us with pleasant lessons and choice tunes, and with them many more to know what rest we took'. Or there is the Lady Brilliana Harley's gardener who, being sent as a messenger to her son Ned at Oxford, 'fell so in love with travel that he would fain be sent again'.

The book is a conservative book: it stands by the values that have lasted so long in country life, and it is all the better witness for coming from the outside. These antique standards of conduct, the friendliness, hospitality and mutual courtesy of great and small folk alike, still exist, if only in part, in the forgotten background of the English countryside.

## III. Santayana on England

Are we to regard Santayana as American or no? He is usually thought of as half-American, Spanish on the other side. In fact he was a full-blooded Spaniard — it happened that his mother married a Sturgis and George Santayana was brought up in the purple of old Boston. That gave an edge to his temper about America, with which he was never in love. He detested New England Puritanism, always self-righteous, which had filtered down into doing good to all the world (whether the world wanted it or no), into an irremediable ethical superiority intolerable to those more deeply and richly cultivated — Latins, for example, with a far longer and instinctive knowledge of what mankind really is, what it is capable of, and particularly what it is not capable of.

This background made Santayana all the more appreciative of Anglo-Saxon qualities in their English environment, i.e. their original, more catholic, more human, environment. After all, New England, perhaps America in general, culturally speaking, is an extrapolation of only one side of the English spirit, and that the less attractive — the Puritan not the Anglican, the strait-laced, the serious-minded, the ethical: Milton not Shakespeare, sermons instead of drama, Roger Williams, Cotton Mather and Increase Mather (or, perhaps, cotton-mouthed Mather) rather than Ralegh or Bacon, Richard

Hooker or Marlowe, Ben Jonson, Inigo Jones, Nicholas Hilliard or Nicholas Stone, Donne or George Herbert.

Santayana tells us, in the Prologue to his *Soliloquies in England*, that he was predisposed to regard England with sympathy, especially after coming to spend the first free holidays of his youth there from studying in Berlin. Before this, 'admiration for England, of a certain sort, was instilled into me in my youth. My father had a profound respect for British polity and British power.' Santayana makes it clear that it was the intelligent foreigner's one-sided conception, rather than a misconception, of Britain's achievement in the nineteenth century. 'It was admiration for material progress, for wealth, for the inimitable gift of success; and it was not free, perhaps, from the poor man's illusion, who jealously sets his heart on prosperity and lets it blind him to the subtler sources of greatness.'

The son, an altogether subtler person — one of the subtlest minds to express itself in the language in this century, and one of the finest writers in its prose — makes it clear that this does not speak for him. Not for him the conquests of British commerce, the delights of parliamentary government, or even the glories of the Navy — and perhaps it was as well! These things pass — have passed into history. No: 'what I love in Greece and in England' — Santayana wrote while in England during the first German war — 'is contentment in finitude, fair outward ways, manly perfection and simplicity'. He thought of the England of 1914 as the ancient Greece of the modern world; as he wrote, 'the images were English images, the passion was the love of England and, behind England, of Greece'. Love of one's subject is no bad preliminary qualification for writing about it; but Santayana had other, more critical, qualifications. It is obvious that his appreciation of England was, in the first place, a scholar's appreciation; in the second, a philosopher's; in the third, a poet's. He was, above all things and everywhere, an outsider; he was nowhere at home; he was a singularly free spirit, totally disengaged, untethered, without possessions or prepossessions, without illusions or hopes. What better state of mind could there be for an observer?

But he was not only an observer, a philosophical intelligence of acute sensitiveness and understanding, his portrayal of the

English soul in his *Soliloquies* is the most naturally penetrating to be written, as is his portrayal of the German soul in *Egotism in German Philosophy* — a cardinal work, insufficiently known.

Santayana happened to be in England when the war broke out, and he remained there, chiefly at Oxford, until the days of the peace. A celibate, something of a solitary, something of the medieval peregrinating scholar, he had lodgings at first in the High, afterwards in Beaumont Street — in those days when it was possible to have lodgings in either, now institutes, offices, welfare centres. From those comfortable digs, outwardly detached, inwardly anxious and apprehensive, he sauntered out alone to think his thoughts. 'During those five years, in rambles to Iffley and Sandford, to Godstow and Wytham, to the hospitable eminence of Chilswell [where Robert Bridges lived], to Wood Eaton or Nuneham or Abingdon or Stanton Harcourt,

> Crossing the stripling Thames at Bablock-hithe,

these Soliloquies were composed, or the notes scribbled from which they have been expanded. Often over Port Meadow the iron whirr of aeroplanes sent an iron tremor through these reveries, and the daily casualty list, the constant sight of the wounded, the cadets strangely replacing the undergraduates, made the foreground to these distances.' Alas, owing to the mania of the Germans, we have been through all this a second time; as for the Oxford countryside, still so fresh and sweet in those days, anyone who knows the hideous urban sprawl that has devastated it for miles around, has one clue to the horror of our time.

What was he so apprehensive about? — himself so detached that he could live under any domination, uncommitted to anything human save the love of truth and beauty? In a letter he confesses that during the first two years of the war he expected a German victory — as the Germans themselves did — and that made him 'very miserable'. Even at best he feared that 'Germany might become unconquerable, and the war might have to end in some arrangement not unfavourable to her, because she would be free to prepare even more thoroughly for the next against weakened opponents'. One sees how perspicacious this man without illusions was — these are the rewards of prophetic insight that come from real philosophic detachment: it was precisely what came about. So different from the liberal illusions of Keynes, the unphilosophic lack of detachment of Bertrand Russell and Santayana's Cambridge friends! Santayana had a deeper insight into the real nature of Germany and what was to be expected from it: 'in its heart it never believed in another world, but always looked forward to a sort of heroic suicide or "twilight of the gods": for the very people who are now planning a great German era for the whole world are perfectly conscious that that era, too, must pass away in time. It will be merely a *beau geste*, lasting a thousand years ending in the tragic and romantic extinction of the race and its glorious *Kultur.*'

The astonishing thing is that that was written in 1914 — such clairvoyance, such insight, undistorted by illusions! We were always hearing about the thousand years of the Third Reich under Hitler; the 'heroic suicide' was precisely what came about in 1945. It is evident that what this outsider has to say about Germans or English is infinitely more worth while than all the clap-trap we had to put up with from Keynes about the Treaty of Versailles, Russell about universal disarmament, Lowes Dickenson and Brailsford about the blamelessness of the Germans for the war and all those who, with the best will in the world, only encouraged the Germans to try it again. Santayana has a passage about political perversity to which I can wholly subscribe, pointing out why nonsense in the realm of politics is less tolerable than nonsense about religion or metaphysics. 'If one were not governed in religion by emotion and imagination one could have no religion at all — for imagination and emotion are the substance of it. It is to be tolerated and respected nevertheless, because men have no adequate knowledge and no trained courage in respect to their destiny: they therefore have to make believe something or other, and that is their necessary religion. But politics is a matter of fact, of history, of morals; perversity in that is intolerable. See how people have to die for it.' In his Letters he has a penetrating sentence that goes right to the heart of the matter with Bertrand Russell, whom he knew intimately. 'There is a strange mixture in him, as in his brother, of great ability and great disability: prodigious capacity and brilliance here — astonishing unconsciousness and want of perception there. They are like creatures of a species somewhat different from man.' It is enough to the historian to say that they are Russells. The great ability, of course, was for mathematics and philosophy; the great disability for human affairs. So what value have Russell's opinions about politics? As G. M. Trevelyan used to say to me, 'he may be a genius about mathematics, but he is a goose about politics'.

These amiable and high-minded persons were engaged in applying to themselves the martyr's crown of 'conscientious' objection — as if they were the only persons to possess a conscience — while their younger comrades were dying in their thousands to resist the first onrush of the Germans who have ruined this century for us, and for themselves. Santayana at first tried to keep his mind outside the conflict, and then found that he couldn't: the holocaust of youth deeply affected him — especially with his sensibility and response to youth, its spirit and looks — the lengthening list of casualties, the constant sight of the wounded being brought back to Oxford. (One remembers that secret place in the garden of New College where the ancient wall was broken through to make a passage from the Examination Schools, then a hospital.) It was a massacre of a whole generation; the casualties were far worse in the first war than the second: it was the whole future leadership of the nation that was obliterated, for — since there was no conscription till 1916 — it was the best, the elect, who went and were lost. As Harold Macmillan — one of the few to survive, himself thrice wounded — has said to me, it led to the fearful loss of nerve and leadership between the wars, and that encouraged the Germans to try it all over again.

What was it in that blithe young generation that so appealed to the disillusioned philosopher? Here was that glorious, never-ending, poignant summer of 1914 (like 1940 again): 'I was soon satisfied that no climate, no manners, no comrades on earth (where nothing is perfect) could be more congenial to my complexion. Not that I ever had the least desire or tendency to become an Englishman ... My own origins were living within me; by their light I could see clearly that this England was pre-eminently the home of decent happiness and a quiet pleasure in being oneself. I found here the same sort of manliness which I had learned to love in America, yet softer, and not at all obstreperous; a manliness which when refined a little creates the gentleman, since its instinct, is to hide its strength for an adequate occasion and for the service of others ... These self-sufficing Englishmen, in their reserve and decision, seemed to me truly men, creatures of fixed rational habit, people in whose somewhat inarticulate society one might feel safe and at home. The low pressure at which their minds seemed to work showed how little they were alarmed about anything: things would all be managed somehow. They were good company even when they said nothing. Their aspect, their habits, their invincible likes and dislikes seemed like an anchor to me in the currents of this turbid age. They were a gift of the gods, like the sunshine or the fresh air or the memory of the Greeks: they were superior beings, and yet more animal than the rest of us, calmer, with a different scale of consciousness and a slower pace of thought. There were glints in them sometimes of a mystical oddity; they loved the wilds; and yet ordinarily they were wonderfully sane and human, and responsive to the right touch.'

Santayana was puzzled by what governed the English character; it was not at all self-evident. It was something secret — hence the misconceptions foreigners are liable to, who judge by what is on the surface — especially the Germans, who are above all obtuse. It was analogous to the England foreigners do not much see — nor, increasingly, the English themselves, we may add, for there is less of it: 'a beautifully healthy England hidden from most foreigners; the England of the countryside and of the poets, domestic, sporting, gallant, boyish, of a sure and delicate heart, which it has been mine to feel beating, though not so early in my life as I could have wished'. Still, 'what is it that governs the Englishman? Certainly not intelligence; seldom passion; hardly self-interest, since what we call self-interest is nothing but some dull passion served by a brisk intelligence. The Englishman's heart is perhaps capricious or silent; it is seldom designing or mean.' Santayana goes on to answer his

s

question descriptively, rather than abstractly, and that is better. 'What governs the Englishman is his inner atmosphere, the weather in his soul. It is nothing particularly spiritual or mysterious . . . The secret of English mastery is self-mastery. The Englishman establishes a sort of satisfaction and equilibrium in his inner man, and from that citadel of rightness he easily measures the value of everything that comes within his moral horizon. In what may lie beyond he takes but a feeble interest.'

That last stricture is true, too — one reason why the English had no conception of the depths, or the capacity for evil, in the German soul. What irritated the Germans more, as Santayana also saw, the English simply were not interested. Why should they be? They were themselves a contented people, contented with themselves — too contented, indeed — and with things as they were. Things have the defects of their qualities: the defective side to the contentment of the English is that it runs to smugness, they simply will not look ahead. When the nation's very existence is at stake — whether it is a threat from some foreign power or the undermining of their whole economy — they will not see the writing on the wall till they have their backs to it. It is only when they are interfered with that they are aroused. 'As the Englishman disdains to peer and is slow to speculate, so he resents any meddling or intrusion into his own preserves.'

One example of that smugness, that lack of interest in foreigners, Santayana says nothing about, though he was piqued by it — during all the years that he was there Oxford took no notice of him, the dons simply didn't know who he was. As it happened there was living in Oxford at that time a philosopher of greater originality and importance than Santayana, and at least his equal as a stylist — F. H. Bradley; but he lived a life of complete seclusion and talked to no-one. Eliot came all the way from America to Merton to study him; there is no evidence that Santayana so much as saw him. Robert Bridges made friends with Santayana, but then he was a superior spirit. It was not a question of a university chair, for, as Santayana says, he never cared much for 'academic straw', but they might at least have offered him a seat in a common-room. It was the same smug Oxford that allowed Rostovtsev and Einstein to pass on to America, or, for that matter, let Namier and C. S. Lewis pass to Manchester and Cambridge, or that led All Souls to reject Eliot.

Santayana observed a paradox — 'that the English people who have invented the word home should be such travellers and colonists, and should live so largely and so contentedly abroad'. He has a suggestive explanation: 'home is essentially portable; it has no terrene foundation, like a tomb, a well, or an altar; it is an integument of the living man, as the body itself is . . . From the tent we can imagine the cart developing – one of the earliest of human habitations — and from the cart the boat: tents, boats, and carts (as the Englishman knows well) are in a manner more human than houses; they are the shelters of freemen.' This leads to some of the most penetrating observations on English architecture that I have ever read. It is, of course, derivative. 'But how thoroughly and admirably domesticated! How entirely transmuted inwardly from the classic tragic monumental thing it was into something which, even if in abstract design it seems unchanged, has a new expression, a new scale, a new subordination of part to part, and as it were a new circulation of the blood within it! It has all been made to bend and to cling like ivy round the inner man; it has all been rendered domestic and converted into a home.' And he points the contrast with the grander, nobler, more sublime architecture of the Mediterranean originals, essentially military, religious or civic, and its tragic spirit when one looks into it. 'It dominates the soul rather than expresses it, and embodies stabilities and powers far older than any one man, and far more lasting.'

This sense of inner equilibrium, of instinctive rather than external balance, leads Santayana to an appreciation of compromise remarkable in a Latin, and to do justice to the English Church, perhaps its most idiosyncratic expression. This is rare in a foreigner: foreigners naturally understand either Catholicism or Protestantism better, they are apt to belong to one or the other. It is more difficult to understand an institution that is a good deal of both; yet it is the Church of England — and neither Protestant Nonconformity nor the Roman Church in

England — that carries the character of the English people. Compromise is of its essence, and 'compromise is odious to passionate natures because it seems a surrender, and to intellectual natures because it seems a confusion. But to the inner man, to the profound Psyche within us, whose life is warm, nebulous and plastic, compromise seems the path of profit and justice.' Even Santayana does not get the Church of England quite right, for instance he calls its scholarship 'mincing'; whereas one of the finest things about it has been its eminent tradition of scholarship all the way along, from Richard Hooker to Dean Inge.

However, he sees that the English Church is still fundamentally Catholic, while he has a good word even for Puritanism. 'The Puritan stiffening was essential to raise England to its external dignity and greatness; and it was needed to fortify the inner man, to sober him, and persuade him to be worthy of himself.' Candour compels me to admit that this is true; Santayana convinces me, when no-one else could. He sees that Shakespeare, being anti-Puritan, or possibly pre-Puritan, is 'in some respects not like a modern Englishman'. But the reason is not owing to the exuberance of the comic spirit in him, but to his being willing to let himself go in all directions, his ruthless and unlimited probing of the passions. Modern Englishmen, formed by the public school and geared to government, knew instinctively that in order to govern others one had first to govern oneself, and therefore one could not give way to the passions or even afford to explore them too deeply — it was liable to be too disturbing, to upset the equilibrium. This was a gain to government, but a loss to literature; it accounts in part for the superficiality of our modern drama compared with the power and licence of the Elizabethan. The victory of Puritanism twice over — in the seventeenth century and in the Victorian age — has supervened.

No-one has ever written more perceptively about Dickens than this highbrow philosopher. At first his enthusiasm seems surprising. 'Love of the good of others is something that shines in every page of Dickens with a truly celestial splendour. How entirely limpid is his sympathy with life — a sympathy uncontaminated by dogma or pedantry or snobbery or bias of any kind! . . . I think Dickens is one of the best friends mankind has ever had. He has held the mirror up to nature, and of its re- flected fragments has composed a fresh world, where the men and women differ from real people only in that they live in a literary medium, so that all ages and places may know them.' What Dickens had above all was 'a vast sympathetic partici- pation in the daily life of mankind'. Vulgarity? — we are sur- prised to hear this elect spirit answer, 'and what can we relish, if we recoil at vulgarity?' We begin to appreciate what it is that appeals so much to Santayana in Dickens — as against all the counts against him, the absence of any *ideas* as such, the lack of taste (as with Balzac); in fact 'almost everything is left, almost everything that counts in the daily life of mankind, or that by its presence or absence can determine whether life shall be worth living or not'.

In short, the concrete joy in life allied with a superlative gift for rendering it in all its manifestations was what drew this ascetic aesthete in Dickens. 'Walt Whitman had a sort of transcendental philosophy which swallowed the universe whole, supposing there was a universal spirit in things identical with the absolute spirit that observed them. But Dickens was innocent of any such claptrap, and remained a true spirit in his own person . . . Walt Whitman, in his comprehensive democratic vistas, could never see the trees for the wood, and remained incapable, for all his diffuse love of the human herd, of ever painting a character or telling a story; the very things in which Dickens was a master. It is this life of the individual, as it may be lived in a given nation, that determines the whole value of that nation to the poet, to the moralist, and to the judicious historian. But for the excellence of the typical single life, no nation deserves to be remembered more than the sands of the sea; and America will not be a success, if every American is a failure.'

The warning here is equally valid for the British as well as the Americans, in the circumstances of mass-civilisation, as things have turned out. Political and philosophic liberalism, even at its least attractive — as with the Utilitarians and Philosophic Radicals — seems to have an irresistible attraction for Anglo- Saxons; though, as Santayana points out, Bentham and Mill,

'who talked about the greatest happiness of the greatest number . . . might have been chilled to the bone in their theoretic
love of mankind if they had had the wit to imagine in what, as
a matter of fact, the majority would place their happiness'.
Santayana sees perfectly that to the superior liberal 'the direction in which many, or even most, people would like to move
fills him with disgust and indignation. He does not at all wish
them to be happy, unless they can be happy on his own diet;
and being a reformer and a philanthropist, he exerts himself to
turn all men into the sort of men he likes, so as to be able to
like them.' In short, the conclusion is: 'No man, accordingly,
can really or ultimately desire anything but what the best
people desire. This is the principle of the higher snobbery;
and, in fact, all earnest liberals are higher snobs.'

After the war was over Santayana had a comment on those
earnest, high-minded persons: 'it must have been a painful
surprise to them, and most inexplicable, that hardly anybody
who has had a taste of the liberal system has ever liked it'.
Santayana's judgment, as against that of his disastrous Cambridge friends, was almost immediately borne out by the way
things went in Italy and Germany. In his Letters Santayana has
a phrase about the war having at least the advantage of ending
'the fatuity of liberalism'. (Unfortunately in Britain it did not.)
I see what he means by it: the superficiality of its rationalist
assumptions, the vulgar assumption of progress in regard to
values (e.g. there may well be progress in dentistry, but can
there be any progress upon Sophocles or Socrates, or Michel-
angelo or Phidias?), the triviality of its optimism, its cheap
hopes compared with the mingled tragedy and splendour of the
human record. Progress, if it is to please the high-minded
liberal, 'must continue in the direction in which the nineteenth
century progressed, towards vast numbers, material complexity,
moral uniformity, and economic interdependence'.

Santayana wrote, 'this war will kill the belief in progress, and
it was high time'. But it did not: in all those ways we are still
progressing, until there will hardly be standing room on the
planet, quite apart from the quality of life lived upon it. A little
later he confessed that in those Soliloquies written at Oxford
under the impact of the first war, he had been cherishing a

dream. It was his dream of the generation of 1914 to 1918, the generation that was lost. 'I saw in my mind's eye a manly and single-minded England, free, candid, poetical, akin to feudal France, beauty-loving like old Italy, the Benjamin of the Roman family of nations, adding to the dignity and disinterestedness of the Castilian character only a certain blond charm, a certain infusion of northern purity, and of sympathy with the wild and rural voices of nature.'

It was, of course, an ideal England, an England that is lost, and for ever.

# INDEX

*Printed in Great Britain by Richard Clay (The Chaucer Press) Ltd., Bungay, Suffolk*